The Political
State of
New Jersey

THE POLITICAL STATE OF NEW JERSEY

edited by
GERALD M. POMPER

Rutgers University Press
New Brunswick, New Jersey

Second paperback printing, 1989

Library of Congress Cataloging-in-Publication Data
Main entry under title:

The political state of New Jersey.

    Includes index.
    1. New Jersey—Politics and government—1951-   —Addresses, essays, lec-
tures. I. Pomper, Gerald M.
JK3516.P65   1986   320.9749   85–26183
ISBN 0–8135–1150–X
ISBN 0–8135–1151–8 (pbk.)

Contents

Figures

Tables

Preface

This book is the joint effort of fourteen New Jerseyans. Most were born elsewhere, yet all have chosen to live in the Garden State. All have observed and participated in its political life, learning much and experiencing varying emotions—frustration, humor, and astonishment, as well as satisfaction and pride. All have become convinced that New Jersey has much to interest citizens here and in other states.

The Political State of New Jersey has two related objectives: first, to describe the politics and public policies of the Garden State; second, to evaluate the quality of the state's governmental institutions, political processes, and policy products. This book is written primarily for an audience of citizens, not experts, in the hope that it will help New Jersey's residents, voters, and students of all ages better understand the government and politics of the state.

This book was developed during two years of informal seminars at the Eagleton Institute of Politics at Rutgers University. Through monthly meetings and the circulation of chapters, the political practitioners and academicians in the seminars taught each other. As the group talked and wrote, four common themes emerged, which now run through the chapters that follow.

The first and most important theme is the development of the state government as a significant factor in the politics and public policy of

New Jersey. Although New Jersey has a long history, only recently have *state*—rather than local or private—institutions become major influences. This trend is evident in the political culture; in the political parties; in the formal institutions of the legislature, governor, and courts; in the state's finances; and in public policies concerning education, environment, and economic development. This change did not occur miraculously or spontaneously, but through the political process.

The second theme of this book is the inevitable prevalence of politics—the clash and reconciliation of ideas, interests, parties, and individual men and women—in the development of public policy. In other words, to understand the actions of the legislature or the governor regarding public education or the environment, one must understand not only the formal structure of governmental institutions but also the subtleties of human philosophy, faction, and personality.

The third theme is the fragmentation of New Jersey as a political entity. Clashes between economic interests, governmental jurisdictions, institutions, and personalities complicate policy-making. Trends such as the decay of partisan loyalties and the growth of bureaucracy make New Jersey politics both more complicated and less personal. Today even in the best of circumstances, government can provide only limited solutions to tough problems.

These needs lead to the final theme—the critical role of political leadership in the development of the state. New Jersey has had its share of rogues and bumblers, but it has also benefited from the efforts of some unusually astute and foresighted leaders who have made a major difference in the government of the state and the welfare of its citizens. In large part, the events analyzed in this book are a testament to their efforts.

The twelve chapters of this volume are divided into three sections. The first deals with basic factors that establish the framework of New Jersey's public life. Cliff Zukin describes the political culture and self-image of New Jersey, comparing them to other states. He then employs survey data to analyze the electorate's attitudes toward political institutions and major public policies. George Sternlieb and James W. Hughes examine the state's demography and economy. They look at such changes as the dispersion of housing and industry, the development of a high-tech economy, and the aging of the population. Maureen W. Moakley examines New Jersey's political parties. She points to the decline of the county party organizations, while assessing their continued viability both as electoral and legislative groups. Stephen A. Salmore analyzes campaigns and election patterns. Tracing political campaigns over three periods, he emphasizes the shifts toward more individualistic candidates and independent voting.

The second section of the book deals with the formal institutions of New Jersey government. Donald Linky turns to the governor and executive staff. After describing the unique individual characteristics of the chief executive's life, he examines the techniques and resources used in gubernatorial leadership. Alan Rosenthal describes the state legislature—as a place, a political institution, and a policy–making body. His analysis underlines the ways in which both conflict and cooperation are inevitable in a democratic system. Eleanor V. Laudicina analyzes the state bureaucracy. She points to the critical role of professional administrators in the lives of New Jerseyans and examines problems in the management of the state's enhanced functions. John C. Pittenger devotes himself to the courts, particularly the New Jersey Supreme Court. He shows how the New Jersey judiciary has played a leading role in shaping the state's identity and developing public policy in education and housing.

The third section focuses on selected major areas of public policy in the state. Susan S. Lederman deals with the fundamental policy area of finances. She details the increasing impact of state taxing and spending and the recent changes that have made New Jersey's state government more active. Albert Burstein analyzes the most costly state function, public education. He explores the political groups and leaders active in this area, and examines policies directed toward equity in the schools. Richard J. Sullivan focuses on the newly prominent area of environmental policy. Tracing the development of these programs, he describes New Jersey's leadership in improving the use of our critical resources, water, air, and land. And finally Carl E. Van Horn examines the state's economic development policies. Underlining the political importance of economic growth in all states, he analyzes the varying strategies pursued in New Jersey in recent years.

The volume concludes with an analysis of trends in New Jersey politics over the past two decades. It points both to the emergence of a stronger state government and to continuing problems of political conflict. To provide background for contemporary politics in New Jersey, a chronological listing of recent major events is appended.

This book is the joint effort, and responsibility, of its authors. We owe much, however, to many people. Of these, Edith Saks of the Eagleton Institute is our foremost creditor. She coordinated the entire project, typed much of the manuscript, and communicated much of her own poise and good humor to a collection of individualists.

Many persons aided our work, by providing interviews, commenting on our drafts, or doing research. Particular thanks are due to George Albanese, Patrick Brannigan, Clifford Goldman, Edward Hofgesang, Dina Moakley, Terry Perretta, Barbara Salmore, Robert Sommer, and Chris Wakeley. Connie O. Hughes provided much of the socio-economic data used in Chapter 2. Thomas O'Neill partici- pated in our early seminars and stimulated our thinking.

We also gladly acknowledge the insights we received from the two editions (published in 1975 and 1979) of an earlier Eagleton study, *Politics in New Jersey*. They were edited by Alan Rosenthal and by John Blydenburgh and Richard Lehne respectively. At Eagleton, we received important administrative and secretarial help from Chickie Charwin, Chris Lenart, Judy Lucas, Joanne Pfeiffer, and Sandy Wetzel. Marlie Wasserman, Editor-in-Chief of Rutgers University Press, has been essential in bringing this volume to completion and publication.

When finished, a book no longer belongs to its writers, but to its readers. We want *The Political State of New Jersey* to be used by our audience. New Jersey, like her sister states, needs active and in- formed citizens who will enrich the common public life. Such involve- ment would both enliven the participants and enhance the com- monwealth. It would also fulfill the fondest hope of the authors of this volume.

The Political
State of
New Jersey

ONE
THE
NEW JERSEY
POLITICAL
ENVIRONMENT

FIGURE 1.1.   NEW JERSEY MAP

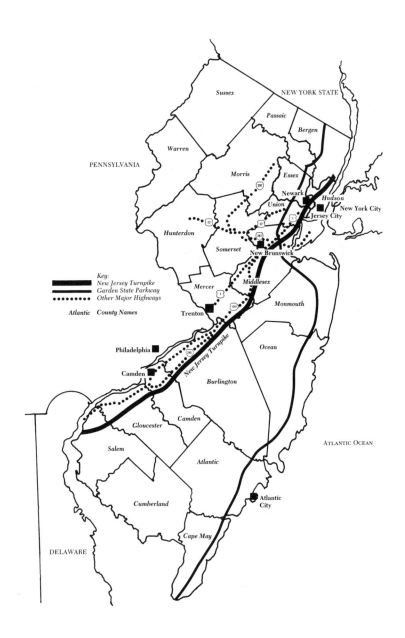

1

CLIFF ZUKIN

Political Culture and Public Opinion

New Jersey is something of a jigsaw puzzle—and not an easy one to put together. When all the pieces are spread out, it seems hardly possible that they will ever fit together into a coherent whole. This is true partly because New Jersey is a magnificently diverse state of great extremes. Consider these unexpected contrasts:

Although the most densely populated of the fifty states, New Jersey has a vast acreage of undeveloped land and open space.

New Jersey's public image is split between the blight of the turnpike and the beauty of the shore.

The state is home to some of the most affluent communities in the country as well as some of the most impoverished.

The northern part of the state is heavily industrialized and cosmopolitan; the southern part is rural and quiet.

The largest city in one of the most metropolitan of states has a population of just slightly more than 300,000.

In one sense there are [many different New Jerseys.] Each has its own culture and values; each makes its unique contribution to politics and the quality of life in the state. But in another sense, there are some common experiences and ways of looking at the world that most New Jerseyans share. These shared beliefs and values make up the political culture of the state.[1]

Political culture cannot be seen or directly felt, but, like the air, it is an element of daily life. Sometimes the values in a culture are so strong they are taken for granted. Consider, for instance, one part of the national political culture: almost all Americans believe that democracy is the best form of government and would agree that it is the responsibility of a good citizen to vote. This is not necessarily the case in other countries. There are also regional differences in political cultures among the fifty states. Citizens of some states, for example, value strong political parties and believe each party should control the selection of its own candidates by holding closed primaries, in which only registered party members are allowed to vote. Citizens in other states place a higher value on promoting widespread participation and demonstrate their belief that Independents should not be disenfranchised by holding open primaries, in which people may vote in the party primary they choose.

An understanding of political culture is important for a number of reasons. The general culture provides a common ground on which individuals relate to society. Most Americans take pride, for example, in being American. [Do residents of New Jersey take equal pride in being from New Jersey?] Cultures also set expectations about how citizens *should* behave. For example, most people stop at stop signs at one o'clock a.m., even when no one is looking. However, in Oregon a yellow traffic signal means stop; in New Jersey it means, hit the gas or you might get hit from behind! Political culture sets the boundaries for what is acceptable political behavior for both citizens and governments.

This initial chapter examines the underlying political culture as revealed by public opinion in the Garden State. First, a general discussion profiles the people who live in the state and examines what they think of their home. Then attention turns to politics, with a description of the state's political culture and an examination of citizen involvement in politics. Finally, specific attitudes of New Jersey residents about their public officials, institutions, and important contemporary issues are illuminated.[2]

THE PUBLIC LOOKS AT ITSELF

Who are New Jerseyans? How are they different from people in other states? How do they view their state?

A DIVERSE PEOPLE

New Jersey is a populous state—ninth largest in the country—with almost seven and a half million residents packed into a relatively small area. Even with its farmland and open space preserves, New Jersey is far and away the most densely populated state in the nation. Yet strangely enough only four cities in New Jersey—Newark, Paterson, Elizabeth, and Jersey City—have populations over 100,000. Only two out of every ten New Jerseyans live in these cities. Seven out of every ten live in the suburbs. One out of every ten lives in the country. New Jersey is largely a suburban state.

In keeping with its suburban nature, New Jersey has a well educated and affluent citizenry, ranking in the top five states in per capita income. Two-thirds of the state's adults are high school graduates; one-fifth have completed college. New Jersey is also an "old" state—only Florida has a higher median age.

Compared with other states, [New Jersey does not have a high proportion of native born residents,] which is one reason there are so many different cultures represented within its borders. Forty-four percent of all New Jerseyans were born outside the state. In fact, about 10 percent of all state residents were born outside the United States, making New Jersey fifth among the fifty states in foreign born population. Thus, it should not be surprising that New Jersey is a state with great ethnic diversity—about one in five claims to have some German, Irish, or Italian ancestry, with lesser numbers boasting of some English or Polish blood. Blacks account for about 13 percent of the New Jersey population and Hispanics for 7 percent.

AN AMBIVALENT ATTITUDE

Statistical descriptions can only go so far. What is it like to live in New Jersey? What do its citizens like and dislike about their state? In fact, New Jersey residents commonly recognize a number of both attractive and unattractive features about their state. At the top of the list of positives are the state's natural environment and its location (see Table 1.1). The state's beauty and natural resources—the shore, open land and wilderness, recreational areas—are dearly valued by the public. While residents in South Jersey and rural areas are more likely to extol these virtues, these features of the Garden State are well recognized by almost all state residents. The state's natural environment is viewed as both a resource to be used by residents and as the one unqualified source of state pride. People also view their close proximity to recreational areas in the state and the easy access to cultural and recreational activities in neighboring states as positive features of life in New Jersey.

TABLE 1.1   WHAT THE PUBLIC LIKES ABOUT NEW JERSEY

Characteristic	Positive First Responses (as a percentage)
Location	33
near metropolitan areas and cultural centers	14
near recreational areas	8
convenient for shopping	4
general "close to everything"	5
other	2
Environment	29
countryside/open land	8
the New Jersey shore	7
good climate	6
likes changing seasons	4
other	4
Quality of Life	20
likes own living area, neighbors, feels secure	9
born here, close to family	4
sports, recreation	3
other	4
Economy	8
good job, job opportunities	6
other	2
Politics, Government Services, Taxes	2
Other	2
Nothing (or no response)	6
TOTAL	*100*

New Jerseyans speak with an equally clear voice about what they do
not like about living in New Jersey (see Table 1.2). It is the man-made
environment that most detracts from the quality of life in the Garden
State. Pollution, overindustrialization, and congestion—people and
traffic—are the primary complaints. Further down the list is dissatis-
faction with governmental performances, a concern treated in greater
depth later.

Specific characteristics aside, New Jersey is a state with an unusual

TABLE 1.2   WHAT THE PUBLIC DISLIKES ABOUT NEW JERSEY

Characteristic	Positive First Responses (as a percentage)
Environment	28
polluted, dirty, unhealthy environment	13
poor climate	6
chemical wastes	4
overindustrialization	3
other environment	2
Quality of Life	15
overpopulation, congestion	6
lacks culture, poor self-image	3
dislikes people	2
racial problems	1
other quality of life	3
Politics, Government	10
poor law enforcement	4
unfair laws	2
dislikes politics	2
other politics/government	2
Transportation/Location	10
heavy traffic, congestion	4
poor condition of roads	3
lacks public transportation	2
other transportation/location	1
Economy	7
high car insurance	3
high cost of living	2
other economy	2
High Taxes	5
Other	2
Nothing (or no response)	24
TOTAL	101

image problem. Perhaps because the state is most often described by those who pass through it rather than by those who live in it, the first thing the words "New Jersey" often bring to mind is the turnpike. This conjures up visions of an overindustrialized, polluted, and congested corridor that runs through urban slums, and exists mainly to get people between New York and Philadelphia as quickly as possible. Other images are of toxic waste dumps, corrupt politicians, and organized crime.

This unflattering view of the state has made New Jersey the butt of many jokes. Indeed, the New Jersey joke is a standard part of every comedian's repertoire, from Johnny Carson's constant cracks to Saturday Night Live's Roseanne Rosannadanna's pronouncement that New Jersey is such a bad place to live "it makes me want to die." The New Jersey jokes generally have one of two themes: New Jersey is an undesirable place to live, or New Jersey is a state without an identity. While neither conveys the whole essence of life in New Jersey, each has more than a grain of truth.

Even politicians perpetuate these negative images of the Garden State. Gary Hart, campaigning for the Democratic presidential nomination in 1984, quipped that his wife was fortunate in being able to campaign in California while he had to tour toxic waste dumps in New Jersey. But Hart had irritated a political nerve; he was never able to get his campaign back on track after that slip. Hart was trounced by Walter Mondale in the primary, leading political reporter Jon Shure to remark that New Jersey had told a Gary Hart joke.

This political anecdote actually illustrates a central fact of state life in the mid-1980s: New Jersey has only recently gained a sense of itself *as a state*. New Jersey is just beginning to escape from the shadows of New York City and Philadelphia and develop a unique identity and a feeling of state pride.

At the start of this decade, about two-thirds of the state's population rated the state positively as an excellent or good place to live. When compared with other Americans' views on their home states, it was clear that Garden State residents were less enamored of their state than might be expected. Out of eight states where identical questions were asked, New Jerseyans ranked only seventh in satisfaction; positive responses in the other seven states averaged 83 percent.[3] In another comparison, 43 percent of the population in the other seven states described their state as an excellent place to live, but only 13 percent of New Jersey residents were this enthusiastic. This is not to say New Jersey citizens felt inferior; few said life in New Jersey was worse than in other states. But neither did they feel chauvinistic. Only about one in four said New Jersey was a better place to live than most other states, about half as many as those living in the other seven states.

The image of the state, however, underwent a dramatic change between 1980 and 1984. The proportion of citizens rating New Jersey as an excellent or good place to live increased from two-thirds to four-fifths; the percentage crowing that New Jersey is better than most other states doubled over the same time (see Figures 1.2 and 1.3). It is true that these new ratings only bring New Jersey residents up to what might be considered normal levels; yet they do represent a fundamental change in one important aspect of the state's political culture.

This dramatic change raises two mirror-image questions: Why was New Jersey so abnormal in terms of state identity and pride to begin with? And, why do New Jersey residents now view their state more favorably than in the past? The answers to these questions are to be found by looking at certain aspects of the state's political culture and media environment that have in the past combined to limit state pride.

POLITICAL AND SOCIAL DIVISIONS

Three characteristic divisions have shaped New Jersey's political culture. The first is that between local and state authority. Many New Jerseyans have a stronger sense of identification with their communities and neighborhoods than they do with the state as a whole. Ethnic and religious settlement patterns led to the development of diverse communities, each with its own customs and traditions. Concerned with protecting their autonomy, few communities wanted to yield power to the centralized state government. Over time, local communities became used to managing their own affairs and jealously guarded a tradition of home rule. Even today, despite the growth of state government, the tension between state control and local autonomy is an important element of the New Jersey political culture.

A second important division is that between North and South Jersey. Somewhat more is involved here than just the obviously different orientations to New York and Philadelphia, respectively. These two regions have fundamentally different personalities. Northern New Jersey is urban, densely populated, and heavily industrialized. Southern New Jersey has a more rural and agricultural economy and incorporates a vast amount of preserved land and open space. The schism between north and south is so deep that in 1981 a number of South Jersey counties voted on a proposal to form a separate state. Few South Jerseyans were actually serious about secession; rather they saw the vote as a way to draw attention to their concerns. A 1981 survey found that by a margin of almost six to one South Jerseyans believed that the New Jersey legislature did not pay enough attention to their concerns. South Jerseyans believe they do not get their fair share of state spending and that they are always outvoted on issues that divide

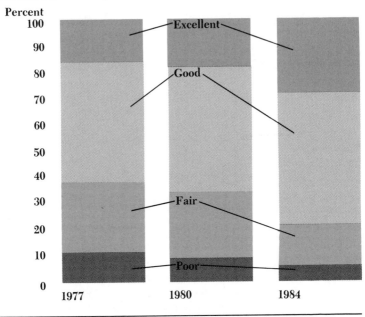

FIGURE 1.2. NEW JERSEY RATED AS A PLACE TO LIVE

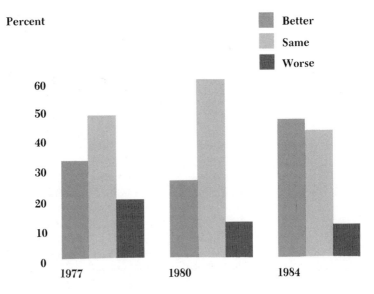

FIGURE 1.3. NEW JERSEY COMPARED WITH OTHER STATES AS A PLACE TO LIVE

along north–south lines. A particularly sore subject is environmental regulation and land preservation. Many southerners complain that the laws made by the state legislature (where the balance of power is tilted toward the north) overregulate them and diminish the value of their land.

The final characteristic division shaping New Jersey's political culture is the division between cities and suburbs. The great disparity between wealthy suburbs and destitute cities is aggravated by New Jersey's reliance on the property tax for a large share of its revenues. (See Chapter 9.) Only New Hampshire gets a larger portion of its revenues from the property tax than New Jersey. With the decreasing tax base in urban areas, many argue that the rich are getting richer while the poor are becoming increasingly unable to maintain or upgrade public facilities in their communities. There is no doubt that the quality of life in urban areas—with a disproportionately higher percentage of minority and ethnic groups—is much lower than elsewhere. There is more crime, poorer quality schools, greater pollution and congestion, and, of course, more poverty. Moreover, as the state's economy shifts from manufacturing to services and high-tech industries (see Chapter 2), there will be fewer jobs available for unskilled workers.

These three characteristic divisions—between home rule and state control, between north and south, and between urban and suburban communities—underlie politics in the Garden State and are essential elements of New Jersey's political culture. They all are part of why it is difficult to identify a single, integrated set of values for all New Jerseyans. And they all help explain why New Jerseyans have had a less developed sense of state identity and pride than is commonly found among residents of other states.

THE MEDIA ENVIRONMENT

New Jersey has also a most peculiar media environment that reinforces the three characteristic divisions just discussed. Media structure has enormous effects upon what citizens know about their state and its politics, as well as upon how citizens view their state. Until the last few years, New Jersey was one of only two states in the country without an in-state commercial VHF television station (Channels 2 through 13). Even now only one commercial station—independent WOR—is licensed in New Jersey, having moved to the state in 1983. People living in the northern part of the state receive television news about New York City, while people living in the southern part of the state receive information about Philadelphia. These out-of-state stations devote only a fraction of their news program time to coverage of

New Jersey public affairs. In 1984, Philadelphia stations devoted only 6 percent of their news broadcasts to news about New Jersey. Incredibly, the New York stations were even worse. Just 2 percent of their stories focused on the Garden State. The average viewer would see one story about New Jersey, lasting thirty to forty-five seconds, every other day.[4]

Out-of-state reporters have neither the desire nor the knowledge about New Jersey to do a good job covering its politics and government. An incident that is sadly too typical may illustrate the point. The day before New Jersey's 1981 gubernatorial primary, which was heavily contested in both parties, a reporter from one of the New York TV stations came to New Jersey for information to prepare an election eve story. His first question, asked in all sincerity, was "What are the names of the candidates?"

Most New Jerseyans do read newspapers published in-state, but even here the unique media environment places a burden on that citizen who wishes to be well informed about state politics. There are over twenty-five daily newspapers in the state, supplemented by a large number of weekly papers. Most are community or county based and their focus is more on local than on state news. The Newark *Star-Ledger* is the closest thing New Jersey has to a statewide paper, but the *Ledger's* circulation is under 500,000 and the paper is not widely read in the southern part of the state.

This media situation has two main consequences. First, it has retarded the development of a state identity, while reinforcing the sense of local community. Second, it has made New Jersey citizens less knowledgeable about their state politics than are citizens living in other states.

A NEW STATE IDENTITY

Despite historical divisions and a disadvantageous media environment, however, New Jersey is changing; the 1980s appear to be a period of increasing state awareness and identification. Why would New Jerseyans now be developing a state identity? Two reasons suggest themselves.

First, there are two new and highly visible features of the state —the Meadowlands Sports Complex and casino gambling. These provide tangible reference points for state residents to share, fostering a sense of identity, and a sense of state pride.

In the late 1970s the Meadowlands development turned 18,000 acres of swampland in northern New Jersey into football and basketball stadiums and a race track. The Meadowlands is home to the New Jersey Nets basketball team, the Cosmos soccer team, the Generals of the U.S. Football League and the Giants and Jets of the National Football League. The Cosmos, Giants, and Jets refuse to use "New Jersey" in front of their team name, and New Jerseyans are getting more upset about this unwillingness to publicly embrace the state. The percentage of Garden State residents who follow Giants football and want the team renamed the New Jersey Giants increased from 53 to 66 percent between 1980 and 1982, testifying to the growth of state chauvinism.

Atlantic City's contribution to the New Jersey image is something of a double-edged sword. It is not entirely clear that New Jerseyans wish their state to be known as Las Vegas East. The public is quite ambivalent towards casino gambling, expressing an attitude that can best be termed uneasy acceptance. On the one hand, casino gambling is a source of pride as a feature unique to the state, and people recognize the financial benefits that come with the industry. On the other hand, citizens are convinced of the involvement of organized crime and official corruption in casino gambling. They are uncertain as to whether Atlantic City will become a tourist/resort center or be known only as a gambling mecca with a tinge of sin. Citizens, however, do know that casino gambling is *theirs*. Thus, although the Meadowlands and Atlantic City have yet to become an unqualified source of state pride, both are clearly cornerstones in the state's new development of a self-image.

The second key ingredient in the growth of state identity and pride comes from political leadership. Only recently have politicians made an issue of the state's image. Senator Frank Lautenberg's 1982 campaign slogan was "New Jersey First." New Jersey and New York City officials have recently been waging a war over common interests such as economic development and trash dumping. These battles, highly publicized in the papers, have doubtless contributed to an "us versus them" mentality. Also, the state government launched an ambitious media campaign extolling the virtues of New Jersey to promote tourism, with Governor Thomas Kean himself appearing in television and magazine advertisements. Thus the general political culture in New Jersey can be said to be evolving in the 1980s. More than a little late, but better than not at all, New Jersey is slowly shedding its inferiority complex and developing a positive image of itself as a state.

THE PUBLIC LOOKS AT POLITICS

How does the public relate to the political system? What are New Jerseyan's attitudes towards their governing officials and various issues of the day?

PUBLIC INVOLVEMENT IN POLITICS

Like people in most states, New Jerseyans follow national and international politics more closely than either local or state politics. New Jerseyans as a group, however, appear less interested in all politics than residents polled in six other states (see Table 1.3). The most significant lack of interest occurs with respect to state politics: only 15 percent of New Jerseyans said they had "a lot" of interest in state politics, half as many as in other states. Only one New Jerseyan out of every two was at least "somewhat" interested, compared with almost three out of every four citizens in other states.

Nor are New Jerseyans highly knowledgeable about state politics. For example, when New Jersey was represented by former U.S. senators Clifford Case and Harrison Williams, each of whom had been in office for over twenty years, only one-quarter to one-third of state residents could name them. In 1984, just three in five knew that their governor was a Republican; only two in five knew that the Democrats controlled the state legislature.

Not all the blame for New Jerseyans' low level of knowledge can be blamed on citizens' lack of interest, however. As noted above, New Jersey's unique media structure makes learning about state government a much more difficult task in New Jersey than it is in most other states. Indeed, lack of knowledge of state politics probably reinforces lack of interest in state politics as much as lack of interest decreases the desire to learn.

States vary tremendously in how their citizens value political participation. In some states, such as Maine and Alaska, over 90 percent of the eligible voters are registered to vote. In others, such as Nevada or Hawaii, only about half are registered. New Jersey is right at the national average. In 1984 about 70 percent of eligible voters reported being registered. Those not registered say they are simply not interested in politics or that they cannot see how government affects their lives, or both. Turnout in presidential elections in New Jersey is also at the national average: about 80 percent of New Jersey's registered adults, representing about 55 percent of all eligible citizens in the state, came out to vote in the Reagan-Mondale election of 1984.

In New Jersey, as elsewhere, far fewer people participate in state elections than in presidential elections. Just over 60 percent of all registered voters may be expected to vote in congressional elections when there is no presidential election; only one in two registered voters takes part in elections for the state assembly and senate when a gubernatorial contest is not at the top of the ticket. As in all states, it is

TABLE 1.3   PUBLIC INTEREST IN POLITICS

	Very Interested	Somewhat Interested	A Little Interested	Not Interested	Total
State Politics					
New Jersey	15	36	31	17	99%
Other States	30	42	20	8	100%
National Politics					
New Jersey	33	36	22	8	99%
Other States	36	40	18	6	100%
Local Politics					
New Jersey	21	28	30	21	100%
Other States	32	34	21	12	99%

NOTE: Other states are the average from polls taken in: Kentucky, Delaware, New Hampshire, Connecticut, Massachusetts and Texas.

the better educated, wealthier, and older citizens who come to the polls most frequently. Most New Jerseyans vote not because they think their one vote may make the difference in who is elected but because they are convinced that voting is a civic duty—a responsibility shared by all good citizens of a society.

POLITICAL ORIENTATION

New Jerseyans are political pragmatists. They are guided less by ideology than by specific cost-benefit calculations concerning the issue at hand. Some evidence of this nuts and bolts approach comes from simply observing how people describe themselves: about 20 percent say they are liberal, a similar number say they are conservative, and the remainder describe themselves as being either moderate or having no particular political ideology.

In line with their nonideological politics, New Jerseyans are politically independent. Official registration figures in 1984 showed that 45 percent of the registered voters were independents, while 34 percent were Democrats and 21 percent Republicans.[5] In actual fact, many of those who call themselves Independents lean toward one party or the other. Still, the point remains that most New Jerseyans like to think of themselves as not tied to any particular party or ideology. Thus, the public's overall orientation to politics in New Jersey does have some clearly identifiable characteristics. It is quite balanced in both partisan and ideological terms, and this often takes the form of an independent approach to politics. (See chapters 3 and 4 for further discussion.)

Political scientists would call this New Jersey attitude "individual-istic," meaning that people focus more on personal goals than on the goals of society as a whole. ⌈Government is viewed as a necessary evil rather than as a tool to accomplish social change;⌉government should regulate, not initiate. Politics is seen as the specialized responsibility of professional politicians, not as the duty of all citizens.

RATING THE GOVERNMENT

Garden State residents do not rank politics high on their list of most respected professions. Public opinion surveys conducted over the past decade lead to three general observations: (1) New Jerseyans view politics and politicians with a great deal of cynicism, and have little confidence in the political system; (2) however, people do not think politicians and government in New Jersey are worse than anywhere else; and (3), more optimistically, citizens' views of their state govern-ment have been improving over the last ten years.

When asked to assess the overall quality of state government in 1980, only one-third of New Jerseyans gave clearly positive ratings of "excellent" or "good," compared with one-half of the people living in six other states where the same question was asked. But, while fewer New Jerseyans rated the quality of their government positively, only 14 percent felt that things were better anywhere else; 11 percent said they were worse. Garden Staters' negative reaction to home state pol-itics grows partly out of a general distrust of government and partly from a view that politics is usually a dirty business.

Yet even some basic values in a culture may change or be affected by current events. Interestingly, just as people rated the state as a place to live more favorably in 1984 than in 1980, so they have also up-graded their ratings of government. Favorable evaluations increased from one-third to almost two-thirds during this period. It remains to be seen whether or not this more positive assessment reflects a real change in the state's political culture; it may only reflect the fresh start traditionally given to a new governor or the state's robust economic health in 1984.

In fact, there is some statistical evidence that New Jersey's more charitable view of government is indeed only a product of the times rather than a fundamental change in perceptions of government. The confidence citizens have in their government, as distinguished from their evaluation of its performance, has not increased to any great ex-tent. Still only 15 percent say they have "a lot" of confidence in their state government. Most (60 percent) have only "some" confidence, and 25 percent have even less. These low ratings extend to national and local government as well, and to interest groups such as organized labor and big business. It should also be noted, however, that New Jerseyans differ little from citizens of other states in these appraisals. (See Tables 1.4 and 1.5)

New Jerseyans have far more confidence in nongovernmental institutions such as organized religion, their schools, the state university, and the mass media than in their government. New Jerseyans' lack of confidence reflects a widespread belief that government is removed from the average citizen. In 1984 only one in ten felt that state government paid "a lot" of attention to the public when deciding what to do. The vast majority felt that government at best paid only "some" attention to their concerns.

While it may be hard to imagine, these cynical views of the New Jersey public actually represent quite an improvement in the image of state responsiveness. The percentage saying government pays "little" or "no" attention declined from 52 percent in 1977 to 42 percent in 1980 before further dropping to the 1984 level of 33 percent.

"Corrupt politicians" are, of course, part of the New Jersey image. Moreover, the average New Jerseyan would probably agree with this characterization quite readily. As a class, politicians commonly are looked upon as contemptible and loathsome creatures. New Jersey

TABLE 1.4   PUBLIC CONFIDENCE IN NEW JERSEY INSTITUTIONS, 1984

Institution	A Lot of Confidence	Some Confidence	Not much Confidence	No Opinion	Total
Church, Organized Religion	40	42	13	4	99%
Rutgers University	35	30	3	31	99%
Local Public Schools	30	41	20	9	100%
Television News	30	54	15	1	100%
Newspapers	25	56	18	1	100%
Own Local Government	16	55	26	3	100%
N.J. State Government	15	59	23	2	99%
National Government	13	57	27	3	100%
N.J. Political Parties	7	48	37	8	100%
Labor Unions	13	40	38	9	100%
Large Corporations	9	46	38	7	100%

TABLE 1.5   PUBLIC CONFIDENCE IN STATE AND NATION,
1984 (as the percentage showing high confidence)

Institution	New Jersey	United States
State government	15	23
Local government	16	23
Newspapers	25	18
Television news	30	28
Labor unions	13	12
Large corporations	9	19
Church, organized religion	40	24

SOURCE: New Jersey data from Eagleton Institute. National Data from Harris Survey (#112) released Dec., 14, 1984.
NOTE: Wording in the two surveys differed slightly. New Jersey entries are expressions of "a lot" of confidence; national entries are expressions of a "great deal" of confidence. NJ entries were asked about "NJ state government" and "your local government;" national entries were asked about "The Press," "Organized Labor," "Major Companies," and just "Organized Religion."

politicians are generally believed to be corrupt (but no more corrupt than those in other states) and motivated more by the desire for personal gain than for public service.

But along with this general view comes a "So what's new?" view of corruption and the belief that "My own representative" is pretty good. In fact, New Jerseyans appear to be quite tolerant of political corruption, accepting shady dealings as political business as usual. Undoubtedly, this attitude dates back in part to old style political machines when powerful parties controlled county politics (see Chapter 3). In those days, the saying went, politicians got investigated, indicted, convicted, and then reelected. Local citizens could sometimes forgive the indiscretions or personal enrichment of their elected leaders so long as there were patronage jobs to dispense and everybody was kept happy. To some extent this mind set is still with us: we expect our politicians to be a little crooked: we are pleasantly surprised when they are honest.

Rating the Legislature

The negative image of government and politicians, rooted in New Jersey's political culture, again appears in differences between ratings of the state legislature and individual representatives in the legislature (see Table 1.6). New Jerseyans may not dislike their legislature, but they certainly do not hold it in high regard. During the eight years of the Byrne administration, from 1974 to 1981, public approval rat-

TABLE 1.6   PUBLIC EVALUATION OF NEW JERSEY BRANCHES OF GOVERNMENT

	Evaluation (as a percentage)			
	Positive	Neutral	Negative	No Opinion
GOVERNOR				
Thomas Kean				
April, 1984	57	31	5	8
October, 1983	52	31	7	10
September, 1982	39	41	5	15
Brendan Byrne				
September, 1980	33	43	21	3
April, 1978	37	40	15	8
April, 1976	21	39	37	3
April, 1974	52	18	2	28
William Cahill				
March, 1973	36	44	14	6
May, 1972	39	39	15	7
LEGISLATURE				
April, 1984	31	45	8	16
September, 1982	32	46	9	14
September, 1980	30	44	15	11
April, 1976	23	48	21	8
April, 1974	27	34	5	34
May, 1972	24	43	12	21
SUPREME COURT				
April, 1984	30	30	8	32
September, 1982	33	35	9	22
September, 1980	34	30	12	23
March, 1976	40	35	10	15

NOTE: Positive category includes ratings of "excellent" and "good." Neutral category includes ratings of "only fair." Negative category includes ratings of "poor."

ings of the legislature stayed remarkably constant. On the average, only one in five New Jerseyans would say the legislature was doing an "excellent" or "good" job. Half would say it was "only fair," some 15 percent would say poor, and about an equal number would have no opinion at all.

The same New Jerseyans, however, are much more positive when asked about the individual people who represent them in Trenton. About 40 percent gave their own representatives positive ratings, with slightly fewer giving them the lukewarm endorsement of "only fair." About one in ten felt their state assembly and senate representatives were doing a "poor" job. This, of course, raises an interesting question: how can a legislature made up of pretty good legislators be only fair as a body?

Part of the answer lies in image and information. The general attitude toward politics and government in the political culture is negative. Because people hear more about crooked politicians than honest ones, and about existing problems than solved ones, negative views become reinforced and stereotypes are developed. But since most people have little interest in and information about politics, these images are not firmly based and can change very easily. When people have direct contact with their own representative, it leads to more favorable views of the legislator than the legislature.

To be sure, the legislature's low ratings are more than simply an image problem. During the 1970s bitter and emotional battles over the state's income tax raged. Many New Jerseyans felt betrayed by Governor Brendan Byrne. As a candidate he had said he saw no need for a state income tax in the foreseeable future, but then as governor he found that his vision had been extremely limited. After that, Byrne was not a popular figure, and the legislature never escaped the stigma of guilt by association with the governor.

The legislature's job performance improved during the first few years of the Kean administration. On the face of it, it is difficult to explain why the job rating of a Democratic legislature should improve when it clashed with a popular Republican governor, but it must be remembered that about half the people in the state do not know either the governor's party or which party controls the legislature. What appears to have happened is that the legislature had the slate wiped clean when Kean replaced Byrne as governor.

Rating The Governor

Evaluations of the governor are of course keyed to a particular individual. Thus they are far more volatile than the ratings for an institution such as the legislature. As with presidents, ratings of new governors are initially quite positive, as people project their hopes onto their chief executive. For example, during Brendan Byrne's first six months in office, before the income tax battle, positive evaluations of the governor outnumbered negative ones by about thirty points. After the income tax controversy, in the summer and early fall of 1974, evaluations of Byrne reversed themselves, with negative job ratings outnumbering positive ones by about twenty-five points.

Byrne's second term was marked by great consistency in the public's perception of him: about one-third rated his job performance favorably and about 60 percent rated it unfavorably. Thus, with Brendan Byrne people formed their opinions based on the major, salient conflict of his administration—his handling of the income tax controversy. With little new information about the governor coming from the impoverished media environment, evaluations changed little during the rest of his tenure (see Table 1.6).

The best thing Governor Thomas Kean had going for him when he assumed office was that he was not Brendan Byrne. People wanted a change, and they wanted their new governor to do well. So Kean received a warm, if somewhat reserved, reception upon coming into office. In fact, Governor Kean's popularity grew steadily through his first term. In February of 1983 positive ratings stood at 33 percent. They increased to 52 percent in October of that year and to 57 percent in April, 1984. By 1985, this popularity had made the governor a strong candidate for reelection.

Political observers, looking back over the 1981-1985 term, generally attributed Kean's popularity to four interrelated factors. First was Kean's personality. He was viewed as a warm person, who genuinely enjoyed meeting the common citizen, especially when compared with his predecessor. Second, Kean generally avoided explosive issues that could have caused a breach of faith with the public. Third, the state's economy was extremely healthy, enabling more groups to have a slice of the budget pie. Finally, the greatest increase in Kean's popularity came when he became more visible, touring toxic waste sites and presiding over ceremonies at various places throughout the state. As Kean's visibility increased, so did his popularity. Thus we can see how the state's chief executive may use the ceremonial powers of office to enhance his popularity, which in turn increases the political power he is able to wield.

Rating The Courts

New Jersey courts are all but invisible to Garden State residents. Fully six in ten report knowing only "a little" or "nothing at all" about how the court system works in the state (see Table 1.6). Thus it is not surprising that ratings of the New Jersey Supreme Court are basically static: about 30 percent rate the court's job performance positively as "excellent" or "good," 30 percent as "only fair," 10 percent as "poor," and about 30 percent offer no opinion. New Jerseyans express about the same amount of confidence in their courts as they do in other political institutions (which is not a great deal), but they generally believe that New Jersey judges are highly competent and that justice is usually well served. These favorable attitudes allow the courts to exercise considerable initiative in public policy (see Chapter 8).

Rating Political Parties

If there is a whipping boy in New Jersey (and probably national) politics it is the party system. Political parties are the most common recipients of the assertions that politics are dirty and corrupt. Most New Jerseyans do not trust the political parties: in 1984 only 7 percent said they had "a lot" of confidence in them. Most likely, this strongly negative image of parties arose when corrupt political machines were a powerful force in Garden State politics.

PUBLIC POLICIES

The evidence presented so far suggests that many New Jerseyans are not vitally interested in the day to day workings of government and that many give less than enthusiastic support to a number of political institutions. However, this does not mean that people are unconcerned about the central issues facing the state or unaware of major actions their government has taken to address these issues. Citizens pay particularly close attention to decisions about taxes and spending. They also expect their state government to maintain a safe and pleasant environment and to provide opportunities for educational and economic betterment.

Taxes

New Jerseyans exert a great deal of influence on the direction of government and the quality of life through their attitudes toward taxes. The state constitution mandates a balanced budget, meaning that revenues raised through taxes must be directly linked to the level of state spending and services provided to the citizenry. The public's willingness to pay exerts major influence on how politicians will deal with such issues as poverty, aging, education, and public transportation.

In keeping with the state's individualistic culture, residents bring a fairly pragmatic approach to matters of taxes and spending—they do not simply oppose all higher taxes as a matter of course. They will consider the situation before expressing their preferences. For example, in early 1982 only about 25 percent of the state's residents felt New Jersey's budget problems were very serious; by a margin of 51 to 32 percent they preferred a reduction in government services and workers to an increase in taxes. Fiscal conditions, however, worsened as the year went on and the governor announced plans to lay off approximately 1,400 state employees. By September almost 40 percent of the state described the budget problems as very serious, and by a margin of 51 to 37 percent they favored an increase in taxes rather than a reduction in services. A clear majority of 56 percent even approved of the tax package passed in late 1982 raising the state sales and income taxes.

The overall pragmatism of New Jerseyans toward particular tax situations becomes even clearer when viewed alongside their general cynicism towards taxes. Most New Jerseyans feel their taxes are too high already (a belief they hold in common with citizens from many other states). Over half feel New Jerseyans pay more in overall taxes than citizens in other states do; about two-thirds think that their property taxes are higher in New Jersey than elsewhere (actually an accurate perception, see Chapter 9). Still, New Jerseyans are able to evaluate tax and spending proposals on their own merits. Such independence is an important part of New Jersey's political culture.

Education

The issue of education arouses intense feelings. Because parents are passionately concerned about their children's future, and because the quality of local schools is heavily dependent on property taxes, education involves just about everybody in New Jersey. Moreover, the policy area of education invites the basic conflict between state and local control. It involves the New Jersey Education Association, perhaps the most powerful interest group in the state, and is given heavy and often provocative coverage by the state's largest newspaper. (See Chapter 10.)

New Jersey's per pupil costs for elementary and secondary education are among the highest in the nation. Most parents, with the clear exception of urban parents, are quite pleased with the quality of their local schools and teachers. In 1983, 72 percent of parents said their local schools were doing an "excellent" or "good" job, and 75 percent gave the same positive endorsement to teachers in their schools. Moreover, parents, as well as state residents as a whole, believe that the quality of the public school system has been improving over the recent past.

New Jersey parents are, on balance, disposed towards educational reform. Various national trends in education have found support in New Jersey. For example, the so-called back to the basics movement has yielded statewide competency tests (High School Proficiency Test). Parents who see drugs and a general lack of discipline as major social problems in the schools have had their supporters too on the state level. And, fully three-quarters of New Jersey parents say that computer literacy is very important to their children's education.

The Environment

New Jersey residents do not like the image of their state as cancer alley, although they do recognize the kernel of truth in that image and are becoming increasingly concerned, and increasingly militant, about environmental protection. A 1984 Eagleton survey asked people to rate the seriousness of a number of issues facing the state, and the cleanup of toxic wastes led the list, with 83 percent finding it a "very serious" problem. Only about half rated such traditional pocketbook issues as unemployment and inflation of similar importance.

Environmental protection will probably be the single most important issue in the state for the rest of the decade (see Chapter 11). The status of the environment bears not only on recreation and the image of the state, but also on perceptions of physical well being. In New Jersey the environment is primarily a health issue. Over 60 percent of New Jerseyans believe that toxic wastes pose a direct threat to their family's health. While most people, however, still feel that environmental hazards are more of a state than a local problem, concern about personal exposure to toxic substances and to air and water pollution has been growing, and there is a clear perception that "things are getting worse." One indicator of the depth of concern over this issue is the public's willingness to accept an increased tax burden to spur environmental cleanup.

Economic Development

New Jerseyans realize that the state's economy is changing from a manufacturing base to service and technology (see Chapter 12). Between 1976 and 1982 the percentage of citizens who felt that it was important for state government to be active in attracting new businesses to the state and in helping old businesses expand grew from 71 to 85 percent. Almost 70 percent favored providing businesses with tax breaks to encourage expansion. However, the public does not believe in growth at any cost. Citizens were only evenly divided on the issue of providing tax breaks to businesses, if such tax breaks would mean an increase in their personal taxes. New Jerseyans have also become increasingly opposed to business expansion at the expense of environmental pollution over the years.

Going Forward

The jigsaw puzzle picture of New Jersey is not simple, for there continue to be many different New Jerseys—rural, urban, traditional, changing, bashful, boastful, mythic, and real. To some extent, which pieces are most important depend upon who is looking. Yet, out of the diversity a whole does finally emerge.

There is little doubt that the state's political and social cultures are undergoing a profound transformation in the mid-1980s. New Jersey is beginning to acquire a new sense of state identity and pride. Politicians are beginning to use this pride for their own ends; it remains to be seen how this development will affect everyday politics in the state.

There have also been changes in New Jersey's goals and concerns. The state is moving from an economic base rooted in manufacturing to a service economy, while the current administration hopes to make "hi-tech" a household word. At the same time New Jersey is fast becoming a state of environmentalists. Demands for clean and safe surroundings will undoubtedly increase in the future.

Yet as the state's political culture evolves, its basic character remains the same. New Jersey cannot deny its history. On the one hand it will never lose its strain of Yankee individualism; and on the other, it will never stop being proud of the ethnic, geographic, and cultural diversity of its citizens or of the honest feelings of community attachment and local identity. The theme of change amid continuity will be easily recognized in the chapters that follow.

Notes

1. See Daniel Elazar, *American Federalism: A View from the States*, 2nd ed. (New York: Thomas Y. Crowell, 1972); Alan Rosenthal, "On Analyzing States" in *The Political Life of the American States*, Alan Rosenthal and Maureen Moakley, eds. (New York: Praeger, 1984), 1–29; and Samuel Patterson, "The Political Cultures of the American States," *Journal of Politics*, 30 (February 1968): 188–203.

2. Statistical information in this chapter comes from U.S. census data and from periodic telephone surveys by the Eagleton Institute, Rutgers University to assess public opinion on a variety of subjects.

3. The seven states were Connecticut, Delaware, Massachusetts, New Hampshire, Florida, Texas, and Kentucky.

4. Roger Johnson, *An Analysis of Television Coverage of New Jersey by New York, New Jersey and Philadelphia TV Stations* (Mahwah, N.J.: Ramapo College, Center for Public Policy Research, 1984).

5. Figures supplied by the Election Division, New Jersey Department of State, Trenton, N.J.

6. Elazar, *American Federalism*, 94–96.

2

GEORGE STERNLIEB AND JAMES W. HUGHES

Demographic and Economic Dynamics

Politics in New Jersey is not an isolated world. Here, as elsewhere, citizens and politicians are affected by their work, their residential environment, and their neighbors.

In New Jersey these social and economic factors are changing. The state's population is getting older and spreading away from urban concentrations. People are living in different places and in different arrangements than they did twenty years ago. The economy has changed its emphasis from manufacturing to services and high technology. With changed jobs have come new communities. These transformations are likely to transform politics as well.

By the early 1980s, New Jersey had endured several economic and demographic shocks. The once unchallenged major industries of the United States and New Jersey were subjected to unprecedented stresses, and compelling demographic changes only worsened the pains of adjustment.

But these pains may be only temporary byproducts of a shift to a new order. The state has made a relatively successful adaptation to the new economy of the nation. New Jersey now fully reflects the major growth sectors of the American economy. Jobs and places of residence are rapidly being linked in new geographic configurations. This chapter reviews the demographic and economic transition of New Jersey, the spatial revolution of the state's social and economic system, and probable directions in the future.

HISTORICAL OVERVIEW

New Jersey's present population and economic patterns mark the latest stage of a long-term evolution. Since its early days, New Jersey has come nearly full circle: a dispersed rural agricultural population shifted to a highly centralized industrial society, only to evolve into a dispersed, exurban post-industrial state. Profiles of four pivotal periods of demographic and economic change will set the context for understanding New Jersey in the 1980s.

THE RURAL SETTING (1790–1800)

At the dawn of the nineteenth century New Jersey and the United States both were rural societies; there were few population centers to compare with the great urban concentrations of Europe. Dispersed rural populations and small towns and villages were the primary features of the human landscape. The towns and villages were commercial centers, providing services for farmers and miners. These centers were founded to meet trade and transportation requirements, and their locations often depended on proximity to rivers, canals, bridges, and road networks.

Thus, the Great Falls of the Passaic River provided power for one of America's first large industrial cities, Paterson, while Newark's location downriver on the Passaic facilitated water-borne transportation. The Indian trails of pre-Colonial times became the main streets of the older New Jersey settlements. Those who today shop or work on Albany Street in New Brunswick, or Broad Street in Newark, or Nassau Street in Princeton, tread ground that has served as main routes for three centuries.

THE RISE OF THE INDUSTRIAL CITY (1850 to 1870)

By 1850 the United States and New Jersey began to experience the effects of the emerging industrial era. The clearest result was the rise of the industrial city. During the broader forty-year period between 1840 and 1880, New Jersey's urban-industrial civilization blossomed. The basic population statistics provide startling evidence: the six largest cities contained only 40,000 people in 1840, compared with 410,000 in 1880.

Between 1800 and 1850, the population density of New Jersey doubled. It took only 20 years for it to double again. In 1800, almost the entire population of the state lived in rural areas. By 1850, over 17 percent resided in urban areas; and by 1870, almost 44 percent of the state's population was urban. At the same time, population declined in agricultural areas such as those which now comprise Hunterdon, Sussex, and Warren counties.

EARLY METROPOLITANIZATION (1920 to 1940)

By 1920 a new pattern of spatial location—as well as a suggestion of future dispersion—began to come into focus: the industrial metropolis. Out of the massed worker populations of the preceding era, a middle class developed. At the same time, residential clusters developed outside the cities but still dependent upon them for most economic and social functions. The city, in other words, still dominated New Jersey's economic and social reality, and 1930 probably represented the pinnacle. Newark's population, for example, reached over 442,000 people in that year, followed by a half century of decline. At the dawn of World War II, over 60 percent of the state's economy was dominated by manufacturing.

POST-WAR SUBURBAN DYNAMICS (1950 to 1970)

After the war, dispersion surged to full force. Populations moved out from the cities along the highway network established during the 1920s and 1930s, along the new toll roads, and along the interstate system set into place in the 1950s and 1960s. Post-war affluence loosened the pent-up demands for housing of the Depression and World War II, which could only be satisfied swiftly by accelerated suburban development. New housing was soon to be followed by economic decentralization.

Life throughout New Jersey was being transformed. Cities lost their functions. Cultural and economic advantages once unique to the central city became dispersed throughout the surrounding, and expanding, suburban zones. The results of this dispersion are also visible in the new structure of the state's population. As the constraints of depression and war disappeared, new households formed and birthrates skyrocketed. The now heralded baby boom of the 1950s generation arrived, and as it matured, it altered the state's age profile.

The gathering momentum of this era established strong influences on the 1970s and 1980s. While the general direction of this momentum was predictable, the scale of the change had been completely underestimated.

The Exurban Present

The present era reflects not only the maturation of the forces of the post World War II years, but also their interaction with new economic dynamics: the rise of world economic competition, accelerating industrial change, differential regional growth and evolving demographics. Four characteristics are significant in New Jersey today: shifting age structures, new household profiles, economic evolution, and new geography of residences and jobs. Population trends will be considered first, and then economic developments.

POPULATION MOMENTUM

The pattern of rapid population growth in New Jersey was abruptly truncated in the 1970s (see Table 2.1). For most of the post-war period, the state's rate of population growth was far in excess of that experienced by the United States as a whole. Then, during the 1970s, birth rates, which had begun to drop earlier, fell precipitously, reducing population growth. Moreover, great shifts of America's population to the south and the west clearly began to take their toll. New Jersey's relationship to national population trends changed markedly. Population growth in New Jersey between 1970 and 1980 was a barely perceptible 2.7 percent; by contrast the population of the nation grew at

TABLE 2.1   POPULATION, 1950–1980

	United States	New Jersey
1950	151,326,000	4,835,000
1960	179,323,000	6,067,000
Change: 1950 to 1960		
Number	27,997,000	1,232,000
Percentage	18.5	25.5
1970	203,302,000	7,171,000
Change: 1960 to 1970		
Number	23,979,000	1,104,000
Percentage	13.4	18.2
1980	226,546,000	7,365,000
Change: 1970 to 1980		
Number	23,244,000	194,000
Percentage	11.4	2.7

SOURCE: *Statistical Abstract of the United States: 1985* (Washington, D.C.: U.S. Bureau of the Census, 1984), 12, 13.

four times that rate. Thus New Jersey moved from very rapid growth to relative maturity.

Equally important were changes in the age structure of the state's population. Three trends are important for the nation as well as New Jersey. First is the incredible impact of the baby boom generation—the completely unexpected increase in birth rates that started shortly after World War II and continued until approximately 1960. Second is that group's replacement by the baby bust generation—an equally precipitous decline in births after 1960. And third is the soaring growth of the elderly population. Each of these trends is visible in the data of Table 2.2, which lists changes in New Jersey's age structure from 1970 to 1980. The maturing baby boom is gauged by the very rapid expansion of the population aged twenty to thirty-four. The baby bust is marked by the depletion in the ranks of people under fifteen years old. The rise of the elderly is reflected in the growing mass of those over sixty years of age.

The forces represented by these data have enormously altered the political fabric of the state. Whereas, a decade or two ago, the major suburban issue was expansion of education, today's major issue is

TABLE 2.2   NEW JERSEY AGE STRUCTURE, 1970–1980

| | Population | | Change: 1970 to 1980 | |
Age (years)	1970	1980	Number	Percentage
0- 4	589,801	463,289	− 126,512	− 21.5
5- 9	693,364	508,447	− 184,917	− 26.7
10-14	711,132	605,841	− 105,291	− 14.8
15-19	612,405	670,665	58,260	9.5
20-24	509,667	614,828	105,161	20.6
25-29	463,624	574,135	110,511	23.8
30-34	403,858	563,758	159,900	39.6
35-39	414,326	479,749	65,423	15.8
40-44	465,907	400,074	− 65,833	− 14.1
45-49	478,417	394,038	− 84,379	− 17.7
50-54	439,472	432,520	− 6,962	− 1.6
55-59	381,013	430,048	49,035	12.9
60-64	314,332	367,660	53,328	16.9
65 and over	693,794	859,771	165,997	23.9
TOTAL	7,171,112	7,364,823	193,711	2.7

SOURCE: *State of New Jersey Census Trends, 1970-1980* (Trenton, N.J.: N.J. State Data Center, Office of Demographic and Economic Analysis, Dept. of Labor, 1984).

which school to close. Similarly, much of the emphasis on employment and job generation results from the enormous increase of the twenty to twenty-four-year-old age group. For every five such individuals in 1970, there were six in 1980.

Clearly the center of political attention has shifted radically with the coming of age of the baby boom generation. The last three gubernatorial campaigns have been marked by a concentration upon job-related issues, with much less attention being paid to the care and feeding of those who have fallen off the economic train. Urban aid continues, but is far outpaced by the need to create a good climate for business in New Jersey, i.e., by lowering specific business-related tax rates, and, most currently, by hitching the state onto the high-tech locomotive.

At the other end of the spectrum, the rise of the elderly is epitomized by the increase in retirement communities in the southern part of the state. The growing number of senior citizens has injected a serious and potent element into discussions of health care costs and general income tax rates, promoting conservative attitudes on some issues. Whether debate centers on housing production or employment efforts, homestead exemptions or school aid, the changes in demographics are forceful realities in shaping both the politics and the policies of the state.

NEW HOUSEHOLD PROFILES

A different change, of equally compelling proportions, has occurred in America's and New Jersey's households; its implications for state politics are equally potent. Households are more numerous, smaller, and less traditional. The total number of households between 1970 and 1980 increased by 330,000, while the total population gain of the state was only 194,000 persons. The state secured almost two households, and two housing units, for every person added during the decade.

This growth in households is largely the result of altered living arrangements (see Table 2.3). Generally, the pattern has been one of household fragmentation and greater diversity in households. Increasingly prominent are arrangements once considered distinctly atypical. Family households (two or more related individuals), once the norm, grew by only 98,000 during the decade of the 1970s. Nonfamily households (singles or two or more unrelated individuals) grew by over 232,000.

Among family groups, the number of married couples (the classic image of the typical living arrangement) actually declined, with their share of total households contracting considerably. New fami-

TABLE 2.3   NEW JERSEY HOUSEHOLDS BY TYPE, 1970 AND 1980

	1970		1980		Change: 1970 to 1980	
	Number	Percentage	Number	Percentage	Number	Percentage
Family Households	1,833,423	82.7	1,931,578	75.8	98,155	5.4
Married-Couple Families	1,573,056	70.9	1,553,090	60.9	−19,996	− 1.3
Male Householder, no wife present	57,157	2.6	73,251	2.9	16,094	28.2
Female Householder no husband present	203,210	9.2	305,237	12.0	102,027	50.2
Nonfamily Households	384,759	17.3	617,016	24.2	232,257	60.4
Single Person	351,545	15.8	537,510	21.1	185,965	52.9
Two or More Persons	33,214	1.5	79,506	3.1	46,292	139.4
TOTAL	2,218,182	100.0	2,548,594	100.0	330,412	14.9

SOURCE: See Table 2.2.

TABLE 2.4 NEW JERSEY EMPLOYMENT STRUCTURE, 1970–1982

| | New Jersey Employment (in thousands) | | Change: 1970 to 1982 | | Distribution as a Percentage | | | |
| | | | | | New Jersey | | United States | |
	1970	1982	Number	Percentage	1970	1982	1970	1982
Goods Producing	985	837	−148	−15.0	37.8	27.1	33.2	26.7
Manufacturing	863	728	−135	−15.6	33.1	23.6	27.3	21.0
Mining	3	2	−1	−33.3	0.1	0.0	0.9	1.3
Construction	119	107	−12	−10.1	4.6	3.5	5.0	4.4
Service Producing	1,623	2,249	626	38.6	62.2	72.9	66.9	73.4
Transportation and Public Utilities	182	196	14	7.7	7.0	6.4	6.4	5.6
Wholesale and Retail Trade	538	698	160	29.7	20.6	22.6	21.2	22.9
Finance, Insurance, and Real Estate	118	167	49	41.5	4.5	5.4	5.2	6.0
Services	410	662	252	61.5	15.7	21.5	16.4	21.2
Government	375	526	151	40.3	14.4	17.0	17.7	17.6
TOTAL	2,608	3,086	478	18.	100.	100.	100.	100.

SOURCE: *Employment and Earnings* (U.S. Department of Labor, Bureau of Labor Statistics, 1970, 1982).
NOTE: Data refer to nonfarm payroll employment. Data also represent annual averages.

ECONOMIC GROWTH ZONES

New Jersey's cities have been left as monuments to advanced indus-
trialization. The new economy is dispersed throughout the state. Diverse communities are now emerging as powerful forces in the state's
economy and social system. In an earlier era, barge canals, waterways, and railroads defined the economic map. Today, highways, and
particularly the interstates, provide the framework for the economy of
the state.

The New Jersey Sunbelt

The first of these emerging areas is a ring of communities that have
gained the popular sobriquet of the New Jersey Sunbelt. This area follows the route of Interstate 287, which runs the circumference of the
New York metropolitan region. This corridor is also sometimes known
as the Communications Corridor because of the size and quantity of
development devoted to AT&T activities.

This area has been building economic momentum for over twenty
years, since the completion of the first stages of I-287 in the early
1960s. It now encompasses and influences large parts of Middlesex,
Somerset, and Morris counties, and is growing at a rate equal to or
surpassing that of the southern or western United States. In the last
several years, development has intensified within this corridor, particularly between the Raritan Arsenal in the south and Morristown in
the north. It appears to be evolving along the model of Route 128, the
freeway that rings Boston, is often labeled Electronics Highway,
and is sometimes credited with starting New England's economic re-
surgence during the past decade.

Sunbelt Outgrowth

In a somewhat more adolescent state of development are parts of
New Jersey that can be designated Sunbelt outgrowth or ring city
diffusions. These are essentially defined by the radial corridors extending outward from their intersections with the I-287 ring road.
Presently, four distinct outgrowth corridors can be defined. First is
the Route 1–Route 130 Outgrowth, encompassing southern Middlesex and suburban Mercer counties. It stretches from a revitalized
New Brunswick in the north to Lawrence Township in the south. A
second major diffusion is the Garden State Parkway Corridor Outgrowth, which affects large sectors of Monmouth County. Another AT
& T element, Bell Labs in Holmdel, stands as an early benchmark of
the shape of present and future economic activity here. A third outgrowth extends along Interstate Highway 78 into Hunterdon County

and is symbolized by the new Exxon facility in Clinton. This corridor, particularly, will see added growth toward the end of the decade when direct interstate highway connections are completed to Newark Airport. The final outgrowth, defined by <u>Interstate Highway 80</u>, still in an earlier stage of development, is evident in northwest Morris County and Passaic County.

Trans-Hudson Manhattan

Other powerful transformations are also taking place. One can be designated <u>Trans-Hudson Manhattan</u>, the geographic expansion of Manhattan westward. This is represented by massive Bergen County office and high rise residential developments, riverfront or waterfront developments proposed along the Hudson River in Hudson County, and economic activity in the Meadowlands in the vicinity of the Sports Complex. The latter also could be set off as a separate entity, nicknamed Sports City.

Recognizing the vigor of these developments, New York City's Mayor Ed Koch attempted to end federal aid toward Jersey City's revitalization as an office center. The mayor feared that Manhattan would move westward over the Hudson in search of lower-rent, secondary office facilities and relatively inexpensive land. He viewed this development as directly competitive with the revitalization efforts in other boroughs of New York City.

New Jersey has become an increasingly formidable competitor, whether for service facilities or for sports. Only a generation ago, the principal baseball teams of New Jersey were the Triple A contestants of the Jersey City Giants and the Newark Bears, farm teams for the old New York Giants and Yankees, respectively. The Giants now occupy Candlestick Park in San Francisco and the tenure of the Yankees in their Bronx stadium is increasingly threatened by the allure of a proposed major baseball facility in the Meadowlands, which already houses two major-league football emigrees from New York City, the Jets and the Giants.

Trans-Delaware Philadelphia

There is an equivalent to Trans-Hudson Manhattan in the southern portion of the state—Trans-Delaware Philadelphia, an area that includes suburban Camden, Burlington, and Gloucester counties. This territory is the primary recipient of the eastward dispersion of businesses from Philadelphia. It might be called New Jersey's Sunbelt South, since firms locate on Interstate 295 and the turnpike just as corporations in the northern portions of the state cluster near Interstate 287.

Las Vegas East

This area, also known as Recreation City, features 30,000 new jobs in the casinos created in the last five years in Atlantic City. The gross win for the casinos in 1983 stood at $1.8 billion. To the bewildered observer of a half decade ago, it would have been incredible to suggest that the proceeds could so soon rival those of Las Vegas.[2]

Retirement City

The development of retirement communities in the southern shore counties also merits notice. Economically, retirement communities are similar to export industries. Money exported from the rest of the nation in the form of pension and Social Security payments flows into retirement areas; that money is spent on consumer goods and supports a host of secondary economic activities such as recreation, building, and medicine. Such an economy is strongly evident in Cape May, Atlantic, and Ocean counties.

URBAN DECLINE

New Jersey has long been known as the most urban of states. Today this is a misnomer, given the location of its growth zones. Rather, New Jersey is basically a suburban and exurban state, with its major cities now representing a relatively small (and decreasing) proportion of its population and economic activity. Indeed, there are few states of equivalent size within which major cities play so small a role. As late as 1940, the big six New Jersey cities—Camden, Elizabeth, Jersey City, Newark, Paterson, and Trenton—had a total resident population of nearly one and a quarter million people, representing nearly 30 percent of the state's total. Their share of the population, both as a percentage and in absolute numbers, has since declined dramatically (see Table 2.5). By 1980, fewer than one million of the state's seven million population (or only 13 percent) resided in the six cities.

The dynamic of shrinkage opened up urban housing opportunities for minorities (undoubtedly aided and abetted by suburban racial exclusion) and, in common with most of the nation's older cities, made them increasingly a refuge for blacks. In 1980 both Camden and Newark had black majorities, with Trenton rapidly approaching that status. And the increasing presence of Hispanic citizenry further underscores this pattern of differentiation.

Black Americans now represent the most urbanized of America's ethnic groups. Blacks moved from south to north, from farm to city and created one of the most massive demographic shifts in world history. New Jersey's cities exemplify this historic migration.

TABLE 2.5   POPULATION OF NEW JERSEY'S LARGEST CITIES,
1940–1980 (Numbers in thousands)

| | *Total Population* | | | | |
	1940	*1950*	*1960*	*1970*	*1980*
Camden	118	125	117	103	85
Elizabeth	110	113	108	113	106
Jersey City	301	299	276	261	224
Newark	430	439	405	382	329
Paterson	140	139	144	145	138
Trenton	125	128	114	105	92
	Black Population as a Percentage of the Total				
Camden	*10.6*	*14.0*	*23.4*	*39.1*	*53.0*
Elizabeth	*4.5*	*6.5*	*10.9*	*15.5*	*18.2*
Jersey City	*4.5*	*6.9*	*13.3*	*21.0*	*27.7*
Newark	*10.6*	*17.1*	*34.1*	*54.2*	*58.2*
Paterson	*3.1*	*5.9*	*14.7*	*26.9*	*34.1*
Trenton	*7.5*	*11.1*	*22.5*	*37.9*	*45.4*

SOURCE: *New Jersey Population Trends 1790 to 1980* (Trenton, N.J.: N.J. State Data Center, Office of Demographic and Economic Analysis, Dept. of Labor, 1984).

These new entrants into urban economy, however, have found the cities much less hospitable in terms of jobs and social services than in the past. New Jersey's major cities historically have been focal points of employment. In 1946, the big six cities accounted for nearly half a million jobs, or 37.5 percent of the state's total. Cities actually had more jobs proportionately than their share of the population. By 1982 the situation had changed. Jobs in New Jersey's cities had declined to just a little over 300,000, or only 11.9 percent of the state's total, and a smaller proportion than their shrunken share of the population.

Many remnants of the old industrial order—zones of multi-floored abandoned factories and company housing—take the form of virtual "rust bowls," the present, urban equivalent of the agricultural dust bowls of the 1930s. Only a very few office buildings as yet symbolize the rise of a new economy on the landscape of New Jersey's cities.

Even the largest of the state's cities, Newark, now houses fewer than 5 percent of the state's jobs and shelters fewer than 5 percent of its population. The role of big cities in New Jersey has declined so rapidly that it has endangered their political power. Urban aid has become a moral issue and, in part, a racial issue, but not one that is supported by the muscle of total resident votes—or economic clout.

New Jersey's Supreme Court has long wrestled with the issues of exclusionary zoning and with the problem of providing low and moderate-cost housing in the suburbs. A lengthy series of court decisions, known as the Mount Laurel cases, now explicitly require growing communities to ensure that a fifth of all new housing is available for rent by low and moderate-income households (see Chapter 8).

It remains to be seen whether substantial socioeconomic shifts will follow the court decisions. Perhaps the relatively lily-white character of affluent suburbia, already somewhat speckled by fair housing legislation, will alter substantially in the future.

A LOOK TO THE FUTURE

Predictions of the future are always dangerous. Unforeseen events can quickly alter things that appear firmly established. Nevertheless, it seems clear that the course of New Jersey's future must be shaped by certain aspects of its current demography and economy.

THE DEMOGRAPHY OF THE 1980s

One of the few areas of forecasting that lead to reasonable anticipations are projections of the future population's age and structure. Although abrupt shifts can occur in future birth rates, all individuals who will be five years of age or more by 1990 have been born. Most are likely to stay in their home state. For the coming years, the maturing baby boom and baby bust generations will dominate the age profile of New Jersey, as well as the nation.

Census bureau projections for New Jersey from 1980 to 1990 are presented in Table 2.6. Overall population is expected to grow about 2 percent, repeating the basic pattern of the 1970s. Within this trend, however, there can be great variation among age groups. Again, the major factor will be the baby boom generation. By 1990, it will have reached full adulthood, as shown by.the bulge in the 30 to 44 year old segment for that year. Housing opportunities, and certainly the vigor of the economy as a whole, are traditionally of great importance to this group. Moreover, as the baby boom generation reaches childbearing age, there will be a growth in the under-five-year-old

TABLE 2.6   POPULATION PROJECTIONS FOR NEW JERSEY, 1980-1990

| Age (years) | Population in 1980 | Population in 1990 | Change: 1970 to 1980 | |
			Number	Percentage
0- 4	463,289	511,300	48,011	10.4
5- 9	508,447	488,600	− 19,847	− 3.9
10-14	605,841	464,700	− 141,141	−23.3
15-19	670,665	473,900	− 196,765	−29.3
20-24	614,828	518,000	− 96,828	−15.7
25-29	574,135	631,600	57,465	10.0
30-34	563,758	665,700	101,942	18.1
35-39	479,749	593,500	113,751	23.7
40-44	400,074	560,200	160,126	40.0
45-49	394,038	463,000	68,962	17.5
50-54	432,520	378,000	− 54,520	− 12.6
55-59	430,048	352,100	− 77,948	− 18.1
60-64	369,660	363,800	− 3,860	− 1.0
65 and over	859,771	1,048,700	188,929	22.0
TOTAL	7,364,823	7,513,100	148,277	2.0

SOURCE: "Provisional Projections of the Population of States, by Age and Sex; 1980-2000," Current Population Reports, Series P-25, No. 937 (U.S. Bureau of the Census, 1983).

population, caused not by an increase in the birth rate but simply by the existence of more potential mothers in the population.

Projections can also be made for the baby bust generation. By 1990, the oldest persons in this group will be well into their college years. Their imprint on the age profile is a deep indentation between ten and twenty-four years old, with a decline of nearly 97,000 persons. In the fifteen to nineteen-year-old group that shrinkage doubles to 197,000. Between 1970 and 1990 a decline of almost 350,000 school age children (ages five to nineteen) is expected. This 25 percent drop will create compelling challenges for the state's entire education infrastructure.

At the other end of the profile, those 65 years old and over represent the fastest growing age group in New Jersey. By 1990, nearly one in seven of the state's population will be 65 years old or more; this is half again as many as in 1970.

Unanticipated events and developments will certainly alter the scale of each of these projected shifts, but the basic pattern will not and cannot change.

THE NEW ECONOMY

Less certainty exists in predicting the state's future economy and possible population migration. Throughout the recessions of 1980 and 1982, New Jersey's unemployment rates were far below the national averages, and even below those of Texas and California, two bell-wether Sunbelt states. This result was partially due to the state's de-creasing dependence on uncertain manufacturing activities, and to its greater reliance on service activities, which tend to be much more sta-ble during recessions.

Employment was also sustained by the slow growth in population and labor force during the preceding decade. New Jersey had more people moving out of the state than moving into it, thus easing the strain on the entire economic fabric. This pattern could well be re-versed in the rest of the 1980s, if the New Jersey economy continues to expand. New jobs could be absorbed by newcomers, leaving resid-ual unemployment. Migration into the state would also alter the scale of the population projections, although not their basic age distribu-tion, and would enlarge future housing requirements.

Economic growth will certainly spawn a range of problems, but such problems are far more welcome than their no-growth counterparts. In New Jersey, the performance of the following industries will be criti-cal: high technology in general, and pharmaceuticals and medical and biological sciences in particular; communications and information pro-cessing; the broad range of services; and gambling, sports, and tourism.

The total dimensions of the state's future economy are uncertain, but its shape is reasonably clear. Adjustments will be made to provide housing near the new locations of growth, suburban and exurban. Economic rationalists may decry the under-utilization of the older ur-ban infrastructures, but despite these protests, pressures to build new highways, water systems, and housing will continue, and even ex-pand. The state's population shifts have not yet caught up with basic economic realities. A housing shortage and related intra-state regional development needs will persist through the balance of the 1980s.

New Jersey's future will accent the crest-of-the-wave developments already sketched in this chapter: sustained vigor in the maturing Sunbelt and trans-metropolitan areas, expanding momentum in the Sunbelt outgrowths, a thickening of the remaining growth zones, and, at least as of this writing, much more piety than muscle in efforts to revitalize the older urban areas, either in terms of jobs or popula-tions. These geographical patterns ultimately will change political bal-ances within the state.

Notes

1. George Sternlieb, James W. Hughes, and Connie O. Hughes, *Demographic and Economic Trendlines: Planning and Markets in the 1980s* (New Brunswick: Rutgers University, Center for Urban Policy Research, 1982).

2. See George Sternlieb and James W. Hughes, *The Atlantic City Gamble* (Cambridge: Harvard University Press, 1983).

3

MAUREEN W. MOAKLEY

Political Parties

A major development in New Jersey politics over the past two decades has been the declining influence of political parties in the state's politics. Earlier, parties directed the state's political development and, over the years, informal coalitions of powerful county parties came to dominate the political life of the state. But this fragmented and parochial party system proved inadequate for meeting the complex demands of modern government, and, as these organizations declined in influence, the state as a collective political entity began to emerge. Hence, the rise *and* decline of party organizations charts the political development of the state.

Given these recent changes, where do parties stand now? Certainly New Jerseyans continue to hold them in low esteem and many think the political process would be better off without them. One difficulty with any assessment of political parties is that the idea of party is a complex one. Party represents three dimensions in the political system. One refers to patterns of identification among voters; another relates to the system of local, county, and state organizations throughout the state; and a third applies to divisions among various elected representatives in government. Each of these dimensions represents a key aspect of party in the political process. This chapter first describes the evolution of party organizations in state politics, and then goes on to discuss the various aspects of parties in the current political system, suggesting that, with all their flaws, parties still perform important functions in New Jersey politics.

HISTORICAL DEVELOPMENT OF NEW JERSEY PARTIES

Although the growth of organized political parties mirrors the early political development of the state, New Jerseyans have always been ambivalent about their role in the political system. During the earliest days of the Republic, norms of civic consensus, which eschewed any notions of mere partisan divisions, characterized most people's ideas about how politics should be conducted. Yet the reality of statewide elections and the struggle among various groups and regions for representation to the Congress and the State House produced, in remarkably short order, strong, competitive political parties. In fact, New Jersey was one of the first states in the Union to organize politics within a two-party framework.[1]

The first popular, statewide contests, the congressional elections of 1789, laid the groundwork for partisan politics. During this election, a group of political leaders from West Jersey (which would evolve into the Federalist party) successfully organized a statewide slate of candidates that became known as the "Junto" ticket. Shortly thereafter, an opposition party emerged in more industrial Essex County, when a group of prosperous Newark citizens organized the Republican Society (which would evolve into the Democratic-Republican party). By 1800 organized parties dominated the entire electoral process, with thriving local, county, and state organizations established throughout the state.

Population and legal changes in New Jersey after 1840 further strengthened the role of partisan politics, while structuring the party system along county lines. A population boom caused by waves of mostly poor and uneducated immigrants shattered the relative homogeneity of the state. These newcomers initially settled primarily in large, industrial urban centers. Their demands for social services and public facilities expanded the role of county government, while legislation streamlining freeholder boards facilitated partisan domination of county government.

THE GROWTH OF COUNTY ORGANIZATIONS

The freeholder boards, and the public monies and jobs at their disposal, became the power base for emerging county bosses. Most immigrants began by living in squalor and poverty, their integration into the social and political system blocked by economic and religious prejudice. Isolated in urban communities, sustenance and survival, not devotion to the public interest, propelled them into politics. By force of sheer numbers, they acquired political influence through the established network of political parties and became ideal cogs in the emerging political machine.

These machines flourished during the Gilded Age when politics in New Jersey, as elsewhere, was "debased by incredible corruption, subservience to special interests, cynical bargaining and the ruthless use of power."[2] During this time the political institutional position of the governor and legislature remained weak, while informal groups of party leaders ran the state. Although interest groups, such as railroads, banks, and utilities, also wielded enormous power, they usually connected to the system through party leadership, which in turn controlled the governor as well as the legislative delegations in Trenton.

Ethnic rivalries played an important role in the partisan coalitions of that era. For example, the Italians, who comprise one of the largest ethnic groups in the state, arrived a few generations after the Irish. These newcomers were locked out of existing Irish-dominated organizations. Hence, many Italians, who by virtue of their socio-economic status and religion would have normally allied with the Democrats, became Republicans by default. This initial cleavage is still evident today.

In short order ethnic groups supported by county machines broke into state politics. In 1884, Leon Abbot, who came out of the Hudson organization, was elected governor. He brought with him to Trenton men of humble origin who relished their new-found power. This new breed of politician—"barroom loungers" and "creatures of the slums"[3]—was not well received by the old guard in Trenton. Nonetheless, machine governors and their constituencies enjoyed tenure in Trenton with increasing frequency.

Contrary to popular impression, party machines—and the corruption they fostered—were not confined to urban Democrats. Republicans also had their bosses. Indeed, the Republicans originally controlled the political machines in Essex, Middlesex, and Camden counties as well as the infamous organization in Hudson County. Moreover, monolithic Republican parties flourished in more rural areas where they dispensed patronage and material rewards among immigrant farmers and artisans in return for political support. During the Depression, for example, a voucher system for coal and other foodstuffs, based on assessed needs, was established in some rural counties. These vouchers and more generous allotments were more accessible to all "good" Republicans.

Reacting to the excesses of the era, a reform effort that mirrored the Progressive Movement began, appropriately enough, in Jersey City. Between 1890 and 1911 the entire electoral process was overhauled. Reforms instituted more regularized procedures at polling places and legislation attempted to regulate campaign funds and prevent the improper use of street money, which was a cash payment made to party workers on election day. Other changes streamlined the electoral process; the county became the electoral unit for the state senators, assembly members, and freeholders, while the election of municipal commissioners was citywide.[4] These reforms undoubtedly curtailed some of the more blatant abuses of the day, but they also had the curious effect of strengthening the role of the county boss and his organization. The streamlined nomination process was much easier to control than the old municipally-based system, and so successful challenges to the organization candidate became increasingly rare. In effect, these reforms institutionalized an independent power base for county organizations. And it was from such organizationally secure bases that county bosses controlled the politics of the county and, in some cases, the politics of the state.

Counties became autonomous political fiefdoms controlled by the head of the dominant party, and informal and shifting coalitions of these organizations dominated the political life of the state up through the 1960s. During this time, most of the twenty-one counties were solidly one-sided in partisan distribution, providing the dominant organization with a solid base of partisan support in a noncompetitive environment. The party virtually controlled access to nomination and election at the municipal level as well as the county level. As county functions increased over the years, the jobs and appointments this expansion created facilitated a vast county patronage system, which the party controlled.

County organizations extended their influence to the State House primarily through their legislative delegations. Until the reapportionment decisions of the 1960s, state senators and assembly members were elected from within each county. Thus, the county party also controlled nomination and election to the state legislature, and legislators, for the most part, did the bidding of the party boss. There are colorful accounts of turn-of-the-century legislative sessions at which county bosses stood in the galleries and literally shouted orders to their delegations on the floor.[5] County leaders continued to exercise their influence till recent years, albeit more discretely. An anec-

dote is told about a state senator who strenuously enumerated his objections to a proposed bill on the floor of the legislature. During this
discourse, a colleague passed him a note explaining that the county
boss wanted his delegation to support the bill. The senator then continued, "Now that I've discussed the bad points of the bill, let me tell
you why I'm going to vote for it."

While such stories of legislative life are not unique to New Jersey,
the significant point is the extent of county influence in contemporary
politics. Until the early 1970s, if a governor wanted something from
the legislature, in most cases he went to the county bosses and struck
a deal. The bosses, in turn, passed their decisions on to their legislative delegation, and the governor had his policy.[6]

County organizations also played a key role in gubernatorial nominations and elections. Frank Hague, with the huge pluralities he
controlled in Hudson County, could often hand-pick candidates for
the State House. From 1919 to 1938, Hague sponsored a series of
successful gubernatorial candidates. The most colorful of these was
A. Harry Moore, an affable and kindly Hague agent who was elected
governor in 1926 and 1932 and 1938. (His tenure at the State House
was interrupted by rules against successive terms.) In 1934, he
obliged the boss by running for a seat to the U.S. Senate, but dutifully
resigned that seat three years later when Hague decided he should be
governor again![7]

Even as the power of individual bosses began to wane in the 1940s,
informal coalitions of county leaders continued to dominate politics at
the statehouse. A candidate for governor still had to procure the endorsement of several key county chairs in order to make a viable bid
for the nomination, and even the most prestigious candidate for
governor was dependent on the nod of the county organizations and
the votes, money, and campaign workers they controlled. Richard
Hughes, a distinguished candidate and outstanding leader, could not
have won office in 1961 without his county chairmen's backing; even
as late as 1973, Brendan Byrne acknowledged that he would not have
attempted his first bid for the State House without the backing of the
Hudson organization.

THE DECLINE IN COUNTY POWER

The fortunes of county parties have declined dramatically in recent
years. While these organizations remain influential at the local level,
they are now only a minor factor in state politics. In a remarkably
short time, demographic shifts, reapportionment decisions, changing
campaign methods, and the emergence of a more professional ethic in

government have eroded the influence of these organizations and their leaders at the state level. These developments have ushered in a new era of politics in New Jersey.

By the 1960s, the post World War II building boom began to change the political complexion of many counties (see Chapter 2). Middle income, suburban housing development created demographic shifts throughout the Garden State. Upwardly mobile, middle-class residents left the cities and migrated to the suburbs, which were now often located in rural strongholds. Suburbanization had two effects. First, it tended to diminish the solid partisan base of many county organizations, since in many cases these new residents brought their own partisan preferences with them. Monmouth County, for example, was a solid Republican bastion up through the 1960s. Then many upwardly mobile urban residents from Hudson and Essex migrated there, bringing with them their Democratic leanings. Monmouth is now considered the most competitive county in the state, and Republican party leaders caustically refer to it as Jersey City South. The second effect of suburbanization is the change in political expectations of the population. The growing middle class, with its higher educational and income levels, found many of the rules and incentive systems of typical organization politics either at odds with its political ideals or irrelevant to its life style.

Although the organization of the parties conformed to the formal statutes, the law did little to control their internal workings. Charters were not required and procedures were informal at best. The law mandated only that an annual reorganization meeting be held in each municipality and county following the primary election. Quorums or secret ballots were not required and, in most cases, meetings were little more than *pro forma* endorsements of the agenda of the leadership. Such old-style or machinelike operating procedures tended to alienate an emerging middle-class constituency which expected more participatory involvement.

Reapportionment decisions of the late 1960s and early 1970s were an equally critical factor in the decline of county influence. Previously, representation in the state legislature was apportioned on the basis of one senator per county regardless of population; assembly districts, based on population, were also drawn within county boundaries. Hence, nomination and election to the state legislature was virtually locked into the county system. In 1966 the state judiciary enjoined further legislative elections. Then at a special constitutional convention, the structure of the legislature was changed to forty state senators and eighty assembly members elected from forty legislative districts. More important, perhaps, was the 1972 state supreme court decision that mandated that county boundaries be ignored in devising state legislative district lines.[8]

These decisions radically changed the structure of legislative politics: county parties no longer dominated the process. Although in most cases, legislators still require support of various county and local parties for nomination and election, they are no longer locked into a monolithic system. Many legislative districts now extend over county lines and, in a few cases, legislators are able to run their own campaigns outside the organization. In all cases, legislators now enjoy considerable independence in Trenton.

These changes also affected the county parties' influence in executive politics. First, as legislators became disengaged from the county system, governors became less dependent on the county leaders' influence to work their will in the state legislature. Second, and perhaps more critical, public financing of gubernatorial primaries and elections, instituted in 1977, and changing campaign techniques (see Chapter 4), relegated the county party to a minor role in the statewide electoral process. County leaders no longer picked gubernatorial nominees, since they no longer controlled either the financial resources or the blocs of voters and the campaign organizations that were needed to deliver the election to a chosen candidate. Given their diminished influence, the parties' access to the state patronage system substantially eroded.

More subtle changes were also occurring in state politics. Initiation of broad-based state taxes signalled an enlarged role for state government in the policy process. The enactment of a statewide income tax in 1976 shifted the balance away from home rule, and state government began to assume broad responsibility for public policy and public services. In this new milieu, executive management became more professional. Formerly, most of the key actors in state politics had been dependent on their county base. Hence, they had tended to view the political world from a decidedly parochial perspective. A growing number of the political elite, however, facing the complex and technical demands of modern government, rejected these orientations. Now standards of efficiency and effectiveness and a more modern notion of the public interest characterize key participants in state government.

These trends crystallized during the tenure of Brendan Byrne. Byrne probably owed less to the county bosses for his nomination and election than most of his predecessors, and throughout his first term executive politics took on a different cast. Byrne dealt more directly with the legislature and relied less on the bosses for support. When the Democratic county leaders arrived in Trenton with their "favor baskets," they were often sent home empty-handed. By the end of his first term, Byrne had alienated most of the Democratic bosses; yet he went on to win renomination and election without their support. His reelection in 1977 signalled the end of the county parties' dominance in state politics.[9]

PARTIES IN MODERN POLITICS

Where do parties fit today? Given the rapid political change of the past two decades, their place in the present political process is both difficult to ascertain and the subject of considerable debate. Voters continue to regard them with suspicion and many political observers argue that the political system would be better off without them.

Yet, relative to other states in the Union, politics in New Jersey remain a highly partisan affair. Local and county party organizations continue to structure the electoral process, recruiting candidates and conducting campaigns. Over 80 percent of the state's voters still express some predisposition toward one of the two major parties and presumably act on these cues in many of their electoral choices. And, at the State House in Trenton, the day-to-day operation of government reflects basic party divisions. The New Jersey legislature is considered one of the most partisan legislatures in the nation,[10] and party remains a dominant motif of politics in the governor's office.

One difficulty in placing political parties in perspective is that the idea of party has meaning at several levels of politics. "Party" refers to the voters in the electorate who consider themselves oriented or inclined toward the candidates and politics of either the Democrats or the Republicans. "Party" applies to the network of working organizations that exist at the local, county, and state level. "Party" also refers to the basic operating and organizing divisions among elected officials in government throughout the state. A systematic consideration of parties on all these levels suggests that, although they no longer dominate politics, parties do remain an important component of the political system.

PARTY IN THE ELECTORATE

New Jerseyans, like their counterparts across the nation, no longer display monolithic attachments to either of the two major parties. The erosion of the New Deal coalition and the increase of civic individualism encouraged by a mass media environment has led to growing political independence among Garden State voters, especially during the 1970s. Yet the idea of party has a curious resilience in the voters' minds. When asked in 1984 to express a preference for one party or another, only about a third of the voters claimed to be Democrats, a fourth considered themselves Republicans, while the rest of the voters initially called themselves Independents. When pressed with a follow-up question, however, about towards which party they leaned, the number of confirmed Independents dramatically declined. Then the shape of the New Jersey electorate became 49 percent Democratic and 38 percent Republican, while only 11 percent of the voters retained their independent status.[11] In a series of polls over the past few years, the data indicate a decline in the number of Democrats and Independents with a slight increase in the number of Republican identifiers. (See Chapter 4.)

Who are these partisans? Are there any significant ideological, social, or economic differences between those who consider themselves Democrats and those who identify themselves as Republicans? (See Table 3.1.) For the most part, New Jersey partisans resemble their counterparts in other states. Democrats in the Garden State are an ideologically diverse group. Just over half of all Democrats consider themselves liberal, while about 40 percent consider themselves conservative. On the other hand, Republicans are much more ideologically cohesive. About 70 percent of all Republicans consider themselves conservative, more than twice the number who consider themselves Republican liberals. Although there are certain differences among the socio-economic characteristics of partisans, in most cases these are not highly pronounced. Democrats tend to have less income and less education and are slightly older than their Republican counterparts. Democrats are more likely to reside in center cities while Republicans are much more likely to live in the newer suburbs.

When one considers sex and race differences, however, Garden State partisans evidence some interesting patterns, also mirroring national trends. New Jersey appears to have a pronounced version of the gender gap. There is a notable difference within both parties between male and female identifiers: Democrats enjoy more support from women while men comprise a significant majority of Republican identifiers. Race is also a factor in partisan divisions: almost 20 percent of the Democratic party is nonwhite, but only 5 percent of Republicans are black or Hispanic.

How do the party preferences of different identifiers translate into votes? In all statewide contests and in a few congressional races, the

TABLE 3.1   DEMOGRAPHIC CHARACTERISTICS OF NEW JERSEY
PARTISANS

Characteristic	Democrats (as a percentage of total party)	Republicans (as a percentage of total party)
Liberal	53	29
Conservative	43	69
Age		
18-29	27	28
30-49	31	35
50-64	26	20
Over 65	16	17
Education		
Less than high school	31	22
High school graduate	36	41
Schooling after high school	32	38
Income		
Under $15,000	33	20
$15,000-$30,000	32	32
Over $30,000	34	48
Place of Residence		
Center city	16	7
City and older suburb	23	21
New suburb	26	42
Rural	35	31
Race		
White	81	95
Nonwhite	19	5
Sex		
Male	44	56
Female	56	44
Occupation		
Blue collar	33	30
White collar	26	30
Self-employed	5	11
Retired	18	18
Unemployed	18	12

SOURCE: Eagleton Poll, Rutgers University, August 1984.

link is tenuous. Extensive and expensive media campaigns, controlled by individual candidates and not by the party, create a volatile political environment where money and media count. In these contests, voters rely less on their partisan predispositions and are likely to make choices on the basis of perceptions about individual candidates. In most other electoral contests, however, party preferences heavily affect the outcome. While the typical New Jersey partisan may cast a ballot for a popular president, governor, or U.S. Senator of the opposite party, that same voter will usually vote along party lines in most congressional, legislative, county, and local races, thereby providing a decided stability to these elections.

Out of the forty legislative districts in New Jersey, there are only about seven that are considered competitive. In the remaining thirty-three, one party or the other controls both the senate and assembly seats, and successful candidates from these districts usually win by substantial margins. The results of the 1983 legislative races underscore the partisan character of electoral politics at this level. Republican Governor Thomas Kean, enjoying unprecedented popularity and voter approval in the state, appealed to the voters to elect a more Republican legislature. Arguing that the Democratic–controlled legislature was obstructing his policy agenda, he and his party spent considerable time and money attempting to unseat key Democrats in various districts. But he failed. He was unable to translate his personal popularity into votes; indeed, the Democrats actually gained seats in that election. (See Figure 4.1.)

While to some, voting merely on the basis of party preference may appear to be uninformed, such choices among voters make a good deal of sense in the context of New Jersey politics. The party divisions among most congressional, legislative, and county governing bodies generally reflect the partisan orientations of their constituencies. And these divisions, particularly beyond the local level, usually translate into distinctive policy orientations among those candidates that the voters elect.

In New Jersey, discernible political differences between Republicans and Democrats in office manifest themselves in broad policy areas. Republicans tend to support more business and development actions, a less restrictive role for government, more conservative approaches on social issues, and more regressive revenue raising measures such as the sales tax. Democrats, on the other hand, are likely to support more spending on social services, more government intervention, more liberal approaches on social issues, and more progressive tax policies such as the income tax. Hence, partisanship in the electorate provides a measure of political stability and policy coherence in

Garden State politics. This linkage is established and maintained through party organizations.

PARTY AS ORGANIZATION

"Party as organization" applies to the vast network of municipal and county party organizations throughout the state and to the thousands of individuals who hold official positions in these organizations. The present status of these organizations presents an interesting paradox. While the political influence of parties is suffering a decline, organizationally parties appear to be experiencing a measure of growth and regeneration. While increased competition and the influx of middle-class voters contributed to the decline of many monolithic party organizations, it also prompted the rejuvenation of many established organizations as well as growth and vitalization of other normally moribund minority parties. Thus, as organizations, parties are alive and well. Indeed, New Jersey's local and county parties are considered to be among the most organizationally developing parties in the nation.[12]

Party Structure

The formal structure of the state's party organizations is prescribed by Title 19 of the New Jersey Statutes and illustrated in Table 3.2. The law provides for four levels of organization, based on the state's 5,597 election districts, 567 municipalities, 21 counties, and the entire state. The official party structure begins at the electoral district level. Election districts are determined by population, the law allowing that each district should have as close to 750 voters "as practicable," although it is not unusual for some districts to have as few as 300 or as many as 1,500 voters. Each party's members annually elect in the primary one committeeman and one committeewoman from each election district. These committee members become the grassroots representatives of the organization in each municipality in the state. These members meet the first Tuesday after the primary and elect a municipal chairman and vice chairman of the opposite sex.

The second Tuesday after the primary, all municipal committee members from a given county meet at their annual county reorganization meeting to elect a county chairman and vice-chairman of the opposite sex. It is at these meetings that the competition for party leadership in the county is played out. The county committee is the largest working organization of the party apparatus; it varies in size from barely one hundred to well over a thousand. Municipal chairmen usually are the working core of the organization under the direction of the county chair.

TABLE 3.2   NEW JERSEY STATE PARTY ORGANIZATION

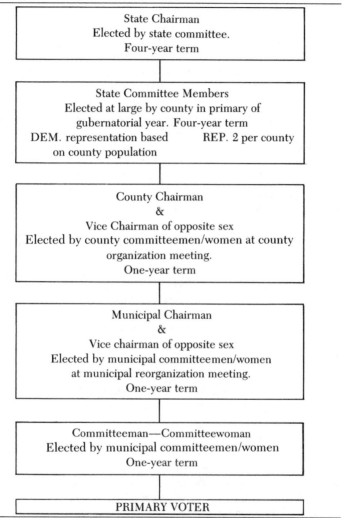

State Chairman
Elected by state committee.
Four-year term

State Committee Members
Elected at large by county in primary of
gubernatorial year. Four-year term
DEM. representation based   REP. 2 per county
on county population

County Chairman
&
Vice Chairman of opposite sex
Elected by county committeemen/women at county
organization meeting.
One-year term

Municipal Chairman
&
Vice chairman of opposite sex
Elected by municipal committeemen/women
at municipal reorganization meeting.
One-year term

Committeeman—Committeewoman
Elected by municipal committeemen/women
One-year term

PRIMARY VOTER

SOURCE: Mauren Moakley & Gerald Pomper, "Party Organizations" in *Politics in New Jersey*, p. 87.

In large and well-organized cities, which produce critically large blocs of voters, the relationship between the municipal and county chairs can be an uneasy alliance, given the keen competition for power and position within the county.

Party politics varies among municipalities and counties. Many vibrant and active parties have detailed charters and by-laws, which provide for secret ballot party elections, mandate quorum rules, and specify monthly or bi-monthly meetings where party business is coordinated, debated, and resolved. At the other extreme are the moribund party organizations, usually of a minority party, where vacancies are common, rules and procedures are nonexistent, and only a few members meet to decide questions of the leadership and then lapse into dormancy until, possibly, the next election. Another variant of party organization common in New Jersey is the old-style machine. This organization is generally characterized by a powerful chairman and a small core of notables, who monopolize control of the party. Committee members may be active and allegiant, but they are given little access to the decision-making process. Although such machine operations are more typical in older Democratic urban areas like New Brunswick, they still exist in some rural Republican strongholds like Somerset and Hunterdon counties.

At the state level, the party's representatives comprise persons from each county chosen in the state primary for a four-year term that runs concurrent with the governor's. The state committee is a loose organization that acts as a liaison between the twenty-one county units and the state party as well as between the state and the national party. Formerly, Title 19 mandated that each state committee should consist of one male and one female member from each county. A revision of the statutes in 1978 allows each party the option of basing representation to the state committee on county population instead. Presently, the Republican party retains the two per county rule, while the Democrats have opted to apportion membership on the committee on the basis of county population.

The organizational position of the state committee and state chairman might suggest a hierarchical structure in which the state committee enjoys considerable political influence, but the actual politics of the situation is quite different. New Jersey never has had strong state party organizations. Indeed, up until the recent past these committees did the bidding of powerful county chairmen. Since election to the state committee is determined by rank and file voters in the primary election and not by the party network, elected members to the committee are often considered outsiders in regular party circles. The state chair, although officially the choice of state committee members, is actually the pro forma representative of each party's gubernatorial candidate. Hence, the municipal and county party structure is relatively isolated from the state committee, and state committee members traditionally exercise very little influence on regular party affairs.

Of late, however, the state committees are playing a more prominent role in county, legislative, and local fundraising and campaigning and are beginning to emerge as more visible actors in party politics throughout the state.

Party People

Who are these people who support the party effort in New Jersey? Why do they give their time and energy? And perhaps most importantly, what do they accomplish? The diverse character of party organizations in the state is reflected in the diversity of the participants and the variety of their motives.

Although party workers generally reflect the demographic composition of their communities, they usually include a core of local notables—real estate and insurance brokers, attorneys, bankers, business people, and various elected municipal employees. In addition, other community activists, housewives, and politically-oriented students are likely to be committee members. Especially in older cities and towns, party activity can be a family tradition, as younger people become active in the party because their parents had been involved.

Why do they join? In most cases, they join for multiple and overlapping reasons. Probably the most common motives for party service, however, are social. Local parties in many municipalities are akin to other civic, service organizations in which like-minded folk with an interest in public issues can socialize and gossip about local politics. Social rewards include "inside dopester" status about political people and events in the town and county and participation in party socials and fundraising events. The distinct difference between parties and other civic associations, of course, is the political contest that occurs at election time. A member of Common Cause, for example, may occasionally garner a measure of satisfaction when a particular policy that the group supported is accepted. But for the regular party worker elections provide frequent, direct, and measurable opportunities for satisfaction. Indeed, most party people, as distinct from other civic-minded activists, relish the game or contest of elections where there are clear winners and losers.

Although social motives may be the most common denominator, prestige, influence, and ambition are also important to many party workers. Once they get a taste of party activity, many workers strive for increased influence. Loyal and active workers may be given more responsible assignments or positions. One common reward is a seat on the municipal party's screening committee, which recommends candidates for elective office.

Party work is also considered a prerequisite for elected office. An ambitious individual with an eye toward electoral politics will usually build a network of support through the party organization. Formerly, of course, party work was the only route to elected office; without the support of the organization, candidates stood little chance of success. While the current system is much more fluid in that some individuals are successful running for office outside the organization, access to most local, county, and legislative positions is still controlled by the party. Even if a given individual is initially successful outside the organization, party support becomes essential if that candidate wants to solidify a base of support and run for higher office. One party leader once described a popular and aspiring elected official in the following terms: "This fellow has a lot of potential; he could do our party a lot of good, but he always runs outside of the organization. I told him, if he wants to go any higher in this state, he should either join his own organization or take it over. Otherwise, we won't touch him." One can come up through the ranks, join the ranks, or take over the ranks, but at some point, integration into the organization is considered essential.[13]

Material incentives represent another motive for party work. The rich folklore about New Jersey's parties include stories about buckets of coal, turkey, and other foodstuffs, as well as cash advances for needy party workers. Certainly prominent among those rewards were extensive patronage positions that were at the disposal of local and county organizations. Those days are over. Nonetheless, there are still some material rewards for loyal members of the organization. Jobs remain a key incentive. As one county chairman noted, "I'm a full-time employment agency." Summer jobs for teenagers are made available to some municipal and county organizations. These jobs are sought after by party workers of all socio-economic strata. Even professional people with substantial incomes are likely to want summer jobs for their children. The party leader knows that "the money the kid will earn will probably finance a trip to Europe rather than college tuition, but what can I do?"[14]

Party access to full-time public jobs, however, is much more limited than it used to be; party workers are more likely to be rewarded with opportunities for economic gain in the private sector. Appointments to boards or commissions may enhance professional activity or visibility. "The party can promote the fortunes of lawyers who seek probate cases, of contractors eager to build public structures, of merchandisers who want to sell to government, of craftsmen who want to work on government projects, or of researchers who want a state grant."[15] Hence, while the folklore about party patronage may no longer strictly apply, material rewards still do play an important role in party service.

Ideology appears to be the least important motive for party service, at least at the local grassroots level. Although party workers are likely to hold views consistent with most other members of their party and view the political world from this perspective, particularly when considering broad state or national issues, internal organizational politics rarely involves ideological positions. Normally, local debate focuses on the quality of the schools, business development, ratables, taxes, and services. While concern about such questions might motivate a citizen to work for the party, rarely are these concerns partisan in nature. In this context, the adage that there is no Democrat or Republican way to clean a street seems to apply: organizational positions on most local issues reflect strategical rather than ideological concerns.

Party Functions

What do these people who work for the party accomplish? Again, following folklore about parties, the average citizen generally assumes that this invisible cadre of activists is made up of inept and self-interested individuals who promote corruption and inefficiency and deter good and fair government. Hence, the words "partisan" and "party politician" evoke negative connotations, reflecting the basic ambivalence most Americans feel about parties and their role in American politics. Even though a measure of self-interest, inefficiency, and corruption may characterize some aspects of party life in New Jersey, the fact remains that these organizations and workers do perform necessary functions in the political system.

As already noted, candidates for the vast majority of elected offices in the state are recruited and nominated through the party system. Most local council members, mayors, sheriffs, members of the freeholder boards, and state legislators are dependent on the party for a place on the ballot. Whether it be through a party screening committee, which endorses a given candidate, or through an open primary, in which party workers often staff campaigns, few candidates are successful without the support of an organization. Parties and their workers conduct and run the campaigns for these elected offices in both the primary and the general election. Especially in recent elections, party activists have also mounted extensive registration drives to bring new voters into the system. And party workers conduct fundraising campaigns usually around the primary and general election.

Party organizations also structure electoral choice by providing cues or labels for the voter. It would be unrealistic to expect that most voters would know much about the political experience or the issue positions of the vast array of candidates on the ballot. Most electoral choices depend on party cues: the voters make a reasonable choice on the basis of a partisan inclination toward one party or another. While this situation is less than a civic textbook ideal, parties do provide a measure of rationality to what otherwise would be a series of random choices.

Hence, party organizations and the cadre of activists that works for the party have a meaningful place in the electoral system. By recruiting and nominating candidates; by conducting local, county, and legislative campaigns; and by structuring electoral choices and debate, these organizations provide an institutionalized link between the individual voters and their elected representatives in government.

PARTY IN GOVERNMENT

The vast majority of elected representatives in New Jersey serving in office are members of one of the two major parties. This fact provides not only an essential coherence in the representative process but also an important principle of organization within government institutions at all levels, but particularly at the county, state, and national levels. Because the members of a political party share both common attitudes towards important policy issues and common loyalty to the party that supported their election efforts, they tend to stick together during all their government activities.

Freeholder boards are intensely partisan. These governing bodies, with operating budgets in the millions, administer a network of community services that include hospital and social services, the county courts, community colleges, vocational education programs, and parks and other recreational facilities. Seats on these boards are the party's route to political influence and patronage within the county. Elected representatives, mindful of their dependence on the party for nomination and election, generally operate on a strictly partisan basis. While the party position on any vote will reflect the tactical concerns of party leaders on substantive policy questions, this position will also reflect the needs and interests of the party's constituencies in the electorate.

Although state legislators now enjoy a measure of independence from local party organizations at the State House in Trenton, the basic operation of the legislature still remains structured around party. Certainly much of the partisan maneuvering in the legislature is strategic, as Democrats and Republicans jockey for power and influence in state affairs. (See Chapter 6.) Most legislators of a single party share a com-

mon political perspective on public policy questions, a like-minded-
ness that makes them tend to stick together on most public issues.
Moreover, since even individual legislators cannot be expected to be
current and expertly informed on all issue areas, they rely on the
party and its leadership in the legislature for cues that structure a
good deal of their voting. Party leadership in general over the past decade has become more stable and influential, particularly among
assembly Democrats; the party caucus has become an essential feature of legislative life.

Even the operation of the bureaucracy in Trenton exhibits a partisan cast (see Chapter 7). Although most employees are ostensibly removed from party influence by virtue of civil service, appointments
for upper level positions with any policy discretion are still made with
an eye toward the party leanings of the appointee. An ideal policy
level appointee should not only exhibit the appropriate professional
qualifications but also share the ideological perspective of the current
administration. Illustratively, during the Kean administration, one
highly qualified applicant who was to administer social service grants
had to repeatedly assure his interviewers that although he was a Democrat, he was "not one of those liberal types who would start spending
a lot of money."

Partisan maneuverings and conflicts are particularly evident
when the governor and the majority in the legislature are of different
parties. Hence, during Kean's first administration, the Democrats in
the legislature routinely faced off against the governor and the Republicans, especially on issues of taxes and spending (see Chapter 6).
Even mundane affairs are administered with an eye toward party.
During his tenure, Brendan Byrne announced that the summer jobs
program would be controlled by his office and administered on the
basis of partisan considerations. This policy was continued by his Republican successor. During the summer of 1982 (when youth unemployment was at an all time high) Kean announced that consideration for summer jobs would first be given to loyal Republicans and
their families.

THE FUTURE OF PARTY POLITICS

Parties in New Jersey are in transition. Although the political
changes of the past two decades have left the role of the party somewhat uncertain, parties are likely to remain an essential aspect of Garden State politics. While parties will never dominate the political life
of the state as they did in former years, party will continue to be im-

portant both for the electorate and for the organizational structure of the political system.

At least in the near future, voters in New Jersey are likely to retain their attachments to the two major parties. Although party loyalty may never be as strong as it was during the New Deal era, the movement away from the parties appears to have bottomed out. Since 1976 the number of Independents at the state and national levels has steadily declined. State and national polls also indicate an increase in the number of Republican identifiers. To what extent the current influence of a popular Republican president and governor will affect the long-term fortunes of the Republicans in New Jersey, however, remains to be seen. In any case, although media and personality will continue to play an increasingly significant role, especially in statewide and congressional races, party cues are sure to remain an essential ingredient in most voters' views about politics.

Increasingly competitive environments should assure that party organizations continue to enjoy a measure of growth and regeneration; these organizations will remain the key to local and county nomination and election. Party organizations are also likely to experience a measure of integration and centralization in that the state parties are becoming increasingly important actors in the electoral process. State conventions, held annually by each party, are taking on added importance, attracting candidates, elected officials, and party workers from every level of government. In addition to adopting a platform that consolidates the party's position on key issues, the conventions now spend considerable time dispensing campaign and fundraising techniques to party workers. For example, the 1985 Democratic convention ran a series of policy and campaign workshops, which were enthusiastically received by every strata of the party membership. As campaign techniques become more sophisticated and fundraising needs more extensive, the state committee will assume an even more central role in legislative as well as local races. Finally, proposals for giving pre-primary endorsements at the state conventions are now being considered and, if adopted, would give the state committee additional clout and visibility.

Given these trends, it is unlikely that partisanship in government will diminish. Although questions of public policy may become increasingly complex, action and debate on most public questions will still reflect, in broad terms, partisan positions of Democrats and Republicans—especially when the subject is budget and taxes, social services, business growth, or the *Mt. Laurel* court decisions. While the era of party dominance in New Jersey clearly has passed, the party is not over.

Notes

1. Richard McCormick, "An Historical Overview," in *Politics in New Jersey*, rev. ed. Richard Lehne and Alan Rosenthal, eds. (New Brunswick: Eagleton Institute of Politics, 1979), 1.

2. *Ibid.*, 8.

3. William E. Sackett, *Modern Battles of Trenton* (Trenton, N.J.: J.L. Murphy, 1895), 305.

4. McCormick, "An Historical Overview," 12–15.

5. Sackett, *Modern Battles of Trenton*, 292.

6. Maureen Moakley, "New Jersey", in *The Political Life of the American States*, Alan Rosenthal and Maureen Moakley, eds., (New York: Praeger, 1984), 234.

7. Duane Lockard, *The New Jersey Governor: A Study in Political Power* (Princeton: D. Van Nostrand Company, Inc., 1964), 89-93.

8. Stanley Friedelbaum, "Constitutional Law and Judicial Policy Making," in *Politics in New Jersey*, 212.

9. Moakley, "New Jersey," 273.

10. Alan Rosenthal, "Dimensions of Partisanship: Exploring Legislative Parties in the States" (Draft paper, Rutgers University, April 1984).

11. Data from Eagleton Poll, May 1984.

12. Kenneth Gibson, et al., "Whither the Local Parties?: A Cross-Sectional and Longitudinal Analysis of the Strength of Party Organizations" (Paper delivered at the Western Political Science Association meeting, March 1982).

13. Maureen Moakley and Gerald Pomper, "Party Organizations" in *Politics in New Jersey*, 100-101.

14. *Ibid.*, 104.

15. *Ibid.*

FIGURE 4.1. THE POLITICAL MAP OF NEW JERSEY

Districts are classified on the basis of average vote for State Assembly
from 1979 to 1985. The ten Competitive districts had an average Democratic vote between 42.5% and 57.5%; 15 Republican districts an average
Democratic vote below 42.5%; and 15 Democratic districts an average
Democratic vote above 57.5%.

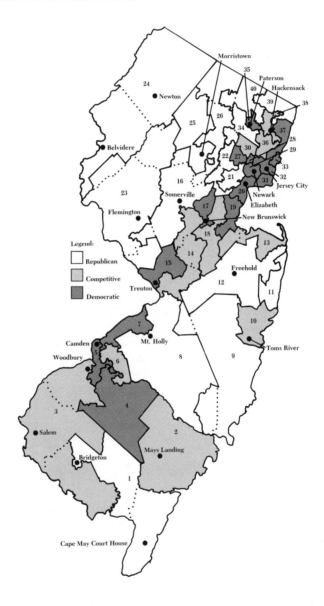

4

STEPHEN A. SALMORE

Voting, Elections, and Campaigns

Elections in New Jersey, as in most states, reflect both local and national factors. Periodically tides sweep the country, altering not only the balance of partisan forces but the very nature of elections and campaigns. Local variations due to economic, demographic, or historic differences, however, can alter or mute the effects of these national tides. In addition, localities have acted, with varying degrees of success, to blunt or deflect the impact of national forces. The net result is an electoral process that, while basically similar across the country, varies significantly from state to state. This chapter first describes national changes and trends, and then discusses the changing nature of electoral politics in New Jersey, away from party-based politics towards candidate-centered politics.

NATIONAL TRENDS IN ELECTIONS AND CAMPAIGNS

The national elections of 1980 and 1984 may have signalled a change in the broad patterns of American politics, patterns that for the last half century have remained fairly constant. Between 1928 and the electoral landslide of 1936, the Democratic Party, led by Franklin Roosevelt, became the majority party in the country. Under the banner of the New Deal Roosevelt forged a coalition that united urban, ethnic, blue-collar voters in the North with the historically Democratic voters in the South. In most parts of the country this coalition regularly prevailed over rural, small town, and Protestant Republicans. During the fifty years following the inception of the New Deal, the Democrats almost always controlled the House of Representatives and, until 1981, the U.S. Senate as well. At the presidential level, Republican successes came only when the party ran personally popular and attractive candidates or faced particularly weak and unattractive opponents. However, the Democrats' general success nationally since the 1930s has not always translated into state and local victories. Although the Democrats elected a majority of the governors and state legislators during this period, there remained many places where the New Deal coalition was in the minority and Republicans usually prevailed. In fact, until the last twenty years, most of the country was divided between Democratic and Republican dominated areas with relatively few jurisdictions exhibiting close and continuing competition between the two parties.

For much of this period, politics and elections can best be described as party dominated. Most voters identified with one of the parties. For most people partisan attachment developed early and rarely changed. Only in unusual circumstances would partisans stray from the fold and vote for the opposition. Concentrations of strong partisans provided the foundation for strong local party organizations. In urban areas, Democratic political machines maintained a tight control over most city governments by mobilizing the faithful on election day and providing rewards to their supporters in the forms of material and emotional satisfactions and personal access to government. In rural areas, Republicans maintained a somewhat looser, but just as effective, control over county governments. Whether a state tended to be Democratic or Republican was largely determined by the balance of urban and rural forces and the strength of party loyalty.[1]

In order to maintain control of their respective areas, local party organizations controlled most aspects of the electoral process. They selected the candidates, organized their campaigns, turned out to vote on election day, and often were instrumental even in determining ballot position and counting the votes through their informal control of boards of elections. In return, parties expected loyalty from the public officials they helped elect, and usually they received it. Only in exceptional cases could politicians maintain their hold on elective office without the active support of their party. (See Chapter 3 for a discussion of how this process occurred in New Jersey.)

This party-dominated electoral system depended both on most voters choosing the party rather than the specific candidate and on the concentration of each party's supporters in different geographical areas. These conditions started to break down, however, as a result of social and demographic changes that began after the end of World War II.

Although these changes were many and varied, two important and somewhat related ones bear mention here: the growing suburbanization of the country, and a decline in voter turnout that has persisted since 1960. Suburbanization weakened party organizations in several ways. Democratic city organizations were hurt as their adherents moved to the suburbs. Most former urban residents retained their party affiliations, but did not become part of the local organizations in their new suburban hometowns, which often had at least nominally nonpartisan governments. On the other hand, the increasing numbers of exurbanites weakened what were once largely rural-based Republican county organizations. The net result was an increase in self-styled independents and in ticket-splitting.

At the same time, voter turnout fell. This decline had many causes, but it was at least partially related to the reduced impact of party loyalty, which had given more reason to vote, and to greater mobility, which now made it more complicated for voters to register. As a result of these trends, parties had less control and fewer people to influence. Candidates could count less on party-based voting and also less on the ability of the party organizations to produce on election day. Through necessity, they began to devise new ways of communicating with, and persuading, the voters—television, radio, direct mail, and so on.

First used extensively in presidential campaigns, these media techniques soon penetrated to lower-level elections. Such changes mark the shift from party-centered to candidate-centered campaigns; candidates could now do for themselves what they had relied on the party to do. As candidates became more autonomous, they increasingly appealed to the electorate in personal rather than partisan terms. These appeals in turn were more effective as the electorate itself became less partisan and more independent.

The effects of this shifting emphasis in the conduct of elections— from party to candidate—can be seen most strikingly at the presidential level. Republican candidates have succeeded by running image campaigns, while Democrats have lost by trying to retain the New Deal coalition. Below the presidential level, the effect has been to decrease the number of areas of complete dominance by one party. Increasingly, candidates win in hostile territory by making personal, nonpartisan appeals directly to voters. While Democratic dominance continues below the presidential level, there is a great increase in voter volatility and a decline in the influence of party organizations.

DEVELOPMENT OF ELECTORAL POLITICS IN NEW JERSEY

These changes did not occur uniformly throughout the country or evenly across different levels of office. Historically, New Jersey has responded to national trends imperfectly and sluggishly. Part of the reason is that New Jersey differs from the country demographically; part of the reason is that certain features of the state's political system have been obstacles to change, indeed were sometimes deliberately designed to blunt the impact of national trends on the state.

In analyzing electoral politics in New Jersey, it is useful to divide the time between the New Deal realignment and the present into three periods. The first, through the end of World War II, was a period of consolidation. The second, from the end of the war to the middle of the 1970s, was a transitional period, during which certain fundamental changes began to occur but were not fully realized. The third period, the mid-1970s to today, is the era of candidate-centered campaigns. The timing of these stages has been different in New Jersey from the rest of the country, mainly in the longer time the transition has taken in this state. Factors peculiar to New Jersey have retarded change, factors such as its media situation, its electoral structure, and its election calendar. New Jersey until 1984 was one of only two states in the nation without a commercial television station within its borders, and it still has no network outlet based in the state. This deficiency has made it more difficult for politicians to become known to the state's citizens (see Chapter 1). Additionally, the county-based system of representation and the schedule for electing the state legislators and governor have served to insulate state politics from national politics to an extraordinary degree.

THE ROOSEVELT ERA

The New Deal alignment was slow in fully establishing itself in New Jersey. As seen in Figure 4.2, the state's Democratic vote for president during the Roosevelt era peaked in 1940, but remained consistently behind the national vote. Moreover, aside from 1964, New Jersey has remained less Democratic than the nation in presidential elections to the present day, with the gap widening again after 1976.

Congressional voting shows a similar pattern. By and large the state has followed national swings, but lagged behind the national Democratic performance—particularly during the Roosevelt era and the

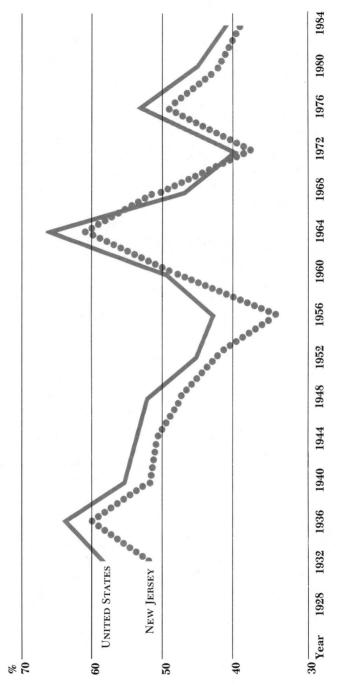

FIGURE 4.2. THE DEMOCRATIC VOTE FOR PRESIDENT, 1932–1984 (AS A PERCENTAGE OF THE TWO-PARTY VOTE)

Democratic Vote for President

years immediately following it. In more recent elections, Democratic congressional incumbents have done well in the off-years when they did not have to contend with an increasingly Republican presidential vote.

While the Democrats did not establish themselves as a majority party during the 1930s and 1940s, the state did sort itself out along the lines of the New Deal alignment in terms of Democratic and Republican areas of strength. Anchored in Hudson County, Democratic strength was to be found in the line of urban counties running from Hudson to Mercer. Republican strength was in the rural counties on either side, particularly in the northwest and along the shore. Overall, however, the state remained about 5 percent more Republican than the rest of the country, because of the narrow base of the Democratic party: the Democrats controlled the cities, but the six major cities in New Jersey contained only 30 percent of the population during this period (see Chapter 2).

Although the Democrats during the Roosevelt era could usually mount a competitive campaign in statewide contests, the Republicans nevertheless continued to dominate the state legislature, the governor's office, and the congressional delegation. This pattern reflected, in addition to demographics, the insulated electoral structure of the state. The timing of elections for governor every three years, for example, meant that these important elections coincided with the presidential election only once every twelve years. The gubernatorial election of 1940 (a presidential election year) produced one of only two Democratic victories in all the governors' races between 1934 and 1949.

A more serious impediment to Democratic success below the statewide level was the use of counties as the basic unit in creating electoral districts for the Legislature and Congress. The effect was most pronounced in the state senate, which was comprised of one senator from each county, regardless of population. Since Democratic strength was confined to relatively few, mostly urban counties, the Republicans were, in essence, ceded a majority of the legislative and congressional seats. The distribution of party strength by county also meant that the Democrats had to win approximately 60 percent of the total vote to gain only half the seats in the state assembly; control of the senate was entirely beyond reach.

In sum, in statewide races, there were sufficient Democratic votes for the party to be competitive. Below the statewide level, however, since they controlled a majority of the counties, the Republicans won most of the elections for legislature and congress. This pattern of competition between one-party areas both reflected the national pattern and made the state peculiarly resistant to Democratic gains. Without regular prospects of winning in the majority of Republican-dominated counties, the Democratic party was unable to build an organization and, therefore, was not in a position to mobilize its limited supporters effectively. Party competition took place *between* areas of one party dominance, not *within* them. Elections reflected a rigid division of the state between the two parties that strongly favored the Republicans.

THE TRANSITION PERIOD

The second period, from 1947 to the middle of the 1970s, marked a transition from rigid party politics to more fluid competition. Democratic strength increased and spread as Republican strength weakened. During this period the strength of the parties also declined due to demographic changes and reforms in the system of representation. The full impact of these changes, however, did not develop until the 1970s; only then did the accumulation of demographic and legal changes overwhelm the ability of the parties to control the electoral process.

Demography

The rapid growth of the suburbs following World War II was particularly strong in New Jersey. The years from the end of the war through the mid-60s marked a rapid increase in population, almost all of it in the suburban areas between the Democratic cities and the Republican rural areas. The new suburbanites often brought their party loyalties with them and, since they came from cities, these were often Democratic. Thus, although the growth of the suburbs extended Democratic influence beyond the city limits, these new residents proved to be less intense partisans and much more independent in their voting patterns.

Surveys of voters during this period (see Table 4.1) demonstrated that New Jersey voters were much more likely to be independent than voters in the rest of the United States. Since 1972, the percentage of voters calling themselves independents has ranged from five to eight points higher in New Jersey than in the country as a whole.

Beginning in the fifties, these changes facilitated growing Democratic success in state level races. Democrats won every gubernatorial election from 1953 to 1965, for instance, and increased their strength in the legislature, even taking control for brief periods. (See Figure 4.3.) In the presidential elections, the state's Republican tilt also

TABLE 4.1   PARTY IDENTIFICATION 1972-1984
(as percentage of total population)

	1972	1976	1980	1984
New Jersey				
Democrat	29	34	35	30
Independent	42	43	39	38
Republican	25	18	23	26
Don't Know	4	5	3	5
United States				
Democrat	40	40	41	48
Independent	35	36	34	30
Republican	23	23	23	28
Don't Know	2	1	2	5

SOURCE: for New Jersey: Eagleton Poll, Rutgers University, for United States: 1972-1980, NES/CPS Surveys, University of Michigan 1984, CBS/ N.Y. Times Poll.

abated, largely because of John Kennedy's popularity among the large Catholic population in 1960 and the strong rejection of Republican candidate Barry Goldwater in 1964. Republicans continued to do well at the congressional level, however. The nature of the state's population (affluent, conservative, Catholic) also made for a state Democratic party whose leaders tended to be more moderate in ideological tone than the national party. The success of the party in this transitional era depended upon success in attracting the moderate, independent vote of the suburbs, not upon the more liberal voters of the shrinking cities.

The Electoral System

The full impact of these demographic changes was not felt immediately because of the state's electoral structure. The 1947 state constitution changed the term of the governor and state senators to four years and of assembly members to two years. State elections were to be held only in odd-numbered years, when no federal elections were being contested. The new charter preserved the county basis of representation, thus continuing the bias towards the more rural and Republican areas of the state. However, in a series of court decisions between the mid 1960s and the early 1970s, this county bias was overturned as violating the principle of one person, one vote.[2] By the end of the transitional period, in the mid-1970s, both legislative and congressional district lines had been drawn without regard for county.

FIGURE 4.3. THE DEMOCRATIC VOTE FOR GOVERNOR AND ASSEMBLY MEMBERS, 1930–1983
(AS A PERCENTAGE OF THE TWO-PARTY VOTE)

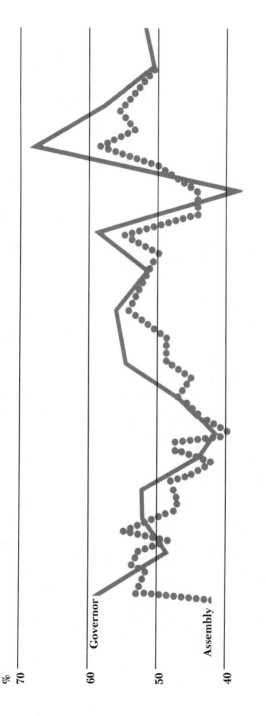

The political significance of this change was twofold. Rather than the county parties naming candidates, candidates had to put together a coalition of party activists in a number of counties. Additionally, because these changes in the system of representation did not occur until the late 1960s, the main beneficiaries were the suburbs, not the urban areas that earlier had been underrepresented. By 1970, the six large cities in the state had lost half their 1930 population and provided only 11 percent of the statewide vote.

Decline of County Organizations

These changes generally weakened the county-based party organizations (see Chapter 3). The decline in the parties' base is indicated by the decline in participation in party primaries. During the Roosevelt period, before the court-ordered changes, turnout in primaries generally was close to 30 percent of eligible voters. By 1952, it had dropped into the 20 percent range, where it has remained ever since. Primary voting turnout during this period also illustrates the decline in Republican strength and relative Democratic gain. In the Roosevelt era, Republican primary turnout was consistently higher than Democratic; however, in the mid-1950s, the turnout for both parties became virtually equal.

Turnout in primaries for the highest state office—governor—has been lower in New Jersey than in almost all states which have had contested gubernatorial primaries. Between 1951 and 1982, the percentage of the eligible population voting in gubernatorial primaries in New Jersey was 17 percent, barely more than half the national average of 30 percent. This primary vote represented only 37 percent of the general election vote compared to 57 percent in the nation generally.[3] These figures show that most New Jerseyans stayed out of the primaries, thereby restricting the mass base of the state parties.

Another indication of the decline of party organizations can be seen in the rise in the number of contested primaries in both parties during this period. In the period from 1949 to 1973, five of the seven Democratic primaries for governor were contested, as compared to none in the years from 1933 and 1946. The number of Republican primary contests for statewide office also more than doubled during the transitional period. These increases illustrate the inability of the party organizations to retain control of the nomination process.

By the end of the transition era, party competition had spread and elections had became more competitive (see Table 4.2). During the transition era, as compared with the earlier one, the number of Democratic counties increased from two to five; the number of competitive

TABLE 4.2   PARTISAN ALIGNMENT OF NEW JERSEY COUNTIES, 1927-1983 (by Democratic percentage of the vote)

		1927-1947		
Strong Republican	*Republican*	*Competitive*	*Democrat*	*Strong Democrat*
(<40%)	(40-44%)	(45-55%)	(56-60%)	(>60%)
Atlantic	Camden	Hunterdon	Middlesex	Hudson
Bergen	Essex	Mercer		
Burlington	Monmouth	Warren		
Cape May	Passaic			
Cumberland	Salem			
Gloucester	Sussex			
Morris	Union			
Ocean				
Somerset				

		1949-1973		
Strong Republican	*Republican*	*Competitive*	*Democrat*	*Strong Democrat*
(<40%)	(40-44%)	(45-55%)	(56-60%)	(>60%)
Atlantic	Bergen	Burlington	Mercer	Hudson
Cape May	Essex	Camden	Salem	Middlesex
Morris	Hunterdon	Cumberland	Warren	
Ocean	Monmouth	Gloucester		
Somerset	Sussex	Passaic		
		Union		

		1975-1983		
Strong Republican	*Republican*	*Competitive*	*Democrat*	*Strong Democrat*
(<40%)	(40-44%)	(45-55%)	(56-60%)	(>60%)
Cape May	Somerset	Atlantic	Camden	Hudson
Hunterdon		Bergen	Essex	Middlesex
Morris		Burlington	Gloucester	Salem
Sussex		Cumberland	Mercer	
Warren		Monmouth		
		Ocean		
		Passaic		
		Union		

NOTE: The counties were classified according to the average Democratic vote cast in the elections for the General Assembly during each time period.

counties increased from three to six; and the number of safe Republican counties fell from sixteen to ten. The average county Democratic vote for assembly increased from 42 percent to 46 percent within the competitive counties. Party competition matched the increased voter volatility, as measured by the changes in party shares from one election to the next. In the presidential vote, this volatility rose from 5 to 9 percent, although the volatility of the gubernatorial vote remained at around 4 percent during both the first and second periods, reflecting the way the electoral system helped insulate the state from national trends.

THE CANDIDATE-CENTERED PERIOD

The weakening of the party organizations has resulted in the emergence of candidate-centered campaigns during the last ten years. Parties are no longer able to control the electoral process. Voters have became increasingly independent. They are much more likely to split their tickets between parties in both presidential and congressional elections. (See Table 4.3). Whereas the ticket-splitting in these elections was around 5 percent through 1960, it more than doubled in 1964, and has generally remained at the 10 percent level for the past twenty years.

This trend toward a candidate-dominated, rather than party-dominated, electoral process has occurred within the context of steadily declining voter turnout. (See Figure 4.4.)

The presidential vote in New Jersey, (which is of the least concern to the state parties since it is the election in which they are least involved) has always been higher in New Jersey than in the nation generally. The state has followed the national pattern of long-term decline in turnout since 1960. However, in the last twenty years, the state-national gap has narrowed significantly. This appears to be due to the nation becoming more like the state, rather than the other way around. As the differences among all states in education and affluence have diminished, party competition has grown, and more states provide liberal access to the polls.

In the elections for state offices—governor and the legislature —the decline in turnout has been more precipitous than in presidential and congressional elections. This decline is especially notable in state legislative races. In fact, except in these races, there have been some indications that in the last few years the drop in turnout may be abating.

TABLE 4.3   SPLIT TICKET VOTING IN NEW JERSEY, 1932-1984

Year	Percentage of voters splitting ticket
1932	2.6
1936	6.2
1940	5.4
1944	5.1
1948	3.0
1952	4.0
1956	7.3
1960	3.7
1964	11.9
1968	7.1
1972	11.5
1976	10.5
1980	12.3
1984	13.0

NOTE: The figures represent the difference between the number of votes cast for president and for congressional representative in each county, totalled for all counties, and expressed as a percentage of the total state vote for representative. These figures seriously *under*estimate the amount of actual ticket-splitting since they do not take into account ticket-splitting for offices other than president and representative and are based on county averages rather than data about individual voters. Data for a more precise measure are not available over this time period.

Increased Party Competition

The trend toward greater Democratic strength has continued in this period. After 1975, using vote for assembly as a measure, the number of Democratic counties increased from five to seven, competitive counties increased from six to eight, and Republican counties declined from ten to six. As might be expected Democratic strongholds were the urban areas that crossed the state diagonally from northeast to southwest. Republican strength was in the northwest, led by Morris and Hunterdon counties. The rest of the state was competitive. Bergen County, the shore counties, and much of the south were no longer safely Republican, but rather competitive.

County totals mask variations that emerged, particularly in the large urban counties. While still Democratic overall, counties such as Essex, Mercer, and Camden were developing strongly Republican suburban areas. The average Democratic county vote of 50 percent in

FIGURE 4.4. VOTING TURNOUT IN NEW JERSEY, 1930–1984
(AS A PERCENTAGE OF ELIGIBLE VOTERS WHO VOTE IN GENERAL ELECTIONS)

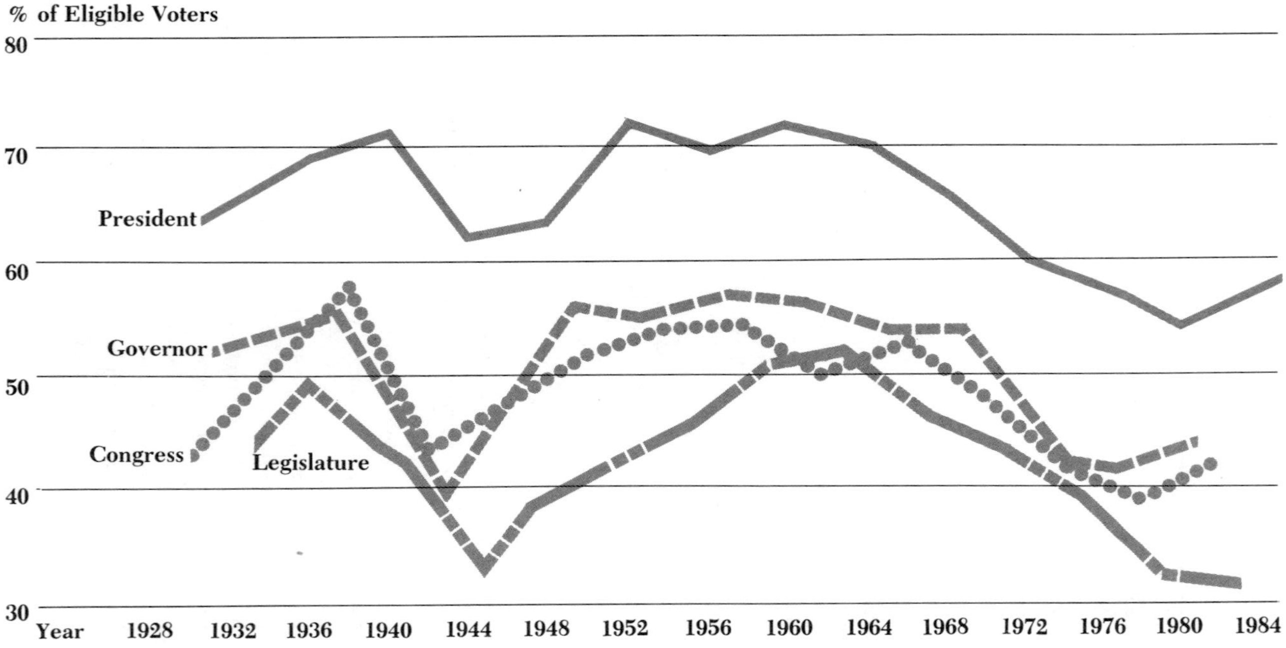

a given election understated the overall Democratic advantage. During this period the Democrats won a majority of statewide elections and continuously controlled both houses of the legislature and the congressional delegation. In presidential elections, however, New Jersey continued to be more Republican than the rest of the country.

Decline of Party Influence

The greater independence of New Jersey voters has continued. Furthermore, the volatility in presidential elections has spread, with a vengeance, to gubernatorial elections. The average change in party share of the vote from one election to the next exceeded 14 percent. Volatility in presidential elections also has continued to increase, exceeding comparable results for the nation as a whole. A vivid example of how the volatility of voters and the staggering of state and national elections can result in dramatic shifts in the political fortunes of the two parties can be seen in the sharply different election results of 1972 and 1973. In 1972, Republican Richard Nixon defeated Democrat George McGovern for President by 63 percent to 37 percent. Just one year later, Democrat Brendan Byrne swamped Republican Charles Sandman in the election for governor 68 percent to 32 percent.

The continued decline in the strength of the parties in New Jersey can best be seen in their complete loss of control of the nominating process for both governor and senator. Contested primaries have become the rule for both parties, and the number of serious contestants in primaries has mushroomed. The nomination of Brendan Byrne in 1973 represented the last time that county party leaders were able to unite on a candidate and enforce that choice in a primary election. In competitive congressional districts, primaries have also become more frequent, although the Hudson County organization was still able, as late as 1976, to force an incumbent congressman to step down by denying him the party's endorsement.

Faced with this situation, candidates have developed their own campaign strategies in order to appeal directly to voters, rather than depend on parties to organize and run their campaigns. This change occurred first at the gubernatorial level but has quickly spread downward. The high cost of communicating with voters in New Jersey, particularly through television, however, has made it difficult for the new campaign technology to spread much below the congressional level. The result has been a two-tiered system of elections. On the top level, particularly among statewide candidates, elections are fought out between individual candidates who are supported by their personal organizations; the party plays a distinctly secondary role. This has become true even in strongly contested congressional elections. For instance, in 1982, Democratic Representative Jim Howard, in the general election, and Republican Representative Jim Courter, in a primary election each spent over half a million dollars on professional media and organizational consultants, professionally produced direct mail, and professional paid telephone banks.

On the lower level of this two-tiered system are local, county, and most legislative elections. The party continues to dominate the electoral process in these elections because it is just too expensive to create a campaign that can replace the local party organization at this level.

CAMPAIGNING IN NEW JERSEY

MEDIA

New Jersey electoral politics is now centered on candidates and not parties. Beginning with the gubernatorial campaign of 1977, politicians discovered that they could bypass parties and appeal directly to the electorate through extensive use of television and radio. Before 1977, the common political wisdom had been that television was too expensive to use in New Jersey. Since the state had no commercial television stations of its own that reached a significant portion of the voters, television time had to be bought on New York City and Philadelphia stations—the first and fourth most expensive media markets in the country. Buying time on these stations was not only costly, but thought to be inefficient, since only a third of the viewers of these stations live in New Jersey.

In 1977, however, Governor Brendan Byrne realized that if he was to be renominated he had to win the primary on his own: he could not count on effective party support. Television out of New York and Philadelphia was expensive, but it was his only option. Running a series of ads designed by David Garth, he turned the liability of being identified with the new state income tax into an asset. Byrne won the multi-candidate primary with just 30 percent of the total vote. He went on to win the general election by the wide margin of 57 percent to 37 percent. From then on, politicians recognized that effective statewide campaigns would require the use of television.

Spending in the three gubernatorial races between 1973 and 1981 provides dramatic evidence of the rapid escalation of mass media usage in campaigns. In 1973, the successful candidate devoted 55 percent of his total spending on communications, both over-the-air and printed; 36 percent of this spending was on radio and television. By

1981, 75 percent of the successful candidate's total budget was devoted to communications, and 61 percent of this money was spent on radio and television. In both 1973 and 1977, the losing candidates devoted similar proportions of their campaign budgets to communications. Between 1973 and 1981, the actual number of dollars spent on communications by the gubernatorial candidates of both parties tripled, rising from approximately $1.2 million to $3.6 million, despite the fact that after 1977 total expenditures were capped by public financing legislation. This 300 percent increase obviously greatly outstripped inflation.

While television is expensive to use in New Jersey, it is also effective. New Jersey voters, precisely because they are forced to rely on out-of-state media for their news, know relatively little about the state, its problems, and its political leaders (see Chapter 1). By placing messages on television candidates can both reach the voters and provide them with a relatively large proportion of their information about the election. Since so many voters are independents and ticket-splitters, this information becomes the principal basis of their vote. The local party organizations are simply not able to compete with television in delivering useful information to voters. The net result is a much more fluid and volatile politics, based more on a perception of candidates that the candidates themselves mold than on underlying partisan loyalties.

INCUMBENCY

With party declining as a voting cue, incumbency has risen in importance. In an environment where voters know relatively little about politics and politicians, incumbents are in a good position to provide voters with positive information about themselves. To the extent that the media—both printed and electronic—cover New Jersey politics, they cover incumbents. Incumbents can also use the power of their office to provide positive impressions about themselves to voters. Unless challengers have the resources to match this built-in advantage that incumbents have, they are doomed to defeat.

Incumbency in New Jersey, however, can be a double-edged sword, as seen in a comparison of the 1982 and 1984 senate races. In 1984, Democrat Bill Bradley coasted to an easy victory over Republican Mary Mochary, despite clear evidence that the public knew relatively little about him. In October, shortly before the election, the Eagleton Poll found that 53 percent of the state's population either admitted knowing little or nothing about Bradley or could offer no opinion about him. His opponent, however, with only limited funds, was unable to mount an effective campaign that could educate the voters about Bradley and herself. While 53 percent may have known little about the Democratic incumbent, fully 92 percent said they knew little or nothing about Mochary.[4]

On the other hand, in 1982, Republican Representative Millicent Fenwick, running essentially as an incumbent, was also initially much better known than her Democratic opponent, Frank Lautenberg—a businessman who had never before sought elective office. However, by effectively spending large amounts of money, mostly his own, the Democratic newcomer was able to define himself positively to the public, change the perceptions of Fenwick, and eventually achieve recognition by 90 percent of the electorate. The lesson is that incumbents may start with a tremendous advantage in New Jersey because they are the only figures the public knows anything at all about, and this often frightens off possible strong challengers. However, incumbents are not as well known in New Jersey as they are in other states, so a well funded challenge can very quickly nullify the incumbent's advantage. The result is even more potential volatility in future elections.

CAMPAIGN COSTS

Candidate-centered campaigns mean that the cost of campaigning has risen dramatically. Not only is television expensive, but so are the other trappings of this style of campaigning—consultants, polling, direct mail, telephone banks, and so on. This increasing cost can be seen at all levels (see Table 4.4). Between 1972 and 1983 the doubling of costs in gubernatorial races, which have been limited by the public financing law since 1977, is dwarfed by the uncontrolled increases for other offices—expenditures about forty times greater for U.S. Senate races, seven times greater for congressional races, and, in the five-year period for which there are figures, more than twice as great for assembly races. Candidates for the U.S. Senate, who were spending just $.07 per vote in 1972, were investing $3.61 per voter ten years later; congressional candidate spending per vote rose from $.45 to $3.09 in the same period. Spending was not much lower for the much smaller constituencies of state assembly candidates, who were investing $2.66 per voter by 1983.

The increase in the cost of campaigning was so sharp, and so alarming to politicians, that public funding of gubernatorial campaigns was instituted in 1977 for both general elections and primaries. In some ways, the state campaign financing system was more generous than the comparable federal program for financing presidential elections.

Once a primary candidate had raised $50,000, he or she is eligible to receive two public dollars for every one dollar raised privately, up to a maximum in 1981 of about $600,000. In the 1981 general election, the two candidates were each limited to spending about $2.1 million, of which half was public funding.

The availability of public monies has changed the way campaigns are conducted. Candidates are no longer dependent on the party for fundraising; and with public monies available, they are less likely to make deals with other candidates. As long as public monies go directly to the candidates, the trend toward candidate-centered campaigns and the declining role of parties is exacerbated. Indeed, the fact that public financing bypasses the parties is testament to their relatively weak position.

Spending in congressional races more than quadrupled between 1972 and 1982 in both New Jersey and the nation. Although New Jersey candidates started out behind the national campaign spending average at the beginning of this period, their spending outstripped both average national increases and total expenditures by the end of it. One notable, persistent difference between New Jersey and the nation is that, nationally, Republican candidates have always spent more on the average than Democratic candidates. In New Jersey it has been just the reverse. The GOP is the smaller spending party. This is largely because the incumbent congressional delegation has been dominated by powerful Democrats—including several senior committee and subcommittee chairpersons—who can attract large amounts of money from political action committees (PACs). In closely contested races, these increased expenditures have mostly gone for the classic elements of the candidate-centered campaign—polling, broadcast advertising, direct mail, and paid telephone banks—all sponsored and directed by the candidate, and not by the state and local parties.

THE NEW ROLE OF PARTIES

Candidate-centered campaigning has made only very limited inroads below the congressional level. The smaller the constituency, the more difficult it is to raise the large sums necessary, and the harder it is to use modern communications techniques. At the local and county level, the party remains the most accessible vehicle for mounting campaigns, and it continues to play an important role in selecting and electing candidates at this level. Indeed, there are some signs that the county organizations are beginning to finance modern media campaigns for local and county candidates. For example, in Bergen

TABLE 4.4 CAMPAIGN SPENDING BY OFFICE, 1972-1983

Year	Senate (U.S.)			Governor			Congress			Assembly		
	Total Spent (×000)	Total Vote (×000)	$'s per Vote	Total Spent (×000)	Total Vote (×000)	$'s per Vote	Total Spent (×000)	Total Vote (×000)	$'s per Vote	Total Spent (×000)	Total Vote (×000)	$'s per Vote
1972	$191	2,707	$.07				$1,274	2,832	$.45			
1973				$2,151	2,091	$1.03						
1974							$1,835	2,084	$.88			
1975												
1976	$684	2,736	$.25				$1,719	2,811	$.61			
1977				$3,309	2,073	$1.60				$2,138	1,986	$1.08
1978	$3,107	1,927	$1.61				$2,450	1,934	$1.27			
1979										$2,993	1,574	$1.90

Year	Senate (U.S.) Total Spent (×000)	Senate (U.S.) Total Vote (×000)	Senate (U.S.) $'s per Vote	Governor Total Spent (×000)	Governor Total Vote (×000)	Governor $'s per Vote	Congress Total Spent (×000)	Congress Total Vote (×000)	Congress $'s per Vote	Assembly Total Spent (×000)	Assembly Total Vote (×000)	Assembly $'s per Vote
1980							$3,876	2,741	1.41			
1981				$4,742	2,290	$2.07				$4,609	2,090	$2.21
1982	$7,810	2,165	$3.61				$6,634	2,146	$3.09			
1983										$4,255	1,602	$2.66

SOURCES: for Senate and Congress: 1972—from Common Cause as reported in Michael Barone, et al., *The Almanac of American Politics, 1976* (New York: E. P. Dutton, 1975); 1974, 1976—from the Federal Election Commission as reported in Michael Barone, et al., *The Almanac of American Politics, 1978* (New York: E. P. Dutton, 1977); 1978, 1980—from the Federal Election Commission as reported in Michael Barone and Grant Ujifisa, *The Almanac of American Politics, 1982* (Washingtin, D.C.: Barone & Company, 1981); 1982, 1984—from the Federal Election Commission as reported in Michael Barone and Grant Ujifisa, *The Almanac of American Politics, 1986* (Washington, D.C.: National Journal, 1985).

For Governor: 1973, 1977—New Jersey Election Law Enforcement Commission, *Public Financing in New Jersey: The 1977 General Election for Governor* (August 1978); 1981—New Jersey Election Law Enforcement Commission, *New Jersey Public Financing: The 1981 Gubernatorial Elections* (June 1982).

For the General Assembly: 1977, 1979, 1981, 1983—New Jersey Election Law Enforcement Commission, *New Jersey Campaign Financing: 1983 Legislative General Election* (January 1985).

County in 1983, the county Democratic party hired media consultants to work for the freeholder ticket, and even ran some television advertising for them on New York stations. In response, in 1984, the Bergen county Republican party not only financed media advertising and heavy direct mail, but also paid for sophisticated polling for its freeholder candidates.

In the legislative races, the state parties are redefining their roles to become brokers for the consulting services needed for modern campaigns. The increase in their role between 1977 and 1983 is evident particularly in campaign financing, as the parties have provided growing proportions of the total spending on legislative races. In the especially critical 1981 race, when legislative control meant control over congressional redistricting plans, both parties contributed amounts approaching or exceeding half of all monies spent. After 1982, Democratic party spending declined to 22 percent of all expenditures, due to the increased difficulty in raising state party funds after losing control of the governorship. This loss was only partly replaced by contributions from Democratic congressional incumbents concerned about the 1981-1983 redistricting battle, and funds raised by committees supporting powerful individual Democratic state legislators. In the case of the Republicans, party aid also declined but still remained at 42 percent of the total, because of decreased support by the Republican National Committee, which had spent heavily in 1981 to support the Republican gubernatorial candidate. In both the 1981 and 1983 legislative elections, the Republicans were able to outspend Democrats only because of party contributions.

State party organizations have spent their money in a variety of ways. In 1983, the Republicans financed a "Republican Legislative Campaign Committee" with a budget of nearly a million dollars, to support legislative candidates in about ten targeted districts. These candidates received extensive polling services from the RLCC, as well as development of media messages, their production and placement, and heavy assistance with direct mail. The development and content of these items was controlled by the RLCC rather than the individual candidates' campaigns, which in many cases were run by party-hired managers anyway. Although the state Democratic party could raise less money both absolutely and proportionally, it also did a substantial amount for its candidates, particularly in the area of party coordination and financing of direct mail.

The spending of political action committees has also increased in significance in state-level elections in recent years, and is often coordinated with party spending. State-level PACs contributed 17 percent of all legislative campaign funds in 1979 and 39 percent of all such funds in 1983. If one includes business contributions that were made directly to the candidate rather than being funneled through PACs, the total rises to about 60 percent of all funds.

THE FUTURE OF NEW JERSEY CAMPAIGNS AND ELECTIONS

New Jersey, thus, has a two-tiered system of campaigns and elections. Candidate-centered campaigns dominate the congressional level upward; parties dominate elections at the local and county level. In between are the legislative campaigns, an uneasy blend of party and candidate dominance.

Candidates running for statewide office—U.S. senators and governors—have campaigns virtually divorced from the state and local parties. Parties contribute nothing of consequence, either financially or in terms of manpower. As a member of the Fenwick core strategy group in 1982 observed of the volunteers who staffed her phone banks, "they were not party people; they were people interested in Fenwick." Moreover, on election day, the get-out-the-vote effort that local parties were to have organized for Fenwick was a dismal failure. Staffers sat in a room at headquarters, waiting for reports of local vote totals from party workers and watching in disbelief phones that never rang. The campaign instead got its information from television and friendly media sources that had access to the television station exit polls. There were no such problems at Lautenberg headquarters, where the paid professional telephone banks operated efficiently.

Most congressional campaigns are also now run with little help from local party organizations. Indeed, many of the newer members of the New Jersey delegation have gained their seats by running in contested primaries without any form of organizational support.

Even in areas where the party still has some say in congressional nominations, the candidates are left to raise their own money after being selected. Candidates benefit from the party's label, but not from its efforts. Indeed the party organizations often base their selection on which candidate seems most likely to attract funds. Bergen Republicans settled on a neophyte challenger to Democratic Representative Bob Toricelli in 1984, because of a pledge (on which he did not deliver) that he would raise $400,000 in cash and in-kind services—a not overly lavish amount for a challenger in that district.

It is below the congressional level—in state legislative and county races—that the state and local parties still play a major role, although that role has changed dramatically over the past half century. Before the candidate-centered period, the state parties were coalitions of county parties, and the modest resources needed for campaigns came from the local level. This gave municipal and county parties a large voice in candidate selection and in the running of campaigns. Today, in state legislative races, and even in some county ones, the technological requirements of campaigns have outstripped local resources. Certainly in many legislative races, and especially but not exclusively in Republican races, the state party has taken over from the local parties by financing the same kind of technology that appears in contests for other higher offices. To generate the needed financial support, the state parties look not to the local organizations, but rather to PACs, gubernatorial candidates, and congressional and legislative leaders who have independent fundraising bases.

Such a system will shortly develop very competitive, fluid, and volatile politics in New Jersey. The continuing role of parties at lower levels will mean that statewide success for a particular candidate will usually not automatically translate into party victories at lower levels. Elections in New Jersey will encourage an essential incoherence and instability in the political system. Inevitably these trends will affect policy-making.

Notes

1. See Joel L. Sibley and Samuel T. McSeveney, eds., *Voters, Parties and Elections: Quantitative Essays in the History of American Popular Voting Behavior* (Lexington, Mass.: Xerox College Publishers, 1972) and Joel Sibley, et alia, eds., *The History of American Electoral Behavior* (Princeton, N.J.: Princeton University Press, 1978).

2. Reynolds v. Sims, 377 U.S. 533 (1964). For a discussion of this and subsequent court decisions that have affected congressional and legislative redistricting in New Jersey, see Stanley Friedelbaum, "Constitutional Law and Judicial Policy Making," in *Politics In New Jersey*, Richard Lehne and Alan Rosenthal, eds., rev. ed. (New Brunswick, N.J.: Rutgers Univ., Eagleton Institute of Politics, 1979), 212–213.

3. Malcolm Jewell, *Parties and Primaries: Nominating State Governors* (New York: Praeger Publishers, 1984), p. 178.

4. These poll results are from an Eagleton Poll conducted in October 1984.

TWO
POLITICAL
INSTITUTIONS

5

DONALD LINKY

The Governor

New Jersey, as one recent governor put it, has been a state so lacking in a collective political, economic, and social identity that it has no ego. When few others thought the task worth the trouble, the state's governors have had to struggle to build support for the recognition of statewide needs. Not all governors have shown equal courage or skill; indeed many have made few lasting marks and one or two may even have been "rogues and thieves."[1] But, to a remarkable degree, strong, personal leadership by some of its governors has made a real difference to New Jersey. Today, New Jerseyans' growing awareness of their state's unique identity must be largely credited to those special governors who labored to build the still fragile and emerging polity —the cohesive political, economic, and social community—of New Jersey.

This chapter assesses the changing leadership role of New Jersey's chief executive. It considers the practical context in which governors work, the evolution of their leadership, and the nature of their modern responsibilities and powers.

THE SETTING AND THE JOB

Only governors can truly understand what it is like to be governor. Governors make decisions and exercise leadership within special contexts and amid unique pressures that accompany the daily job. Governors speak of the ironic loneliness of the public job, and frequently they alone know how they make their most critical decisions.

> When a person is elected governor, there develops within him a need to hold something within himself. It is a trait with all governors I have known. One of the prerogatives of a governor is doing things without explaining why.[2]

There are few positions in our society, perhaps including the presidency, that combine the extent of the governor's decision-making power with his lack of privacy in exercising that power. Even when outside formal public forums, the governor remains the focus of attention, with his casual comments or facial expressions studied for clues about mood or inclination.

> The governor is on stage most of the time. In one sense his role is similar to that of a performer but one who can rarely if ever leave the stage. There is also the special imperial quality to the office. A governor is treated to some extent as royalty, whose person is protected by quasi-military security, whose very arrival sparks attention, and whose personal wishes gain prompt response.[3]

THE SETTING

The governor's office stands at the center of New Jersey state government, literally located nearly under the golden dome, on the ground floor of the State House. Invariably, visitors look through the glass doors marked "Office of the Governor" to see the activity inside, or, perhaps, to view the comings and goings of the chief executive himself.

Veteran State House lobbyists and reporters know that the governor has no private access to his office, and so one sure way to ask a quick favor or question is to loiter at the side entrance to the State House where the governor enters and leaves his limousine. While state troopers provide security, normally only one or two junior staff members travel with the governor to tend to pesonal needs or to fend off unwanted or prolonged questions.

Physically, the governor's office is really a complex of several offices which have spread—first from the north to the south side of the ground floor of the State House, and then in recent years throughout the building's other floors—to accommodate the governor's staff, which has grown from a handful of professionals dealing with legislative matters, press relations, and correspondence to over one hundred people. The once comfortable offices with wood paneling have been subdivided repeatedly in response to staff desires to demonstrate power through physical proximity to the governor. Current renovations of the State House are intended to reverse this trend and to restore the governor's office to its less cluttered appearance of the nineteenth century.[4] As the State House returns to look as it did when the governor's role was that of a part-time executive with only a handful of staff assistants, it will be interesting to note the impact of structural changes on the interrelationships within the enlarged staff bureaucracy of the contemporary governor.

If visitors proceed through the glass doors, they pass down a short corridor flanked by staff offices to a large anteroom, sometimes known as the Reception Room, with its walls lined with portraits of former governors. This room, probably added to the State House in the 1870s, once served as the governor's personal office until further expansion added more space. Here, press conferences, public bill signings, and other routine ceremonies are held, normally toward midday to meet newspaper and television deadlines.

Off the right-hand corner of the anteroom is the governor's small working office, where he goes through most of his daily paperwork, makes phone calls, and performs other routine business. By necessity, relatively few people ever see this office where he spends most of his time, since it is so small that only two chairs can be squeezed in front of the desk. Normally only top staff, cabinet officers, and personal friends are received in this private enclave. The adjacent, much larger room (variously labeled the Private Office or the Cabinet Room) is the setting for most meetings.

The arrangement of furniture in the governor's office may give some indication of an individual chief executive's management style. For some years, the furniture in the governor's Cabinet Room was arranged similar to that in a corporate boardroom, with the governor's desk perpendicular to a long table at which the cabinet or others arranged themselves. This somewhat formal arrangement was inconsistent with the gregarious Governor Cahill, however, and he arranged the room to fit a more informal conversational style with chairs randomly placed around his desk.[5]

The final setting for the governor's day is his residence. For most of New Jersey's history, governors had no official residence, and indeed the part-time nature of the job required only their occasional presence in Trenton. Some governors who lived a distance from the capital would stay in local hotels on those days when they were in the city;

Woodrow Wilson had a bed and small kitchen installed in the governor's office for his occasional use.[6] From 1956 through 1981, however, New Jersey's chief executives officially resided at Morven, the historic Princeton home where Richard Stockton received the news in 1776 that he had been passed over in selection of the state's first governor. Some governors have made extensive use of Morven for private meetings outside the State House and also for entertaining, using the prestige of invitations to the mansion as leverage to gain support for their political or policy objectives. But Morven's cramped colonial dimensions have made it inadequate for most modern functions, so in 1981 the official residence was shifted to Drumthwacket, a larger Princeton mansion.

THE JOB

One of the first, if not the first, things that a governor does in preparing for each day is to review his schedule. Governors vary in how much personal involvement they may wish in setting their schedule, but most recent executives have taken the time to skim written requests and write a short Yes, No, or Send Cabinet in the margins of letters or memoranda to indicate how requests for their time are to be handled.

The individual events on the schedule are accompanied by briefing memoranda, advising the governor of the session's purpose, audience, and background. These memos can enable the staff, particularly those without regular access to the chief executive, to obtain the governor's attention. Similarly, those who have gained meetings with the governor may improve their chances of gaining their ends by first presenting their case to the staff worker preparing the briefing.

Another early daily chore is to review the news reports. Most major newspapers are delivered to the governor's residence, but thorough reading of all but one or two is unrealistic. The press office prepares a one or two-sentence summary of key articles or editorials for distribution to the governor and key staff. Later in the day, the press office supplements the news summary with a file folder of individual newspaper clippings of articles and editorials.

A portion of the governor's day is consumed with signing his name, sometimes several hundred times a day. A few of these signatures are significant, such as those that make a bill the law of the state. Others are on letters to legislators, local government officials, or those private-sector leaders considered sufficiently prominent to warrant the governor's personal signature. Occasionally, the governor scrawls a handwritten note to the recipient to indicate his own interest and involvement in an issue. Other hundreds of signatures are routine but are required by law in the governor's own hand, such as those on warrants to extradite prisoners to or from other states or on deeds or leases to convey the state's interests in real estate or tide-flowed lands. Few homeowners who have built docks or bulkheads realize that the governor has personally set his hand of approval to their project.[7]

The governor also spends much time reading mounds of cabinet and staff memos, letters from key public or private leaders, summaries of meetings, minutes of public authority actions, and commission reports. The paper flow has been screened first by his personal secretary and, possibly, a senior staff person. This control is highly significant; the allocation of information and projects can have major impacts on the changing roles and relative influence of individual staff. Many documents, after appropriate staff review, are returned to the governor with a single-page summary, staff comments, or a recommended response. Papers reviewed by the chief executive may contain brief directions to the staff, such as "OK" or "See me."

Governors spend a great deal of time traveling, and the time when they are relatively secluded in cars and helicopters is particularly useful for reading routine memos and reports or making final changes on a speech. Sometimes, staff or legislators will try to intrude on this seclusion, knowing that the traveling governor is a captive audience who may be approached at this time for decisions without normal distractions of phone calls or other competitors for his time.

On most days, the governor's schedule includes time devoted to his symbolic role as head of state. Thus, he will sign several hundred proclamations during each year recognizing the good works of various organizations, designating days, weeks, or months honoring an assortment of professions, fruits or vegetables, and a range of causes or promotions. While most of this is routine, an occasional political choice may be required, such as when one recent governor declined to proclaim Gay Day for homosexual rights. Occasionally, proclamations create embarrassment: once after an automobile manufacturer had been recognized for creating economic benefits to the state, one of its dealers prominently reproduced the governor's proclamation and picture in its used-car ads.

When ceremonies are public, the governor's outer office conveys a festive air as a variety of ethnic representatives' costumes, beauty queens, and Little League champions wait for their brief time and picture with the governor. These events, which in other states may frequently be handled by a lieutenant governor, may not be an efficient use of the chief executive's time, but they do provide informal contacts with various constituencies, keep the governor advised of special concerns, and help maintain political support.

There is also a certain ceremonial aspect to many of the private meetings that governors hold with representatives of interest groups or other members of the public. On a typical day, a governor may see union leaders seeking support for new highway construction, a veterans' group seeking state funds for a veterans' cemetery, a group of mayors pushing for more state financial aid, and several other public and private representatives seeking support for particular causes. In many cases, the governor already has been briefed on the relevant issues, and usually these meetings serve primarily to demonstrate to interest group constituencies that they have sufficient clout to obtain a personal meeting with the governor. When a decision is announced, it is generally good news; negative results are usually left to the staff or cabinet.

Most gubernatorial workdays and weekends include some portion of time spent outside the State House giving speeches, attending various ceremonies or events, appearing at dinners and political fund raisers. Although only a small portion of invitations received can be accepted, recent governors appear to enjoy this time spent away from the office, perhaps because these events provide generally supportive audiences in contrast to the often critical State House world of legislators, lobbyists, and press. Indeed, as Governor Hughes said with characteristic humor:

> My overall thrill at being governor was the relationship with the people. I got that in many ways. I hustled around the state, probably more than some of the others. . . . My wife says that if I got an invitation to see three Public Service Electric and Gas men open a manhole cover in Teaneck I would go there and say a few words to cheer them up as part of our laboring force.[8]

SOURCES OF LEADERSHIP

The modern governor's leadership role in New Jersey has been shaped by diverse factors. Particularly significant are the methods of selection, the wide scope of formal and informal powers, and the interaction among the people whom the governor needs to implement policies—the cabinet and staff. These factors have limited past leadership, provided new present opportunities, and present possible future problems.

SELECTION

New Jersey's first governor in 1776, William Livingston, was chosen in a "smoke-filled room" by a small circle of the state's leaders.
The next day, the legislature formally ratified the selection.[9] For
much of the state's history, the governor's selection continued to be
dominated by a small group representing the state's political establishment. The interests represented in the group did change—from
the patricians of the eighteenth and early nineteenth centuries, to the
industrial barons of the late nineteenth and early twentieth centuries,
and then to the political bosses of more modern times.[10] But the pattern persisted. As late as 1973, Brendan Byrne conceded that he
would not even have entered the race for governor without the promised formal endorsement of the political boss of Hudson County.[11]
Power in New Jersey was shared, but not widely.

This is not to say that most governors have been lackeys of the elite
that has selected them. The relatively narrow or local concerns of New
Jersey's political power-brokers has helped governors develop reasonable accommodations, with the chief executive allowed a great deal of
independence while the political leaders pursued their own separate ends.

This pattern of restricted involvement has been mirrored to a great
degree in New Jersey's economic and social life. Most of the state's
private sector leaders have had little interest in the affairs of Trenton,
directing their attention outward to the money centers of New York
City and Philadelphia or inward to more local pockets of opportunity. Until quite recently, New Jersey was not viewed as a cohesive
financial, commercial, or communications market for statewide institutions. Leading banks, major corporations, and media concentrated
in regional or local centers nestled at the respective ends of the corridor linking the state's metropolitan neighbors. New Jersey's mass
electorate has been even less involved, showing great indifference to
state politics and much more concern with local issues (see Chapter 1).

For New Jersey's governor, this environment has posed both problems and opportunities. Governors have had difficulty obtaining support for statewide programs or facilities. The state government has remained, contrary to political rhetoric, one of the nation's smallest in
terms of budget or personnel. Governors have struggled to gain approval for barely adequate state hospitals, prisons, highways, colleges,
and other basic facilities. Without the forceful intervention of the New
Jersey Supreme Court, it is questionable whether or not there would

yet be a resolution of the watershed battle over the state's role in financing public education, which produced the first State income tax.

On the other hand, this indifference to New Jersey as a collective entity has given the state's governors a degree of freedom and flexibility rarely found in more politically active states. The governor has had few competitors in setting a statewide agenda. To be sure, implementing that agenda has been a tougher task, requiring the building of fragile coalitions of support from the state's fragmented interests. But even here, the governor has had the advantage of dealing with a relatively select circle of key decision-makers.

Frequently, as Governor Hughes remarked, a governor could insure legislative passage of his program through commitments from a handful of county political leaders (sometimes only one or two) with tight control over their legislative delegations. Similar elites controlled New Jersey's other power sectors. Governors had only to persuade a few newspaper publishers or editors, a handful of labor or business leaders or even some influential career bureaucrats. And when a governor failed to obtain passage of desired legislation, as many did, it was done knowing he had some reassurance that political accountability was largely to a sophisticated elite who generally would understand and credit the governor's efforts even while they withheld support. The governor's task was, while not easy to accomplish, at least manageable in scope.

This special political culture has had a subtle but not consistent impact on the types of people who have been chosen to serve as governor. Selection by a narrow circle of power-brokers has occasionally opened the office to those working outside the normal channels of political advancement—those such as the academic Woodrow Wilson, or those with quite narrow political bases, such as the rural-bred Robert Meyner.

Once in office, New Jersey chief executives have not needed to be particularly charismatic public leaders or dynamic speakers, for these characteristics were of marginal value in a state with both restricted forums for public communication and limited public interest. More important skills have been an extensive knowledge of the state's power structure and some strategic sense of how the key decision-makers could be motivated to act in accordance with the governor's interest. Interpersonal skills in small group settings have been decisive—the arts of persuasion and negotiation, a sense of firmness if not stubbornness, and, above all, an image of personal credibility that reinforced promised rewards and punishments.

While important aspects of this political culture remain today, New

Jersey is changing. Consequently, the way in which its governors exercise power is also changing. The traditional power elites, although not gone from the scene, appear less dominant in gubernatorial politics. Party organizations have declined, ending the past ability of a few county leaders to select party candidates. The governor has become a more "public" official—both more visible to the general public through improved media coverage and more politically accountable to a public, showing new interest in New Jersey affairs. The state appears at long last to be developing a sense of identity, an ego perhaps, as economic, media, and other interests focus attention inward towards the state rather than outward.

FORMAL AND INFORMAL POWERS

The last royal governor of New Jersey was William Franklin, the illegitimate son of Benjamin Franklin. At two o'clock on a January morning in 1776, Franklin's loyal efforts to follow the Crown's orders came to an end, when as he recounted, "I was awakened with a violent knocking at my door, which alarmed my wife so much that I was not without apprehensions of her dying with the fright," and placed under arrest by the colonial militia.[12]

So, in public hostility and resentment, began the history of New Jersey's chief executives. Understandably, the newly independent state provided the governor with only weak formal powers under its first constitution, adopted soon after Franklin's rude awakening. It was not until the 1947 constitution that the state's basic law recognized the need for a strong formal mandate for executive action.[13] Under this charter, the New Jersey governor is today provided with a powerful, possibly the most powerful, constitutional position in the nation. Certainly the power of New Jersey's governor ranks near the top of the scale when compared with the power of other state chief executives—to veto legislation, to control administrative appointments, and to dominate the budget process.[14]

The governor's traditional legislative power was both continued and strengthened by this charter. His veto power was bolstered by the requirement for a two-thirds vote in both houses, instead of the former simple majority, to override his objection. Governors working under the 1947 constitution have rarely been overridden, even though some have made extensive use of the veto power. The governor was also granted the significant tool of the conditional veto, which allowed him to suggest changes in bills passed by the legislature and to return them for reconstruction. The governor was thus allowed, unlike even the president of the United States, to shape legislation to his own desires and to eliminate specific unacceptable provisions even after the critical passage of a bill.

On financial legislation, the 1947 constitution provided more executive authority than either the federal constitution or that of any other state. The governor might eliminate or reduce the amount of spending on specific items through a line-item veto (subject, however, to override by a majority rather than a two-thirds vote of both houses), even while approving the remaining provisions of the legislation.[15] Furthermore, the state constitution prohibited spending that exceeds the governor's estimate of revenues and gave him the considerable leverage of initiating spending through the annual proposed budget.[16]

The governor has broad appointive powers. He names all the judges of the state courts, the department heads of state government, and the members of various bi-state and intra-state authorities, boards, and commissions. The appointive power is particularly valuable for political leverage, and historically has been a useful means for governors to reinforce their political will with legislators, local government officials, and party leaders.

The formal powers of the executive have been protected by decisions of the New Jersey Supreme Court that have generally upheld the strong executive authority when it has been challenged by other institutions or interests. The alliance between the chief executive and the supreme court was visibly forged in the constitutional crisis over the financing of public education, when Governor Byrne personally appeared before the court to argue that it should order the New Jersey schools closed until the legislature had finally resolved this long-deferred problem.[17] Strong ties between the executive and the court have also developed as a result of the propensity of modern governors to appoint members of their own staff to the court. Governors Meyner, Cahill, and Byrne, for example, appointed their counsels and Governor Kean, his policy director, to the court.

Even with the strong formal powers outlined in the 1947 constitution, however, there are times when the governor is frustrated by the limitations of his authority. Throughout New Jersey's history, the formal powers of the governor have been buttressed by the informal assumption of authority by aggressive chief executives. Wilson's activity as a leader of the legislature, including his unprecedented personal appearance in its private caucus, provided precedents for later formal powers. Brendan Byrne used executive orders to impose a building moratorium in one-third of the state's land area, the environmentally sensitive Pinelands. This activity stretched and, in the views of his own legal advisers, exceeded the limits of the governor's formal power, but it ultimately led to supportive legislation.

THE GOVERNOR'S STAFF

Even with the strong formal powers provided the modern governor, successful leadership is largely dependent on an ability to motivate the people theoretically under his control to pursue his goals. As the size of government has grown, the chief executive's personal control of the government has been increasingly exercised through others:

> There has been a diffusion of power to the point where the governor is still trying to impress leadership qualities on a much more complex system. It is not enough to be personally strong, dogmatic, ruthless or whatever. He must understand the complex system of people who have to be sucked into the process to get anything done.[18]

When a governor is elected, his first action is to pick the people with whom he will be working most closely. This selection is both important and highly personal; however it must be done without the luxury of time and reflection. The governor-elect is under great pressure to name those who will speak to the press, sort through the volumes of correspondence, and interview respective appointees. Understandably, most new governors look first to the people who have successfully waged their campaigns for office. These are the people who are most readily available, who have some expectation of reward for service, and who have the strongest interest in making the new administration a success.

As the state government has grown, the governor's staff has changed in structure and significance.

> When Governor Meyner was in office, the size of the state government was so small that it was possible for the governor to know all key decision-makers on a close, personal basis. On the basis of that knowledge, he had an advantage in evaluating the merits of proposals and alternatives coming from the bureaucracy. It is not true today. The growth of state government has made it impossible. The governor can't and doesn't have the same personal grasp of government, and his authority and power must be dispersed over more people.[19]

Increasingly, many decisions are made by senior staff, either expressly or implicitly with the governor's authority. Governors vary considerably in the extent to which they delegate decision-making, but the complexity and scope of the modern state government necessitate that many decisions made in the governor's name are made without his personal knowledge or express consent.

The governor's office is a "wholly different world" from the rest of state government.[20] It has generally attracted a different type of person, maintained a different work style, and operated at a different pace from the permanent bureaucracy. Staffers tend to be generalists rather than specialists, and may well be passing in and out of government from more permanent careers in the private sector. They are likely to be younger professionals with common political experience. Unlike the bureaucracy outside the State House, the governor's staff has traditionally worked in ways that may be inconsistent with structured organizational charts or formal job titles. Press advisers may become key policy operatives; junior staffers hired for travel support may advance rapidly to substantive positions. Under the press of the heavy workload, these conditions can produce an esprit de corps uncommon to larger institutional settings.

The network of personal relationships, both among staff and with the governor, is much more significant for understanding how the governor's office works than any formal structure and organization. As the first person to hold the title of governor's chief of staff said, "A staff whose personalities mesh is both the most important, and the most difficult, task facing any governor in organizing the governor's office."[21]

Personal alliances are formed and broken, sometimes on the basis of opinions on substantive issues, occasionally for reasons of personality alone. Within the office, assessments are continually being made and revised as to the extent of the governor's reliance on particular individuals for information and advice. Hints of the governor's intentions may be gained by those with the most frequent and significant access to the chief executive or by those who seem most able to gain his attention for needed decisions. No matter how senior in title, staff who are unable to keep up with the workload or to deliver results run the risk of being bypassed.

In newly elected administrations, particularly those replacing the opposite party, there may be a natural tendency to centralize decision-making in the governor's staff. The new team's desire to take charge is bolstered by the confidence of a successful campaign and suspicion of the loyalties of the permanent bureaucrats. Arrogance may lead to usurpation of traditional agency responsibilities. As time goes by, however, this centralization may diminish as the newly elected governor's own appointees fill more positions, as members of the governor's staff leave for supervisory jobs in state departments, and as the governor's staff becomes more confident of support within the permanent bureaucracy.

For many years, the governor's office was organized without any formal chain of command. The key staff usually included the governor's counsel, the press secretary, and an executive assistant or secretary (usually concerned with scheduling, patronage, and political matters), with each having direct access to the governor.

At the commencement of Governor Byrne's second term in 1978, this traditional organization was made more hierarchical, with the designation of a chief of staff. The office of policy and planning was also created by Governor Byrne to provide a small think-tank to develop and review new initiatives, focus on long-range projects, and coordinate the planning programs of all state agencies. The Kean administration, while keeping the basic structure of his predecessor's office, has greatly expanded the size of the legal and correspondence staff, implemented sophisticated new word and data-processing systems, and attempted to improve the governor's budget and management capabilities through the creation of a new Office of Management and Budget.

The gradual expansion of staff size and its increasingly hierarchical structure and specialization may eventually undermine the traditional strengths of the governor's staff. "As the staff grows in size, there are more and more people on the periphery who really can't know directly what the governor wants or speak with credibility on his behalf."[22] Efforts to improve the governor's policy and management control of the bureaucracy may bring inevitable trade-offs in creativity and responsiveness. For good or ill, the governor's staff may become more like the bureaucracy it oversees.

THE CABINET

The initial selection of the governor's cabinet is a public statement about a new governor's objectives. The backgrounds of the new cabinet members and their relative acceptability to key constituencies are a first clue to the governor's priorities. Again, however, the process must be hurried, with most governors waiting until after their election to review their potential choices. Excessive delay may give an image of indecisiveness, as well as slow the new administration's assumption of policy and management control. Acting without adequate investigation, however, may risk embarrassment, as the Kean administration discovered when the press reported that its prospective commissioner of education's doctorial dissertation included significant sections of unattributed source material.

Usually, the cabinet contains a mix of political supporters, public administration professionals, and personal acquaintances of the governor. The Kean administration was perhaps unique in using the services of a professional executive search firm to identify potential appointees. Most prior governors have relied on more informal methods such as consulting with party leaders, long-time friends, interest group representatives, or others who may have helpful information.

Although there is no single path to selecting successful cabinet officers,

> the most effective people in the executive branch have been, by and large, those who come immediately from the political environment. The most unsuccessful have been the people from academic positions, think-tanks or the business world who did not have the ability to read the political nature of issues in order to advance substantive policy without political damage.[23]

Once chosen, a governor's interaction with his cabinet as a collective body is generally limited to a monthly meeting. At one time, these were informal sessions where the governor could consult the cabinet on a variety of issues and seek wide-ranging advice on administration goals. The growth of the cabinet and the increasing specialization of departmental roles have made cabinet meetings somewhat more structured, narrower in scope, and generally restricted to topics of collective interest such as budget, civil service, and major legislation.

Some participants in recent administrations have even questioned the continuing value of the full cabinet meeting, describing the typical session as frequently so inconclusive and prone to trivia that it was a "joke" or "farce."[24] However, cabinet meetings do provide an opportunity for the governor to provide internal direction to his administration and allow cabinet officers, particularly those without regular contact with the governor, a forum in which to assess the governor's priorities and evaluate his internal leadership. In recent years, substantive policy development and program management have shifted to smaller subgroupings of relevant cabinet departments that coordinate interdepartmental policies on such issues as economic development or human resources.

A governor's normal relationship with his cabinet officers occurs through individual contacts by memo, telephone calls, or personal meetings. The frequency and nature of these contacts vary considerably. The cabinet officer's institutional role significantly affects gubernatorial access. Key officers like the treasurer meet personally with the governor almost daily during the final phases of the budget or appropriations process. Other, more peripheral, department heads rarely have any contact besides formal cabinet meetings. Governors also vary in the extent of autonomy they allow their cabinets. Governor Byrne appeared typical in his belief that cabinet members should advise him in advance of issues or policies they expected to become the subject of media attention; other than this, however, he relied on few formal guidelines.

Given this rather unstructured relationship, it is understandable that occasional conflicts do occur between the cabinet members and the governor's office staff concerning when and how departmental decisions or announcements should receive the chief executive's attention or approval. In the words of one veteran of both the governor's staff and a cabinet department: "The relationship between the governor and his cabinet officers frequently became adversarial. . . . Certain departments became outcasts to the real policy apparatus of the executive branch and, worse, became internal adversaries to the governor and his staff."[25]

The Governor's Responsibilities

Selected, empowered, and assisted, New Jersey's governor discharges his many responsibilities, which can be grouped into three categories—lawmaking, managing, and communicating.

LAWMAKING

Although the governor's role in legislation is only one of his responsibilities, the public and the press tend to focus primary, if not excessive, attention on legislative performance. Perhaps this is because legislative performance is easier to communicate and understand than the governor's performance as an administrator or a public leader. Legislative success may be quantified simply by counting how many of the governor's bills are passed or how many vetoes are sustained. This so-called legislative scorecard, however, although easy to communicate, may be a highly deceptive standard. There is also a certain drama in the executive-legislative relationship that makes good press copy, particularly when the personalities of governor and legislators are colorful and confrontational.

In the early part of the nineteenth century, governors were quite passive in their relationships with the legislature. They tended to see their job as merely reacting to bills the legislature had passed, giving substantial deference to the legislature's collective judgment. Later, however, and particularly in modern times, the governor has been expected to be an aggressive legislative commander. When the governor has not been perceived as strong, he has come in for criticism not only from the press and the public, but also from the legislature itself. This expectation has resulted from complex factors. Institutionally, the executive has had advantages in policy leadership through the relative clarity and promptness of its decision-making authority, particularly when compared with the extensive negotiation and compromise typical of decision-making in legislative institutions. The relative weakness of the New Jersey legislature, due to its lack of resources, relatively low public esteem, and excessive parochialism, have facilitated gubernatorial dominance.

Sometimes the institutional differences between the way the legislative and executive branches make decisions will generate conflict. Governor Meyner once branded legislators as "prostitutes" for their lack of responsibility in passing poorly conceived bills written to please various special interests, frequently passed with the expectation that the governor would exercise his veto.[26] Other governors, while not as colorful in their invective, nonetheless have pointed to the diffusion of responsibility and authority in the legislature as the cause for their increasing difficulty in obtaining effective commitments from legislative leadership. Individual legislators are less influenced by party discipline, and governors accordingly have been forced to negotiate with factions outside the traditional leadership to generate support for their legislative initiatives.

Newly-elected governors must determine the relative priority to be placed on legislative activity during their administrations. Both political reality and personal style will influence this decision. Governors who face the prospect of repeated rebuffs by obstreperous legislatures, particularly if they are controlled by the opposing political party, may soon come to appreciate and emphasize other aspects of their job. Thus, Governor Meyner's interest in tight fiscal management (derived from his Depression upbringing) was reinforced, particularly during his first term, by a Republican legislature that viewed his election as an aberration, to be corrected at the first opportunity.

The governor's personality also shapes not only the significance placed on the legislative role, but also the style of the relationship. The gregarious Richard Hughes relished the give-and-take of the legislative process and enjoyed the personal byplay of legislative conflict and compromise.[27] The more private Brendan Byrne felt uncomfortable in assuming a similarly personal role; his ultimately impressive legislative record was actually compiled largely after he himself had withdrawn from many routine legislative contacts and delegated significant responsibility to key staff. He found this style not only more compatible with his personality but also more helpful in insulating him from the horse-trading atmosphere that inevitably came with a governor's personal lobbying.[28]

The governor's most formal contact with the legislature occurs at the delivery of the annual message reviewing the state's condition and proposing policy initiatives. Typically, this speech is drafted by the governor's staff after solicitation of ideas from the cabinet. The State of the State address is supplemented during the year by various legislative proposals that receive formal gubernatorial backing as administration bills. These bills are maintained on an administration bill list by the governor's counsel, and their legislative progress is carefully monitored by assistant counsels.

As with most aspects of the governor's responsibility, the governor's formal contacts with the legislature through the annual message and the annual budget address give only a limited picture of how gubernatorial leadership is exercised. Much of the contact is personal, sometimes in meetings with legislative leaders to review priorities, and sometimes privately with individual legislators who control a key bill or vote. Recent governors and legislators have avoided the direct exchange of votes for such favors as patronage or funding for a special project. These negotiations are still basic to the process, but generally the exchanges are more ambiguous and filtered through a network of staff intermediaries to save the governor potential embarrassment.

Throughout the legislative session, the counsel's staff monitors legislative developments. Frequent efforts are made to defer or expedite action on individual bills on the basis of the administration's position. Upon final passage of a piece of legislation, a "passed bill memo" is submitted by the governor's counsel to the governor. This memo, typically one or two pages long, includes a summary of the bill; a review of its legal, fiscal, and political impacts; and a recommendation concerning the governor's appropriate action. It is the single most important, and sometimes the only, document on which the governor relies in making decisions on passed bills. When the governor agrees with a recommendation to sign the bill, he normally writes a simple OK over his initials on the passed bill memo, and the bill is then scheduled for either a private signing or, if the sponsor so requests, a public signing ceremony to which affected interest groups are invited, along with the press.

MANAGING

A central goal of the 1947 constitution was to centralize management and to strengthen the governor's administrative powers through
the consolidation of various agencies.[29] Even with these extensive
powers, however, the governor's capability to exert control over the
state government has remained his most difficult challenge.

Complicating the task are institutional constraints inherent in the
executive branch, the increasing size and fragmentation of state government, and continuing legal impediments to the governor's command over personnel and fiscal resources. Some analysts have even
questioned whether or not key political executives can manage government bureaucracy, at least as management is normally understood
in the private sector.

While the constitution allowed twenty executive departments,
some governors and public administration experts have suggested that
the state government would operate more efficiently with significantly
fewer agencies. Regretting the gradual growth of the number of governmental departments, Governor Meyner said, "I believed in a
strong cabinet such as was called for by the 1947 constitution, which
collapsed eighty-five or more agencies in the executive branch to no
more than twenty departments. I sat in the senate when the cabinet
was reduced to fourteen, and I have been upset over its gradual increase since."[30]

Despite these proposals, the trend since the 1947 constitution has
been toward further fragmentation. The few efforts by governors in
recent years to abolish or consolidate departments have failed, such as
the Byrne administration's attempt to eliminate the departments of
Agriculture and Community Affairs, and to merge the departments of
Banking and Insurance. Consolidation proposals have been weighed
against their relatively small cost savings and the high risk of political failure and embarrassment. It is not surprising, then, that the
comprehensive review conducted under Governor Kean's Management Improvement Plan in 1983 avoided any proposals for departmental consolidation.

As this rocky history suggests, the governor's cabinet officers, while
ostensibly owing their positions and allegiance to their chief executive, are still subject to conflicting pressures from other constituencies. Often, these pressures force an official to balance advocacy for
departmental interests or programs with obligations towards policies
set by the governor. Sometimes, these conflicts are reflected in a cabinet officer's efforts to fight for new or existing turf, to obtain money,

personnel or responsibilities for his or her department rather than another's.

An even more troubling long-term threat to centralized executive control may be posed by the recent proliferation of quasi-autonomous public authorities and commissions. For constitutional purposes, these authorities are statutorily assigned to executive departments, but in practice they possess varying degrees of independence from the governor and his cabinet. Modern governors have utilized the authority concept to implement key policy initiatives, such as development of the Meadowlands and its sports complex, in areas that would otherwise be politically impractical through the existing executive structure. Although the governor is not helpless when it comes to influencing authority actions through his appointive, veto, and budgetary powers, agencies once established frequently develop independent institutional policies that can be difficult for governors and cabinet officers to coordinate with overall administration objectives.

The governor's management capability also concerns his control of both personnel (see Chapter 7) and finance. His fiscal management powers, while strong when compared with those of governors in other states, are also subject to practical constraints. Newly elected governors have little time to influence the budget that is submitted less than a month after their inauguration. Since this budget sets fiscal policy eighteen months ahead, there is a considerable lag time in assuming full fiscal direction of the state government. Moreover, a governor cannot fully control a budget process largely driven by incremental demands of existing departmental programs (see Chapter 9). Despite highly visible efforts to improve management capacity, such as those to pursue recommendations by gubernatorial management commissions during the Cahill and Kean administrations, these inherent barriers to effective management control continue to undermine executive management of the bureaucracy.

COMMUNICATING

The Governor's final and perhaps most difficult responsibility is communicating with the public. Commencing with the initial campaign for office and continuing into the actual administration, a governor must cope with the lack of an effective statewide forum for dialogue with New Jerseyans. As Governor Cahill stated in 1982:

> I firmly believe that the state comes up short in affording a governor the opportunity to utilize the media properly. There is really no way that you can talk to all of the people through any television medium. New

York stations get as far as Trenton and Philadelphia stations get as far as Trenton, generally speaking. We do not—except for educational television, which regrettably does not have the following that the other stations do—have the opportunity to get on television and speak to all parts of the state at once. We also do not have a statewide newspaper. There are people in south Jersey who know nothing about the *Star-Ledger*, and there are people in north Jersey who have never heard of the *Camden Courier*. The regrettable part about it is that our citizens are not fully informed and therefore do not understand the problems and needs of the entire state.[31]

Within the State, the dominant newspaper affecting state government is the *Star-Ledger* of Newark. Other newspapers, particularly *The Record* in Bergen County, may be respected for the quality of reporting and editorial opinion, but the *Ledger*'s wide circulation and geographic coverage makes it the closest thing New Jersey has to a statewide paper.

The *Ledger*'s influence may be seen in various ways in relation to the governor. Most directly, the editorial endorsement of the paper in gubernatorial elections is valued, particularly in closely-contested races. The *Ledger*'s stature and large State House staff, with its extensive personal contacts, also gives it certain perquisites and advantages within State government and the State House. It has been traditional, for example, to leak stories to the *Ledger* in advance of general release to other papers. To some extent, the *Ledger*'s format also leads to special efforts by the governor's office to influence favorable coverage. The paper's tendency, for example, to use banner headlines frequently running across its Sunday front page gives great prominence to the highlighted story. This attention sometimes provokes attempts by the governor's office to leak favorable stories to the *Ledger*'s reporters, with the implicit understanding that the story will be strongly considered by the paper's editors for the front page lead. Another effect follows from the *Ledger*'s recent tendency to feature lengthy multi-part investigative series, often followed by repeated editorial calls for government action to address the conclusions of the story. This treatment builds pressure on gubernatorial administrations for either action or rebuttal.

Apart from this special rapport with the *Ledger*, the relatively informal, almost clublike relationship that some governors used to maintain with the State House press has ended. The general growth in size of the State House press corps, the increasingly rapid turnover in correspondents, and changes in the nature of government reporting have all been factors in the development of the now more formal and professional, if not adversarial, relationship. It began perhaps with the radical national shift in public and press attention generated by the Watergate scandal. As Governor Hughes recently remarked, "Nobody trusts anybody. . . . There is a general letdown in basic trust. When we were young, people in public life had a great deal of respect. Legislators and governors are all in the same boat, judges too. . . . I do not think this should pinpoint governors because in recent times everybody hates almost everybody."[32]

Governors also hold formal press conferences. They rehearse, in advance, possible answers to a list of potential questions—a list usually prepared by the governor's press secretary on the basis of informal talks with the State House press corps. But the value of formal press conferences is debatable. Governor Kean has largely dispensed with formal conferences in favor of individual contacts, and his great accessibility to the press apparently has removed what little objection existed on the lack of full conferences. When held, formal sessions may increase the tendency for "pack" coverage, since the lead story at the conference dominates media coverage and reduces initiatives for independent investigation and reporting. Sometimes, as Governor Byrne has noted, questions can become trivial if press conferences are protracted and reporters seek any opening for a story.

Television too is increasingly important in gubernatorial communication. New Jersey's video coverage has improved recently, through the siting of a commercial VHF television franchise, the growth of cable television and the development, with state support, of the New Jersey Network public television system. Political campaigns are already dominated by broadcast media, with recent gubernatorial candidates vying actively to retain the services of prominent media political consultants. And incumbent governors are also learning how to play by the new rules. The Kean administration, for example, has implemented the most extensive use of broadcast media by the governor in the state's history, scheduling regular televised town meetings, cable television shows, and tourism and lottery commercials featuring Mr. Kean. Indeed, the extent of this use of the media by the governor became a political issue in his 1985 reelection campaign as the Democratic Party sought to limit the frequency of his appearance on state-sponsored commercials, and his Democratic opponent criticized his high-visibility incumbency as "lights, camera, and no action."

As New Jersey's new television world matures, it is likely that future governors will follow the Kean administration's lead. But there may be some costs. One veteran State House reporter has noted that the governor's media presence is becoming increasingly necessary to make a story significant, with frequent efforts to package gubernatorial appearances in visually effective ways. Further, some past governors have decried the superficial nature of television campaigning and reporting, with a governor's message inevitably edited to the tight time and format constraints of the media. As one commentator noted, strong chief executives have succeeded in the past without the aid of mass media skills:

> These governors were all strong leaders who used a variety of personal skills within the structure of government to get things done. None were known for their commanding public presence. None were charismatic folk.[33]

In the future, it is unlikely that New Jersey governors will be able either to win election or succeed in office without some talent for public communication.

THE FUTURE OF GUBERNATORIAL LEADERSHIP

The ultimate test of gubernatorial leadership is the manner in which the individuals serving as New Jersey's chief executive have exercised their authority to set the state's collective agenda. Many factors in the state's political culture have hindered strong leadership on statewide issues, but individual governors have nonetheless risked their political fortunes to set their personal stamp on the future. Some strong individuals have failed, not through lack of personal will, but because the political or social climate of their times was not yet ripe for change. Others have had the benefit of presiding over changes that were more the product of the collective efforts of their predecessors and inevitable trends than their personal leadership.

The gubernatorial selection process will become more democratic as the ability of New Jersey's elite political power brokers to narrow the field of potential candidates is weakened, if not ended, by the undermining of political party organizations and by the public financing of campaigns. Potential gubernatorial candidates will be forced to broaden their appeal to voters outside the narrow circle of the New Jersey political establishment. Indeed, since the introduction of public campaign financing, both major political parties have experienced multi-candidate primaries. As the candidates in these primaries seek support from a wide range of voters, their individual positions on the issues have become increasingly difficult to distinguish and vague media perceptions of personalities have become increasingly important for electoral success. Similarly, as New Jersey continues to develop its independent identity, future governors will find more institutions and interests seeking to influence the setting of the state's agenda. Incumbent governors will be faced with demands from a more independent, factionalized legislature as well as additional constituencies seeking involvement in the policy-initiation process. The mobilization of public support and the effectiveness of an incumbent governor's skills at public communication will become increasingly important in determining the governor's success as a leader and will supplant the traditional small-group persuasive skills needed by earlier governors to gather backing from New Jersey's narrow circles of elite decision makers.

Future governors may also find new problems in implementing their policies. Ironically, some of these problems may be caused by the efforts of governors to extend their personal influence through the creation of new programs or public entities. The proliferation of dedicated funding sources, for example, may constrain the fiscal discretion of the executive; the growth and fragmentation of the state government bureaucracy may confuse management accountability; and the proliferation of special-purpose authorities and similar entities not directly responsible to the chief executive may complicate if not weaken the strong central role of the governor provided by the 1947 constitution.

As New Jersey continues its evolution toward a cohesive political community, the governor's role will change. In many respects, the governor's central position may be weaker in the future as more interests seek to share power. The strong leaders of the past may give way to an executive more inclined towards conciliation, compromise and broader public accountability. Such changes in the governor's role may not be uniformly negative. They may well be the inevitable product of the strong leadership tradition of New Jersey's governors, which has succeeded finally in forging a unified statewide identity from the split personality of the past.

Notes

1. Duane Lockard, *The New Jersey Governor: A Study in Political Power* (Princeton: D. Van Nostrand Company, 1964), 1.

2. Interview with David J. Goldberg, Esq. (former chief counsel to governors Meyner and Hughes), Princeton, April 12, 1984.

3. Interview with Lewis B. Thurston, III (former chief of staff to Governor Kean), East Rutherford, July 31, 1984.

4. See Heritage Studies, *The New Jersey State House at Trenton: an Historical and Architectural Investigation* (Princeton: Short and Ford Architects).

5. Interview with Thurston.

6. Interview with staff of Short and Ford Architects, Princeton, June 10, 1984.

7. On routine public correspondence, an automatic signature machine is utilized. Some governors have also authorized their personal secretaries to sign their name when approved by senior staff.

8. *Three Decades of The Governor's Office: A Panel Discussion* (Trenton: New Jersey Historical Commission, 1983), 19–20.

9. Lockard, *The New Jersey Governor*, 40–41.

10. *Ibid.*, 1–11.

11. Interview with Governor Brendan T. Byrne, Princeton, June 6, 1984.

12. Lockard, *New Jersey Governor*, 33–34.

13. See *Politics in New Jersey*, rev. ed. Richard Lehne and Alan Rosenthal, eds. (New Brunswick: Rutgers University Eagleton Institute of Politics, 1979), Chapters 6, 7.

14. Alan Rosenthal, "The Governor, The Legislature and State Policy Making," in Lehne and Rosenthal, 153–54.

15. *Constitution of New Jersey*, Article V, Section I, Par. 14.

16. *Ibid.*, Article VIII, Section II, Par. 2.

17. See Richard Lehne, *The Quest for Justice: The Politics of School Finance Reform* (New York: Longman, 1978).

18. Interview with Goldberg.

19. *Idem.*

20. Interview with Thurston.

21. Interview with Robert E. Mulcahy, III, (former chief of staff to Governor Byrne), East Rutherford, July 31, 1984.

22. Interview with Joseph W. Katz (former press secretary to Governor), Trenton, June 4, 1984.

23. Letter from Arthur Winkler, Esq. (former assistant counsel to the governor and assistant commissioner of education in the Byrne Administration), dated October 30, 1984.

24. Interviews with confidential sources.

25. Letter from Winkler.

26. Governor Robert B. Meyner, remarks at The Conference on the Future of the New Jersey Legislature, Princeton, September 1984, sponsored by the Eagleton Institute of Politics.

27. *Three Decades of the Governor's Office*, 6.

28. Interview with Governor Byrne.

29. *Proceedings of the 1947 New Jersey Constitutional Convention*, Vol. V, 422.

30. *Three Decades of the Governor's Office*, 5.

31. *Ibid.*, 10.

32. *Ibid.*, 8.

33. Maureen Moakley, "New Jersey" in *The Political Life of the American States*, Alan Rosenthal and Maureen Moakley, eds. (New York: Praeger 1984), 233.

6

ALAN ROSENTHAL

The Legislature

The New Jersey legislature was born in 1776 amidst revolutionary crisis, and it continues to this day to live in a state of recurring, if not perpetual, crisis. The legislature has developed and changed over the years, but it is still the arena where opposing values clash, where conflicts are resolved, and where public problems get addressed. It is the arena in which hundreds of issues are dealt with during a biennial session, including some of the most critical ones facing the state. This chapter explores the people who participate, the processes through which they operate, and the policies that result.

PLACE AND PEOPLE

The oldest part of the State House was built in 1792, which makes New Jersey's capitol building the second oldest in the nation (Maryland's being the oldest). Enlarged from time to time since its initial construction, the State House is now a melange of connected buildings, capped by a gold octagonal dome. Because of its disrepair—a leaking roof, falling plaster, cracking floorboards, and outdated offices and rooms—it is currently undergoing restoration.

The State House is the home of New Jersey's legislature—the New Jersey State Senate and the General Assembly (and the governor and

secretary of state as well)—and the home-away-from-home of New
Jersey's 120 legislators. It is the center of political activity in New Jersey generally and of political activity on West State Street in Trenton
specifically. One side of West State Street is occupied by state office
buildings, including the State House and the State House Annex, the
latter normally providing space for legislative committees and the legislature's nonpartisan staff as well as, temporarily, for the senate and
assembly chambers while renovation is underway. The other side of
West State Street is lined with brownstone townhouses that serve as
the headquarters for various statewide associations and the offices of
contract lobbyists, the "hired guns," representing hundreds of other
groups.

   The capital community is small and manageable, with many of the
principals—the governor, commissioners, executive staffs, and lobbyists—located within a hop, skip, and a jump of the legislature's
domain. New Jersey's legislature is a part-time legislature. It is also a
commuter legislature, with members driving both from nearby and
from the farthest corners of the state to Trenton approximately forty
times a year, and returning home the same day after the session ends.
Sometimes committees meet on other than session days, and this necessitates additional legislator trips to the capital.

   The New Jersey legislature is not like the U.S. Congress, a full-time
body that meets throughout the week, with most members living
nearby and returning to their districts only during recesses and possibly on weekends. Nor is it like most other state legislatures where sessions continue for 60, 90, or 120 days or longer and members spend
consecutive periods of time in the capital. In New Jersey sessions are
normally held on Mondays and sometimes on Thursdays (except during recesses for the budget, the summer season, or election campaigns). For the legislator, life in Trenton is discontinuous, and the
legislative process moves by fits and starts. It is almost impossible for
anyone to give anything much attention for any significant length
of time.

   These commuting legislators have work to do at home and, from
their personal point of view, it is very important work. Indeed, much
of a member's time and energy are spent politicking and servicing
constituents in the district. The state is divided into forty legislative
districts, with three legislators—one member of the senate and
two members of the assembly—elected from and representing the
186,000 persons in each of these districts.

   Legislators take their representational and constituent service roles
quite seriously. Most have a district office and staff to help them han-

dle constituent requests for information and for help. They receive from state funds $6,000 for renting an office, $4,000 for office furniture, and $30,000 a year for staff. In addition, they receive two telephone lines, a telephone credit card, stationery, postage stamps, and an account for office supplies. They also will soon be getting computers in their district offices. They spend their time at home engaging in so-called come-around politics visiting individual constituents and attending such events as a Chamber of Commerce breakfast, a Rotary luncheon, an Italian-American club dinner, or a League of Women Voters evening meeting.

A number of legislators devote themselves to district tasks because they like it. They are people-oriented and enjoy responding to constituents who don't know where to turn, helping constituents deal with bureaucracy and cut through red tape, and being with people and holding their hands, so to speak. Most legislators devote themselves to district tasks, at least in part, because they think they have to—that is, if they hope to get reelected. Members of the assembly serve two-year terms; members of the senate serve four-year terms (except for the senate term at the beginning of a decade, which is only two years). Legislative elections, therefore, are biennial events that command the attention of those incumbents who want to stay in office. And most do. In 1983, for example, out of 119 eligible incumbents (one had been convicted of a felony), only 5 left voluntarily while 114 stood for reelection.

Three-fourths of the legislative districts are relatively safe for one party or the other. Nevertheless, electoral lightning can and does strike. In 1983, for instance, two assembly and four senate incumbents failed to regain their seats. Several were in competitive districts, but one had lost a "safe" seat because he had come to take his district for granted and did not really work it. The lesson that politicians derive from such upsets is that there is almost no district in which you can relax. Even in overwhelmingly Democratic areas such as Hudson County, there is always the danger that another party faction will put up an opposition candidate in the primary. Thus, if districts appear safe, it is because legislators work hard to keep them that way. Early in 1984, just a few months after the November election, one legislator approached another, "You're getting ready for the next election?" His colleague replied, "Aren't you always in this business?" If so many members of the legislature work so hard to get reelected, they must like their jobs. Why? What benefits do they derive from being legislators?

There is the money—a $25,000 a year salary plus fringe benefits and a pension. About one-quarter of New Jersey's legislators are

essentially on the job full-time, but the rest have other employment
—various professions, businesses, selling insurance, or working for a
corporation. Several serve as salaried local officials and some are attorneys whose law firms represent municipalities. Money undoubtedly
matters to the full-time members and even to the part-timers, but
it is probably not as important for most members as are several
other motives.

There are also the perquisites, the perks or side benefits of public
office. Along with other state officials, legislators receive free telegram
service, thanks to a provision enacted in the nineteenth century in return for permitting Western Union to string telegraph lines throughout the state. They receive free railroad passes, a provision written
into the public utilities statutes early in this century as a condition for
granting a monopoly to a small railroad. Perhaps most important as far
as their status is concerned, legislators receive special legislative license plates and can purchase gold seals to affix to these plates. Senators may also request courtesy license plates—distinguished by three
letters and a single or double–digit number—for their constituents.
If assembly members want courtesy plates for a constituent, they
must ask their senate colleague to obtain them.) These perks are
pleasant enough, but hardly sufficient to compel legislators to
seek reelection.

There is the prestige, of course, of being referred to as Assembly-
man or, even better, Senator (according to an old saying, Senators do
not grow in office, they just swell), and it is nice to feel important in
the State House and in one's district. All people require some strok-
ing, and even the slightest deference and the leanest trappings of
office are good for the ego. Politicians, perhaps more than other people, have egos that require gratification. For many legislators, the
prestige of legislative office is one of the major reasons why they run.

There is also the power of public office, the ability to have one's way
and get things done. As one senator stated, "Just being here isn't very
satisfying unless you get something accomplished." What is most important for some legislators is the power to promote certain interests
(whether of labor, business, teachers, or whomever) because they believe in these groups and choose to represent them. For others what
is most important is the power to produce results for particular people
—a job here, an unemployment insurance check there, a new museum or other facility for constituents back home. And, of course,
there is always the power to raise issues and help solve problems. The
desire to exercise power is no doubt a principal motivation of most
members of the legislature.

Finally, there is the process itself, which many politicians find to be challenging and exciting. It has been said that "Unless you've been in politics, you've never really been alive. . . . It's the only sport for grownups—all the other games are for kids." One New Jersey assemblymember resorted to sports to describe legislative life: "It's competition. There's no feeling in the world like competing for something and winning. And once you've tasted victory, you want to taste it again." In the world of sports, there is amateur competition and professional competition, sportsmanlike competition and cutthroat competition. The game can get out of hand. The same can happen in politics, even in a part-time legislature, if an individual's ego depends upon public office. Another New Jersey assemblymember characterized the majority of his colleagues as follows: "It's like their life depends on it. It's their thing. It becomes an obsession, all the politics, the maneuvering, making deals."[1] The latter characterization may be somewhat overdrawn, but legislative life—however confusing, wearying, and frustrating it may be—does have substantial appeal and substantial rewards for most legislators, and it can become an obsession for some of them.

PROCESS AND PARTICIPANTS

Arriving on a typical session day, a legislator normally enters the State House from the parking lot behind the building and walks to one of the party conference rooms in the basement or in the annex (during State House renovations, all activities will be in the annex) for coffee and danish, which may not yet be gone. From the conference room, it is off to the assembly (or senate) chamber to sort through the mail that has piled up on the desk since the week before. Standing committee meetings are scheduled to begin at 10:00 a.m., so the legislator next heads for the committee meeting rooms. Progress may be slow through the corridors, however, as roaming lobbyists buttonhole legislators with whom they have to deal.

Over four hundred individuals are registered as lobbyists, or legislative agents as they are called in the Legislative Activities Disclosure Act of 1971. Many of them are well known to the legislators, and all are readily identifiable because they are required to wear red identification badges when they are in the State House or the annex. Hundreds of associations, corporations, and other groups employ lobbyists on their staffs or contract for their services. Among the largest lobbying groups, in terms of expenditures on lobbying, are the lawyers, dentists, builders, teachers, realtors, and bankers.[2] One or another of the many lobbyists is sure to have a message to communicate or a matter to transact with each legislator.

Although legislators have district offices, unless they are leaders they have no private office in Trenton where they can meet with people. They do their business with lobbyists and with constituents in the open and on the run. And it takes time. No wonder, then, that committee meetings start late. In fact, nothing starts on time. The legislature runs on what has been called Legislative Standard Time, which runs thirty minutes to two hours slower than ordinary time.

When the committee meetings finally do get underway, they tend to be crowded and hurried affairs, attended by legislators sponsoring bills and lobbyists supporting and opposing them. The standing committees, sometimes called standing reference committees since bills are referred to them for disposition, afford the senate and assembly a means of dividing labor, a method of promoting specialization, and a way of facilitating expertise. There are twelve standing reference committees in the Senate and eighteen in the assembly, each with a different jurisdictional domain such as education, transportation and communications, and law, public safety, and defense.

Most of the committees have five members, three from the majority party and two from the minority. But the three most influential committees of the legislature—revenue, finance, and appropriations in each house and judiciary in the senate—have a larger membership. Under the guidance of the chairperson, and with the assistance of the committee staff aide, members go through an agenda that may be either light, with only a few bills to review, or heavy, with twenty to twenty-five bills (although officially no more than fifteen bills are supposed to be considered at a single meeting). The committee will vote to report some bills favorably and pass over the rest.

PARTY LEADERSHIP

Before a bill is taken up on the floor of the assembly or senate, it is brought up in the party conference (or the caucus, as it used to be called). The conference is a party mechanism, and the parties are fundamental units of organization in a legislature as partisan as New Jersey's.

Each party—the senate Democrats, senate Republicans, assembly Democrats, and assembly Republicans—selects its own leaders as the new legislature begins. As of 1985, leadership positions were relatively numerous, reflecting the demands made by individual legislators for positions of some status, if not always great authority. Among majority party Democrats, leadership positions were held by ten members in the assembly and six in the senate. Among minority party Republicans, leadership positions were held by eight in the assembly and six in the Senate. If one includes not only party positions—such as majority leader, assistant majority leader, whip, and so forth—but also the chairperson and vice-chairperson of standing committees, then all but one of sixty-seven Democrats in the 1984–1985 legislature was a leader. There are now so many legislative leaders that Governor Kean once observed that, "When I ask for a meeting with the leadership, there are forty people in this room."[3]

Each party group in the assembly tries to get its conference started after morning committee meetings are over and members have had a bite to eat. In the senate the conference on a session day starts at 11 a.m. after a quorum call. At the conference, which is staffed by partisan professionals, members exchange views, leaders obtain feedback from the rank and file, and the rank and file get cues from leaders. Bills are discussed and party positions are taken on some. For the most part, members work out problems and build consensus for one another's bills. With the day's agenda reviewed, members emerge from the conference for sessions on the floor of the Assembly and Senate.

ORGANIZATION IN THE LEGISLATURE

The assembly and senate chambers in the State House are dominated by the rostrum at the front and center. It is from here that the speaker of the assembly and the president of the senate respectively overlook their membership and preside. The speaker and the president, as presiding officers, are the top legislative leaders, selected in effect by the majority party in the chamber. It is possible, although rare, for a member of the minority to put together a bipartisan coalition and be elected speaker, as was done by Republican Thomas Kean in 1972–1973. Since the 1974–1975 session, however, Democrats have had majorities at each session and have selected the presiding officers and organized each chamber.

In past years the tradition was for the positions of speaker of the assembly and president of the senate to rotate. Until 1971 new presiding officers were chosen every year, and from 1971 to 1979 they normally were chosen every two years. Today, members may serve successive two-year terms, and several have done so. With continuity in office possible, the top leaders are, or at least have the opportunity to be, more powerful today than previously. They appoint chairpersons and members of the standing committees, albeit after consultation with others. They are primarily responsible for referring bills to committees and deciding which ones get taken up on the floor and when. They speak for the legislature to the executive, and they represent their respective chambers with the press and the public. Together with the governor and the chief justice of the supreme court, the speaker of the assembly and president of the senate are the principal government officials of the state.

As one faces the speaker and the president on the rostrum, seats to the right of center are assigned to the majority party and those to the left of center to the minority party. Within these partisan groupings, members are seated by county or by legislative district. The majority and minority leaders have seats on the aisle, so that they can move through the chamber easily. The session, usually scheduled to get underway at 1:00 p.m. in the senate and 2:00 p.m. in the assembly, begins with a prayer, salute to the flag, and the taking of attendance. Next, ceremonial resolutions honoring individuals and groups are offered by members, and the presence of special guests in the galleries—such as state celebrities, beauty queens, high school basketball teams—is acknowledged. Then the senate and the assembly get down to their main business, legislating.

THE LEGISLATIVE PROCESS

The numbers of the bills scheduled for floor consideration at a particular session are listed on billboards on the wall on either side of the rostrum. The first bill of the session is moved. Debate takes place. The voting machine is opened by the presiding officer. Members flip electronic voting switches at their desks. Large monitors at the front of the chamber register the ayes in green and nays in red next to the names of members listed alphabetically. The voting machine is then closed by the presiding officer and the tally announced. A second bill is moved and the process is repeated, again and again throughout the rest of the day. Depending on the length of the calendar, the session lasts until the late afternoon or into the evening. Afterwards most members head home; but a few—those from nearby or those who are especially hardy—remain for dinner at favored restaurants, such as Lorenzo's.

The pace of a session day can be slow, frustratingly slow. More often, however, it is hectic, maddeningly so. Although no more than thirty bills are supposed to be taken up on a single day, the rule is frequently waived and fifty or more are processed. With members and staff milling around on the floor and conferring with one another, the presiding officer calls for order and eventually gets it, for a time. Even on a relatively leisurely day, the enactment of legislation, especially in the assembly (known affectionately as "the zoo"), appears to take place amidst buzzing confusion and with little rhyme or reason. And occasionally—as during the frantic closing days of the legislative session —the legislature passes bills in wholesale lots, "grinding out statutes like so much hamburger meat."[4]

Although dealing with bills and statutes is the core of the legislative process in Trenton, the legislature also performs several other functions. The senate gives (or withholds) advice and consent on gubernatorial nominations. The legislature proposes amendments to the New Jersey Constitution and acts on amendments proposed by Congress to the U.S. Constitution. These functions require relatively little time and energy. The assembly and senate also exercise oversight, checking on the administration and performance of state programs. This function is laborious, has little appeal for members, and consequently tends to be neglected. Legislation, on the other hand, has great appeal for members; when faced with a problem most will respond, "There ought to be a law." Given these predilections of legislators themselves, it is hardly surprising that the legislature's main business—in committee, in conference, or on the floor—is making laws.

Lawmaking is also the principal concern of the legislature's nonpartisan staff, the Office of Legislative Services. With about 250 people on an annual budget of roughly $10 million, the office helps individual members by researching bills, drafting bills, and reviewing bills for proper technical form. Most important, it helps standing committees screen and modify bills by providing full-time professional staff to work under the direction of the chairperson.

In the two hundredth legislative session (1982–1983), approximately 7,100 bills were introduced by the 120 members. That averages out to about 60 bills per member. At the high end, two senators introduced as many as 160 bills each and one assemblymember introduced 150. At the low end, a few members introduced only 9 or 10 bills.

One legislator introduced a bill to designate the striped bass as the state fish and another bill to increase the minimum size at which striped bass might be caught. Two legislators sponsored measures requiring professional teams at the sports complex in the Meadowlands to use "New Jersey" as part of their names. Others introduced legislation regulating sanitary conditions at tattoo parlors, requiring drivers licenses to be in the form of plastic cards, providing a program for the spaying and neutering of dogs and cats, and prohibiting the sale of junk food in the public schools. One bill would have exempted fishing bait from the sales tax, another would have exempted breath analyzers, another kerosene heaters, and another smoke detectors. A number of legislators introduced—and not for the first time—a bill to designate "I'm from New Jersey" as the state song. Indeed, this bill passed the assembly on six occasions and the senate on three and made it to the governor's desk twice, where it died for want of a signature. (Governor William Cahill, according to a *Star-Ledger* article of October 21, 1984, rejected the bill with one of the state's most succinct veto messages: "It stinks.") Still another legislator proposed a bill to amend the state constitution to restrict the number of bills a member could introduce to no more than twenty in a session.

Members sponsor some bills mainly as a courtesy to constituents or simply to take a position, and they may not even press for their passage. Most of what they sponsor, however, they do want enacted into law. Therefore, they work at the task of negotiating passage of their bills through the process—lining up sponsors in their own and also in the other chamber; testifying before the committee of reference; and, if their bill is reported out of committee, supporting the bill in the party conference and arguing its merits on the floor. Nevertheless, most of the bills sponsored by members die along the way, usually in committee. Only one out of every eight or nine that are introduced make it through the process.

POWER AND POLICY

Out of the thousands of bills introduced during a typical legislative biennium, relatively few are of great import. That is to say, relatively few affect large numbers of people, require substantial sums of money, alter the distribution of political power, or arouse the interest of organized groups. How these important bills are disposed of, and what happens as a consequence, usually depends on the power and participation of the interest groups represented in Trenton, the governor and the executive branch, and the legislature itself, each of which is involved in varying degrees according to the issue at hand. Whatever the issue, however, one decision or another has to be made in the legislative arena. The legislature cannot avoid at least some involvement in the process, and its role may range from the most limited—essentially saying yes, no, or some other time maybe to a proposal initiated by others—to the most extensive—full participation in shaping a measure, wherever it happens to originate.

THE GROUP STRUGGLE

Some bills are of relatively little concern to the legislature or the governor, but of major concern to organized groups. Referred to as special interest legislation, these bills affect the members of one or several groups more directly than the general public. With regard to issues of this sort, the legislature plays a reactive role, acquiescing to group requests or refereeing battles fought out between two or more special interests on legislative terrain. Although members take sides and many serve as advocates or agents, the involvement of the legislature overall is relatively slight.

If an organized group pushes a measure in the legislature, if that measure does not require the appropriation of funds, and if no other group rises in opposition, then the chances are good that the measure will pass. Much legislation goes through in this manner. Sometimes, however, the group proposing a measure will encounter opposition from another group that fears its interests may be adversely affected. In such a case, the reaction of the legislature usually is to ask the two groups to try to reconcile their views on the subject. If things can be worked out between the principals, then the legislature usually will ratify the compromise. For instance, occupational therapists tried to have a licensure provision enacted into law, but in order to do so, they had to draft legislation that would reassure physical therapists that their turf was safe. Even then, however, there was a danger that other opposition, specifically by the hospital association, might surface. Despite agreement between two groups, the issue could not really be settled until the hospitals also gave their consent.

When one special interest seeks to expand or protect its economic turf at the expense of another, amicable settlement is seldom possible and so battle is waged. Ophthalmologists, optometrists, and opticians do not see eye to eye on a number of issues. One such issue involves the contact-lens market and the efforts of optometrists to protect their dominant position from challenge by opticians. Another involves a bill that would permit optometrists to treat routine eye ailments with medication, which ophthalmologists strenuously oppose.[5] If the proponent of a measure loses, as happened to the optometrists, whose assault on their ophthalmologist brethren was turned back, there is always the possibility of bringing the measure up at another time. Thus, bills unsuccessful in one session of the legislature keep coming back like an old melody.

On occasion one group wins unequivocally, at least for the moment. The New Jersey Dental Association, for example, was successful in enacting its so-called freedom of choice bill, which allowed patients enrolled in dental plans to go to any dentist rather than only to specified clinics. The dentists' victory was attributable in part to the case they made, in part to their lobbying skills, and in part to their Political Action Committee (PAC) and the campaign contributions it made to legislators.

One of the most contentious, albeit narrow, issues centered on the efforts of the animal lobby to ban leghold traps and the resistance of trappers who maintained that their livelihood depended on keeping them. The battle lasted thirteen years, generating considerable heat and more mail to legislators than many other issues. Finally, a compromise was reached and a bill was enacted that called upon Rutgers University to develop a more human substitute for the steel-jawed traps that were being used by the industry.

Other issues broader in scope also find the legislature refereeing interest group struggles and making decisions on who wins and who loses. Take the right-to-know law, in which labor and environmentalists combined to require industry to notify workers about chemicals and toxic substances that they handled. Or take the plant closing legislation, supported by labor and opposed by business, that required six-months advance notice to workers when management planned to close down a facility. The bottle bill is another example. Here the environmental lobbies back legislation requiring consumer deposits, so that bottles will be returned and can be reused or recycled, while labor opposes it, fearing the loss of jobs in the glass industry, as do food wholesalers and retailers, who are concerned about costs and inconvenience.

Whether issues such as these have narrow or broad ramifications, impetus comes mainly from outside the legislature—from the community of interest groups. This is not to say that the legislative role and the legislative arena are unimportant. In the end, legislators must make their own decisions, based upon the current political climate, their individual connections or commitments, the information available, the arguments presented, the skill and credibility of the lobbyists, a group's legitimacy and political resources, and, more and more, past or prospective contributions from a PAC.

If twenty-one members of the senate and forty-one members of the assembly cast yea votes on the floor, then the group or groups sponsoring a measure emerges victorious. If fewer than the constitutional majority of senators and assemblymen vote yea or, more likely, if a measure does not get out of committee onto the floor or through the second chamber, then the groups opposing it have managed, at least for the time being, to hold the line.

EXECUTIVE AND LEGISLATIVE LEADERSHIP

During the two-year lifetime of each legislature, a number of issues arise that transcend the concerns of particular groups. Although interest groups may also be involved, leadership on these issues is mainly by the governor or the legislature, or the two in combination.

Typically, the initiative for major legislation in New Jersey, as in other states, comes from the executive. Some proposals stem from positions taken and pledges made during the governor's election campaign. Cabinet members also have items to advance, so do legislators, all of whom want their ideas included as part of the governor's program. Finally, a number of initiatives come without prior commitment or planning, in response to unanticipated opportunities, crises, pressures, or political demands.[6]

However positive or negative it may feel, the legislature does respond to measures endorsed and pressed by the governor. Indeed, it is the governor's agenda that normally dominates a legislative session, whether the governor is a Democrat or a Republican and whether the legislature is under control of one party or the other. The record of Governor Thomas Kean and the Democratic controlled legislature during 1982–1985 illustrates how the policy-making process works in New Jersey and with what results.

Although there was considerable partisan conflict during this period, the governor and the legislature managed to agree on a number of significant policies. Urban aid is one example. Kean recommended that $5 million go to the six largest cities of the state so that layoffs of police and firefighters could be avoided. Democrats in the legislature favored $14 million for 325 communities, most of which were suburban in nature. This put the governor in the position of having to oppose a bill that would aid those areas on which Republicans depend for their support. In the end a compromise was worked out, with $7.4 million allocated to help 28 cities.[7]

Another bipartisan accord in this period was reached on automobile insurance, after more than a year of contention during which every plan Kean proposed was shot down by the legislature and every plan proposed by the legislature was rejected by Kean. Finally, when the governor started to put strong pressure on the Democrats by making auto insurance reform an issue in the upcoming legislative elections, he and the legislative leaders at last worked out a compromise package of bills overhauling the state's ten-year-old no-fault insurance laws.

Still another area for Democrats and Republicans to act in bipartisan fashion was unemployment insurance. In this case the governor appointed a commission to make recommendations and to resolve what had been an impasse between business and labor on several problems in the system. The legislature voted unanimously in favor of the commission's recommendations. "This is an example," commented the Democratic majority leader of the senate, "of what can be done when the legislature and the administration see a need to work together."⁸

The construction and repair of the state's highways, bridges, and mass transit systems also provide a case of cooperation between the governor and the legislature. When Kean first proposed his $3.3 billion package, Democratic leaders took issue with a number of provisions. Then, when a coalition of groups ranging from the state AFL-CIO and the New Jersey Business and Industry Association to the American Automobile Association Clubs of New Jersey and the state League of Women Voters, as well as several Hudson County Democrats, rallied in support, the legislative leaders backed off. For a while, however, the details of the package could not be settled and the final package was adopted only after strenuous negotiations. Democratic legislative leaders got some of what they wanted—more public participation by means of a referendum on a proposed amendment to the constitution, a finite term on the life of the independent authority that would administer the fund, and the addition of state aid for municipal roads. And the governor achieved his purposes with the creation of the Transportation Trust Fund Authority empowered to sell up to $600 million in short-term bonds and the dedication of part of the gasoline tax for mass transit.

As Kean's first administration drew to a close, the Republican governor and Democratic legislature managed to get together on a number of additional programs. After lengthy negotiations, they agreed on legislation requiring casinos to reinvest a portion of their receipts in projects to redevelop Atlantic City and other urban areas of the state. After relatively brief discussions, they endorsed legislation empowering the New Jersey Sports and Exposition Authority to operate an additional racetrack, enter the hotel business, establish a cultural center, and build an amusement park, as well as bring a professional baseball team to the state. Finally, they succeeded in placing a $90 million bond issue before the voters to finance industrial and educational high technology facilities, and they spoke out effectively on behalf of its passage in the referendum of November, 1984. By whatever standards, these were significant accomplishments and indicated a productive relationship between the executive and legislative branches of government.

TAX POLITICS

Probably few issues are as important or as perennial as those focusing on revenues. Tax policy as much as anything else illustrates the ways in which the governor and the legislature play their respective roles, generally with the governor proposing and the legislature disposing.

Until recently the history of tax policy in New Jersey was one of gubernatorial leadership thwarted by legislative recalcitrance.[9] (See Chapter 9.) Lately, the balance has shifted, making the legislature virtually coequal with the governor. In the Kean administration, conflict and accommodation regarding taxes has continued. In his first year in office, the governor failed by a narrow margin to win an increase in the gasoline tax in the senate, after the assembly had passed it. The next year, with revenues urgently needed to cover a shortfall in the state budget, the governor insisted on an increase in the sales tax while the Democrats insisted on an increase in the income tax for people in high income brackets. After the two sides had struck their partisan poses, a typical political compromise was effected. The governor got part of what he wanted, as the sales tax went from 5 to 6 percent, and the legislature got part of what it wanted, as the income tax was increased by one percent on income over $50,000 a year.

Even when there is no immediate need for additional revenues, taxes can still be an issue. While most members of the legislature would rather not have to deal with taxes, some are committed to property tax relief and to overall tax reform. Proposals for tax commissions are introduced and measures to shift the tax burden from one group to another are designed. The issues can be portrayed in partisan or bipartisan terms, depending upon the strategic objectives of participants in the process.

Sometimes taxes have to be cut. In 1985 the state had a large budgetary surplus, thanks to a very favorable economy. Democrats and Republicans agreed on a reduction in taxes but disagreed on a specific plan. The governor favored a one-time homestead rebate and the Democrats in the legislature favored a more permanent reduction. Finally the governor gave in and reluctantly signed a permanent tax-relief bill, one that he characterized as "expensive, regressive and cumbersome." In this case the legislature prevailed.

By now it is clear that when the time is right or when a crisis demands action, the legislature will have a large part not only in what revenue plan gets enacted, but also in just how the plan is shaped and put together. Nowadays what emerges at the end of the process may well be closer to the legislature's preferences than to the governor's.

BUDGETARY POLITICS

Although the legislature during recent years has carved out a significant role in the determination of revenues, it has not progressed so far regarding expenditures. By its very nature and position, the executive branch is central to the budgetary process, while the legislature exercises influence only toward the margins.

The budget is formulated in the executive, by the various departments and agencies and by the Division of Budget and Accounting of the Office of Management and Budget in the Department of Treasury. Budget formulation has changed recently, so that the governor currently exercises greater control. Indeed, by the time departmental budget requests are submitted to the legislature, executive negotiations have taken place and basic issues have already been resolved.

Normally the governor's budget message is delivered to the legislature in February. The legislature then recesses and the twenty-five-member Joint Appropriations Committee spends two to three months holding hearings on the budget, making revisions, and preparing a budget act for passage on the floor and signature by the governor before the constitutionally prescribed date of July 1. The hearings give the commissioners an opportunity to describe their departments and programs to members of the JAC and allow these legislators the opportunity to question commissioners, not only about the budgets of their departments but about substantive issues as well. The budget review enables legislators to shift funds around from one function to another or among divisions or bureaus within a department. Finally, and not least importantly from the perspective of individual representatives, the process gives members a chance to add to the budget funds for projects in their own districts. Although only about 5 percent of the budget is ordinarily changed by committee action, a number of JAC legislators by now have developed skill in picking apart the governor's budget line by line.

The constitution requires that the budget enacted by the legislature and signed into law by the governor be balanced, with projected revenues equaling projected expenditures. If expenditures are too high, either they must be reduced or else additional taxes must be imposed. The projection of revenue—an estimate of how much money will be generated by the economy under current tax law—is critical. The more optimistic the estimate, the higher the projected surplus (or the lower the projected deficit); the more pessimistic the estimate, the lower the projected surplus (or the higher the projected deficit).

Whatever the state of the economy, the legislature and the governor are likely to disagree on their revenue estimates. Traditionally, the treasury department projections are on the downside so that the state can wind up with a financial cushion. It is also in the governor's political interest to underestimate any surplus, so that he has the upper hand in spending whatever additional monies are collected. For example, according to a legislative estimate made early in 1985, the surplus in the budget for the fiscal year ending that June would be $800 million, almost $200 million more than the administration's projection.

Whatever the precise amount of the surplus, there is likely to be conflict between the governor and the legislature over how to spend it. One newspaperman referred to this situation as a surplus crisis, the opposite of a deficit crisis.[10] In a surplus crisis, instead of having to figure out what programs to cut, legislators have to choose where to add money. At almost any time, and especially in the wake of lean budgetary years, legislators will have a number of programs and projects that they believe are deserving of support. Everyone wants a piece of an expanded pie. "It is tougher," as the co-chairperson of the Joint Appropriations Committee noted, "to deal with a lot of money than it is to say, 'We don't have it.'"[11] A surplus whets the legislative spending appetite on the one hand, and on the other it affords the governor an opportunity to strengthen his political base.

Both the legislature and the governor have ways to negotiate in a budgetary contest. The former can refuse to adopt a gubernatorial spending proposal, and then funds cannot be appropriated for the desired purpose and the governor is thwarted. The latter can veto a legislative item in the budget bill; unless that veto is overridden, which is very unlikely, the legislature is thwarted. And recently, the state supreme court upheld the governor's line item vetoes of specific provisions in legislative appropriations bills, thereby giving the governor an even stronger hand. Although there is little doubt that his position overall is stronger than the legislature's, the budgetary process is not completely a one-sided affair: the legislature shares power here, and through the budget has its say on state policy.

PERFORMANCE

At about the halfway mark in his administration, Governor Kean happened to take a health test that showed that he was under great stress. When informed of the results, the governor smiled and wryly blamed his condition on the Democratic-controlled legislature. His view was, "If the Legislature will cooperate with me, it certainly will be less stressful for me."[12]

The kind of division and partisanship that Governor Kean held responsible for his stress is by no means new to New Jersey. It has long been an important factor in contemporary political life. Since 1948, the governorship and the legislature have been under the control of the same party only half the time. When both branches are in the hands of the same party, as during the second Byrne administration, there is likely to be substantial agreement. The result is that a number of policies and programs emerge from the process. When the two branches are in the hands of different parties, however, the degree of agreement will be lower and fewer policies and programs are likely to emerge. Exceptions occur, of course, like Governor Hughes, who generally received bipartisan support, even after he lost a Democratic legislature, and Governor Kean, who—as has been noted above—has managed well with a Democratic legislature.

Nevertheless, conflict occurs rather frequently in New Jersey and has been increasing of late. One reason for this conflict is partisanship in the legislature. Recent conflict between Democratic legislators on the one side and the Republican governor and legislators on the other has been heated. Confined to particular areas and involving specific issues, the conflict is primarily over power. What has been happening in New Jersey, and elsewhere too, is that the legislature itself has become an electoral battleground where issues are raised and exploited in order to gain partisan advantage. Both Democrats and Republicans play a very political game, with their eyes on forthcoming legislative and gubernatorial elections.

Typically, when the Republican governor puts forward a proposal, legislative Democrats object, perhaps offering their alternative instead. Debate is engaged and postures are struck. The governor insists on most of his proposal, and legislators insist on some of theirs. As one legislator indicated, during the final stages of negotiating the transportation fund, "We want to get our footprint on this thing."[13] Before the dust settles, a deal is made and a compromise is announced. Legislative Democrats, who appear "willing to do almost anything they can to take the edge off any political triumphs Kean envisions,"[14] manage to share in whatever credit is received and both parties can applaud the final bipartisan product.

Partisanship bears only part of the responsibility, however, for the conflict between the legislative and executive branches. Part is also attributable to the marked growth over the years in the institutional strength and independence of the New Jersey legislature. During the late 1960s and 1970s the legislature increased its capacity markedly and developed as a political institution.[15] Standing committees became significant in the process, specialization began to be taken seriously, the legislative workload grew heavier, and more time and energy were devoted by members to their tasks. As important as anything else in the development of the legislature and its enhanced capacity was the expansion in the size and competence of its professional staff—both nonpartisan and partisan staff for leaders, for party conferences, for standing committees, and for individual members as well. As a result, the legislature today insists on sharing not only in the credit for state policy, but also in its formulation. It no longer tolerates being excluded from the initiative and planning part of the process. Chairpersons of standing committees and legislative leaders have served notice that they want to be in on the development of policy, in addition to rendering a decision on its adoption. Although the governor is still the single commanding figure in the state's policy process, is still expected to chart an overall direction for the state, and is still relied on for leadership,[16] the legislature now has an independent and assertive institutional role. This is a profound change from twenty years ago, when the legislature was contently passive.

The speaker of the assembly recently summed up the achievement of the legislature. "We have taken on all the tough ones," Alan Karcher proclaimed, "The ultimate solution is a compromise, but we don't duck anything."[17] The legislature used to duck more problems then it does now, and that was one of the reasons why the state supreme court took on a legislative role in domains like education and housing. Still, the legislature cannot be expected to face every problem head-on. Where there is little possibility of solution or little likelihood of compromise, and where there is little to be gained while much to be lost, the legislature may decide that discretion is the better part of valor. It will sidestep an issue or at lest postpone dealing with it; that, too, is part of the legislative role.

Despite the transformation of its role, the legislature's image with the press and the public remains largely unfavorable. One perceptive observer speaks for many reform-minded citizens when he criticizes the legislature for not being sufficiently responsive or responsible and for being "as unkempt and as disheveled as ever."[18] There is little new in such criticism. Indeed, since the adoption of the state's third constitution in 1947, "bemoaning the weakness and ineffectiveness of the legislature has been a popular pastime in New Jersey."[19] As for most citizens, however, the legislature is little more than an abstraction. (See Chapter 1.)

Like other representative bodies, the New Jersey legislature is an arena where values clash and accommodations have to be worked out. It is where district is pitted against district, constituency against constituency, group against group. It is where conflict has to be resolved and consensus has to be built. It is a very human institution with all the frailties of such. It is amorphous, unwieldy, messy, disorderly, and at times chaotic. Like most institutions, it is not without its problems and, like everything else, its performance can be improved. But whatever its institutional deficiencies and whatever its image, the legislature's recent record of accomplishment has been commendable. The New Jersey legislature may not be pretty, but it is doing its job.

Notes

1. The two quotations from New Jersey assemblymen are reported in Rick Sinding, "The View from the Back Bench," *New Jersey Reporter*, 12 (March 1983): 14–15.

2. Neil Upmeyer, "The Sunshine Boys," *New Jersey Reporter*, 13 (June 1983): 12–19.

3. Quoted in Rick Sinding, "Fixing up the Legislature," *New Jersey Reporter* 13 (March 1984): 10.

4. *The Star-Ledger*, January 22, 1984.

5. Upmeyer, "The Sunshine Boys," 12–13.

6. Alan Rosenthal, "The Governor, the Legislature and State Policy Making," in *Politics in New Jersey*, rev. ed., Richard Lehne and Alan Rosenthal, eds., (New Brunswick: Eagleton Institute of Politics, 1979), 143.

7. See Harvey Fisher, "Boys will be Boys," *New Jersey Reporter*, 13 (February 1984): 30.

8. *The Star-Ledger*, March 27, 1982.

9. See the historical account of tax policy by Richard Lehne, "Revenue and Expenditure Policies," in *Politics in New Jersey*, 236–239.

10. Jim Goodman, "The Surplus Crisis," *New Jersey Reporter*, 14 (November 1984): 33.

11. *The Star-Ledger*, July 2, 1984.

12. *The Star-Ledger*, November 17, 1983.

13. *New York Times*, July 10, 1984.

14. Jim Goodman, "Taking Credit, Casting Blame," *New Jersey Reporter*, 14 (July 1984): 33.

15. For an account of the development of the legislature see Alan Rosenthal "The New Jersey Legislature: The Contemporary Shape of An Historical Institution; Not Yet Good But Better Than It Used To Be," in *The Development of the New Jersey Legislature from Colonial Times To The Present*, William C. Wright, ed., (Trenton: New Jersey Historical Commission, 1976), 72–119.

16. The characterization (made in Rosenthal, "The Governor, the Legislature and State Policy Making," 141–42, 153, 166) continues to apply today.

17. *The Star-Ledger*, April 7, 1985.

18. Sinding, "Fixing up the Legislature," 7.

19. Short and Ford, Architects, *Legislative Space Study for the New Jersey State Legislature* (Princeton, January 1981), 13.

7

ELEANOR V. LAUDICINA

The Bureaucracy

Early each weekday morning Susan V. Mitchell leaves her home in East Brunswick to travel to Marlboro where she serves as program coordinator in the Department of Human Services. Susan's responsibilities range from development of rehabilitative programs for a "cottage" to oversight of some 150 residents of the state-run psychiatric hospital. Originally trained in social work, she is committed to the clients she serves, but often finds the workload excessive and her initiative limited by complex procedural directives from Trenton. Somewhat later in the morning Jim Sandler leaves his home on the outskirts of Trenton to travel a short distance to his state office in the heart of the city. Jim works for the Casino Control Commission. Unlike some of his colleagues, however, Jim never sees the glitter and glamour of Atlantic City's new casinos. As director of administration for the commission, his job is to maintain the complex administrative network that supports the commission's work. The regular arrival of paychecks —in the right amount and to the right people—the availability of office supplies and equipment, telephone, and computer support, as well as oversight of financial operations, all fall under his official jurisdiction. Arriving in Trenton, at about the same time as Jim, Walter Jensen dons his white lab coat as he enters the public health labs of the New Jersey Department of Health. Walter is chief virologist for the DOH and is responsible for supervising one of five comprehensive analytical and diagnostic services performed by the department for physicians, clinical and hospital laboratories, and local health departments.

These characters are fictional but their jobs and responsibilities are real. What common thread ties them together? Despite the variety of their activities, "Susan," "Jim," and "Walter" are all bureaucrats, administrative functionaries, of New Jersey. They represent only a minute fraction of the approximately 100,000 people who make up the work force of state government, a work force more diverse in its characteristics, more extensive in the scope of its activities, and far more powerful in its impact than most citizens of the state ever imagine.

The influence of bureaucratic activity, in fact, permeates virtually every aspect of everyday life for most residents, although often in subtle and almost invisible ways. In the groggy haze of early-morning preparation for work or school few people ponder the pervasiveness of bureaucratic activity. When switching on the light, who thinks about the Public Utility Commission? Yet that agency has the primary responsibility for monitoring both the availability and the cost of electrical power in the state. People take for granted the absence of odd colors and unidentifiable objects in the water they wash in and use to bruth their teeth, not bothering to acknowledge the state Department of Environmental Protection's water quality control program. The milk poured into coffee or on cereal fosters nutrition not illness, because it meets standards set by the New Jersey Department of Agriculture. While driving to work or school—with both personal and automobile licenses acquired through the Division of Motor Vehicles —people inevitably use a road maintained either by the state or by a locality with assistance from the state. The number of stop signs or traffic lights is determined by the New Jersey Department of Transportation. These are only a few of the most common indicators of bureaucratic activity at the state level.

Before taking up the cudgel against "Big Brother" New Jersey-style, or railing against the intrusions of bureaucratic government, one ought to stop for a moment to consider the origins of bureaucracy and the reasons for the growth in size and scope of governmental activity. Bureaucrats do not materialize out of nowhere, nor do they proliferate, rabbitlike, in governmental warrens. Governmental activity emerges in response to perceived needs and executive and legislative initiatives. As the state has grown and diversified socially and economically, the changing needs and demands of its citizens have been carried to Trenton via media, lobbyists, legislators, even bureaucrats themselves. Every bill passed by the legislature, every executive order signed by the governor, requires some means by which it can be carried out, some bureaucracy. The growth in the size and scope of the New Jersey bureaucracy is nothing more than a reflection of the changing character of the state and of the growing demands on its governmental institutions.

The chapter that follows takes a closer look at that growth. It will examine the current range and scope of activities of the state bureaucracy, as well as the complex pattern of competition and cooperation that characterizes relationships among state agencies, the state legislature, and the multiple components of the executive branch. The chapter will conclude with a look toward the future. What is likely to be the configuration of state government? What forces can we identify now that could change the role of the state bureaucracy?

Growth and Expansion of the Bureaucracy

The New Jersey bureaucracy as we know it today had its origins in the state constitution that was adopted in 1947. One of the new charter's principal accomplishments was modernizing the structure and organization of state government. An incredibly complex and truly unmanageable array of over eighty agencies were restructured within fourteen executive departments and a ban was placed on future growth beyond twenty units. This reorganization reinforced the general thrust of the new constitution towards strengthening the power of the governor in both policy direction and management control. Later legislation, passed in 1970, also enabled the governor to reorganize the executive branch at will, in the absence of specific legislative opposition. Legislative approval, however, remains necessary to create a new department or to abolish or substantially alter an existing department.

Today the number of executive departments has grown to twenty, bumping against the constitutional limit. Despite efforts to streamline the state's work force, "cut the fat," and limit budgetary growth, there is no indication that the volume and scope of demands on the bureaucracy will diminish. In the area of social services, for example, the state has taken up some of the slack caused by a diminished federal presence, and to a limited extent has expanded some of its own programs to make up for the loss of federal funding. The shift from categorical to bloc grant funding has created new roles for state agencies once bypassed when funds flowed directly from Washington to local governments. Executive initiatives in response to technological development, environmental concerns, and transportation needs, demand new roles and new responsibilities.

In keeping with the tenor of the times, Governor Thomas Kean has expressed his commitment to a lean and efficient state work force and to holding the line on both budgetary and staff increases. The 1984–1985 state budget reflects these goals with staff in many agencies either diminished slightly or held constant. Nevertheless, expectations of a greatly shrunken, substantially more limited, bureaucratic presence in the state would be illusory. Given the scope of functions currently being undertaken in the state, the extent to which many citizens have come to depend on state services, and the degree of state regulatory efforts, any substantial alteration would be met with a loud roar of opposition.

The growth of state government, however, undoubtedly has slowed. In recent years, in response to austerity measures, some actual declines have been registered. Between 1974 and 1981 the total state government work force grew from approximately 75,000 to approximately 103,600 (see Table 7.1). Yearly increases generally ranged from 4,000 to 6,000 employees. Between 1981 and 1982, however, the size of the work force actually decreased by almost 2,000 workers. Most of these positions were restored the following year, but the rate of growth in new positions clearly had slowed. By June of 1984 only 100 new employees had been added to the state payroll.

The same trend is evident in the budget. The governor's 1984–

TABLE 7.1   THE NEW JERSEY STATE GOVERNMENT WORK FORCE

Year	State Govt. Employees
1974	75,000
1975	77,300
1976	81,500
1977	87,500
1978	93,000
1979	92,500
1980	97,000
1981	103,600
1982	101,700
1983	103,600
1984 (June)	103,700

SOURCES: New Jersey Bureau of Labor Statistics.

1985 budget represented an anticipated increase of only 4 percent in the cost of direct state services. Except in those areas designated as priority concerns—economic development, environmental protection, some social services, and tax relief—the steady incremental growth of state government has slowed. An era of doing more with less surely has descended on New Jersey state government. The long-range impact of cost cutting on the capacity of the bureaucracy to perform its multiple functions remains to be seen.[1]

When compared with the size and scope of state bureaucracies elsewhere, New Jersey's is neither the smallest nor the largest. In total number of state government employees relative to population, New Jersey ranks eleventh. Virtually every other industrialized, urbanized, and heavily populated state has a larger state government work force. These include California, with the largest number of state employees, New York, with the next largest number, Pennsylvania, Ohio, Michigan, and Illinois. A look at the distribution of that work force across departments and among the various functions of state government, however, reveals some characteristics unique to New Jersey. For example, only five states devote more of their total work force to functions related to the regulation, control, and oversight of other internal agency operations. Similarly only six states use more employees for functions related to financial administration. At the other end of the spectrum, by contrast, twenty-five states have more employees assigned to natural resources, sixteen have more staff working in departments of education and higher education, and thirteen devote more of their work force to corrections. Analysis of these staffing patterns tends to reinforce a number of criticisms frequently leveled at the state bureaucracy. First, the state tends to become mired in its own red tape, devoting enormous time and energy to internal paper shuffling rather than to actual delivery of state services to New Jersey citizens. And second, even more commonly and pervasively, the state consistently has failed to devote adequate resources to such critical areas as conservation, environmental protection, and education.

THE SCOPE OF THE BUREAUCRACY

The twenty departments of state governments vary tremendously in both size and scope. Budgetary allocations for 1984, for example, range all the way from an enormous $543.8 million for the Department of Higher Education to a minuscule $4.6 million alloted to the Department of Banking. Similarly, personnel allocations range from the 22,000 employed by the Department of Human Services to the only 95 in the newly created Department of Commerce and Economic

Development. While the Department of Human Services is generally regarded as the mega-agency of state government, others also consume a hefty portion of the state budget. These include the departments of Transportation, Corrections, and Law and Public Safety. Mid-range agencies include the departments of Treasury, Environmental Protection, Labor, and Health, among others. In addition to those already noted, among the smallest state departments are Agriculture, Insurance, and Defense. (See Table 7.2.)

The historical evolution of the twenty state departments reveals how bureaucracy responds to the changing needs of an increasingly complex economic and social environment. The fourteen departments originally established under the 1947 constitution reflected such traditional concerns of state government as agriculture, civil service,

TABLE 7.2   THE NEW JERSEY BUREAUCRACY

Department	Date Established	1984 Budget (in $ millions)	Employees (1983)
Higher Education	1967	543.8	330**
Human Services	1976	472.1	22,000
Transportation	1966	271.6	7,870
Corrections	1976	206.3	4,500
Law & Public Safety	1948	171.0	7,000
Treasury	1948	77.5	3,990
Environmental Protection	1970	51.1	2,200
Labor	1948	43.5	6,700
Health	1948	30.9	1,500
Education	1967	28.4	1,650
Public Advocate	1974	26.1	800
Energy	1977	16.9	550
State	1948	15.7	105
Community Affairs	1966	14.5	700
Civil Service	1948	13.4	600
Defense	1963	9.6	260
Commerce & Economic Devel.	1981	7.3	95
Insurance	1970	6.4	260
Agriculture	1948	6.2	415
Banking	1970	4.6	160

NOTE: Employment data for the departments of Higher Education and Human Services does not include the approximately 20,000 faculty, administration, and staff of the state's university and college system. Dates include years of reorganizations.

health, and labor. Eighteen years passed with no substantial alteration. The decade from the mid-1960s to the mid-1970s, however, witnessed unparalleled change in the configuration of agencies and departments, as the state attempted to grapple with a host of new demands, new pressures, and the vocal activism of new constituencies.

Within that decade, the following new departments were established—Transportation, Community Affairs, Environmental Protection, the Public Advocate, Energy. Each new department was a response to economic, demographic, or social needs. For example in 1966 New Jersey became the first state to establish a department of transportation. In New Jersey, a state whose highway system has always carried more traffic per mile than any other state, the need for coordinated action was clear. In addition the increasing deterioration of an antiquated mass transit system demanded an enhanced state presence. Subsequent establishment in 1979 of the New Jersey Transit Corporation signaled recognition of the growing inadequacy of existing mass transit facilities. New Jersey, via New Jersey Transit Corporation, became the principal operator of commuter lines in the state.

Another New Jersey innovation came in 1974, when the state institutionalized a new governmental function, the ombudsman, through establishment of the Department of the Public Advocate. This new agency assumed greatly expanded power as a combined public defender, consumer advocate, supporter of citizens in their dealings with other divisions and departments of state government, and counsel for mental patients.

Formation of the Department of Environmental Protection (see Chapter 11) and of the Department of Commerce and Economic Development (see Chapter 12) also signaled significant new responsibilities for the state's bureaucracy.

State administration grows not only by the creation of entirely new departments or substantial enhancement of former functions, it also grows by fragmentation. In some cases older departments have split, amoebalike, to form two new departments. The present departments of Human Services and Corrections are a result of the division in 1976 of the Department of Institutions and Agencies. Concerns over the massive and ever expanding size of the old department and the difficulty of maintaining control over its many components led to restructuring. Even after division, the two new departments both rank among the largest in state government. Another reason for the division was the growing disparity between the human service functions carried out by the state via mental institutions and welfare aid and the essentially policing functions of prisons and correctional facilities.

Growing disparity of functions and activities has resulted in division of other departments as well. For example in 1968 a new (and fleeting) concern with the limited range and scope of higher education facilities in the state resulted in the splitting off of a new Department of Higher Education from the Department of Education. Similarly in 1970, the Department of Banking and Insurance was separated into two component parts, owing largely to the differing regulatory needs of the two constituencies and to pressures for attention from differing clientele.[2]

BUREAUCRATIC ACTIVITIES IN NEW JERSEY

State government carries out an incredible range of tasks and activities, which can be grouped into three major functions—service, regulation, and internal support. Many departments are large, umbrella-like entities that incorporate several of these functions, although they usually have just one primary emphasis. Of the three, service and regulation constitute the major activities of state government, and the ones to which the greatest resources are provided.

SERVICE PROGRAMS

The role of state governments is changing, with an emphasis being placed on "their emergence as providers of specific services for people rather than as forces which shape the economic and social environment."[3] Services are particularly evident in New Jersey. Despite the Kean administration's emphasis on economic and infrastructure development, the greatest share of the state budget goes to an enormous range of services for individuals. The Department of Human Services, for example, offers a wide range of assistance programs to the aged, veterans, the mentally ill, the physically handicapped, and the mentally retarded. A considerable amount of federal money also flows through DHS: its Division of Public Welfare, for instance, administers the federally-supported Aid to Families with Dependent Children program along with many other assistance programs. Other large departments also play a major role as service providers to college students (higher education), prisoners (corrections), commuters (transportation), and the unemployed (labor).

The demand for state services is likely to increase over time. The dominant demographic and economic trends within the state, particularly the aging of the population, the growing concentration of needy people in declining urban areas, and the diminished manufacturing base, will all continue to demand a statewide response. Events outside the state, however, particularly in Washington, appear to have had little impact on determining the nature of that response. For example, the level of services provided by the state, though partially influenced by the changes in federal spending during the Reagan years, was largely shaped by forces within the state itself. The state did move in to fill the gap left by reductions in federal funding for Medicaid and to maintain the existing level of health services. Most of the budget increases received by the Department of Human Services, however, were related to the need to upgrade and update physical facilities, meet institutional accreditation standards, and modernize data processing and information management capabilities. Improved service delivery may constitute an indirect result of this activity, but greatly expanded service to clients excluded from federal benefits was not on the agenda. Although new human service programs have been undertaken, they largely represent a response to particular economic and social problems relatively unique to the state.[4]

REGULATORY ACTIVITIES

Although state activity is most evident in service delivery, regulation is also clearly visible. In fact, the two are difficult to distinguish entirely, since many regulatory activities are designed to serve citizens by insuring safe, comfortable, or relatively hazard-free conditions. Consequently, those departments that are primarily service deliverers also engage in a considerable amount of regulatory activity. For example, the Department of Human Services not only establishes the conditions of eligibility for its multiple individual services, but it also establishes and monitors standards of care at state institutions. Similarly, the Department of Community Affairs primarily performs service functions, but its Division of Local Government Services also heavily regulates the state's 567 municipalities and 21 county governments. The division, for example, must review and approve all local government budgets for conformity to expenditure limitations, format, and other procedures. The division promulgates and enforces guidelines for the conditions under which money may be borrowed and prescribes auditing and financial reporting procedures to which all local governments must adhere. As a result of such regulation New Jersey municipalities, in general, enjoy high bond ratings and are relatively free of the financial emergencies experienced by some cities in neighboring states. (See Chapter 9.)

Other departments are primarily regulatory, with service components of only secondary and indirect importance. These departments include Banking, Insurance, Law and Public Safety, Health, and Environmental Protection. State regulations governing individuals range from automobile driver qualifications to safety standards for model rocket builders; however most regulatory effort is directed toward the establishment of operational and performance standards for particular industries. These efforts range from the rate-setting powers of the Board of Public Utilities, the Department of Insurance, and, recently, the Department of Health to the rules governing betting in Atlantic City, safety standards on the job, high school graduation standards, qualifications for health care professionals, and air and water quality.

The regulatory activities of the state of New Jersey are more extensive, more detailed, and farther-reaching in their impact than those of many other states. For example, New Jersey's environmental standards, particularly those affecting air and water, are more stringent than federal standards, and, as noted above, the budgetary and financial activities of local governments are far more closely monitored in the state of New Jersey than they are in many other states. Elaborate regulations govern even the most minute aspects of casino gambling operations.

Despite federal efforts to stem the tide of regulation in the country, New Jersey's state government appears unaffected. If anything, the political climate of the state favors increased regulatory activity —particularly in such areas as toxic waste disposal, casino gambling, and land-use planning—and will be likely to generate further demands on the bureaucracy (albeit with only marginal increments in staff and budget available).

Whatever the industry that is being regulated, the tensions and conflicts are similar. From the affected industry's perspective, regulations are generally onerous, burdensome, costly in time and money, narrowly focused, and insensitive to the needs of competition and profit-making. Consumer advocates and public interest groups, however, generally find the level of regulation inadequate, with loopholes abundant and often unsettlingly close ties between regulator and regulatee. And the bureaucrats actually charged with implementing regulations complain of being overburdened by legislative mandates, understaffed, and caught between the conflicting pressures of affected industries and public interest groups.

In any specific situation, an objective observer may find the evidence supports one of these positions. Over zealous regulation may indeed impose arbitrary and unnecessary demands on an industry.

Critics of New Jersey's stringent environmental regulations, for example, charge that the Department of Environmental Protections's pursuit of environmental quality has put the state at a competitive disadvantage in attracting new industry. Undeniably, too, representation on regulatory boards and commissions is clearly skewed toward the concerns of regulated industry. Many of the state's professional licensing bodies—from the barbers and hairdressers to legal and medical boards—have been accused of excessive self-protection; membership of these licensing bodies shows too little representation of public interest groups and too much representation of the profession subject to regulation. Finally, it is also true that at least some state agencies are charged with far more enforcement responsibility than either budget or staff can adequately manage. The Division of Local Government Services within the Department of Community Affairs, for example, is hard pressed to oversee adequately the myriad of regulations governing the financial affairs of the more than five hundred municipalities in New Jersey. All of these tensions and conflicts are likely to continue and remain inevitable components of state regulation and oversight.

INTERNAL SUPPORT

The least visible aspects of state government, but the ones most critical to the effective functions of both regulatory and service activities, are the internal support activities. Certain departments, in particular the Department of Civil Service and the Department of the Treasury, provide the people and the money that make things happen in the service and regulatory agencies.

Providing People

The Department of Civil Service is one of the smaller departments of state government, but it directly controls access to all state classified or merit positions. At the present time between 85 and 90 percent of all state positions are considered classified. Nonclassified positions fall into two categories. Most are subject to standard criteria based on merit but not subject to an examination procedure. Faculty appointments in the state college and university system are one example. A relatively small number of political appointments fall into the second category. These are the top-level cabinet, undercabinet, and personal staff positions, which are vacated and refilled with each new administration. Generally these positions are filled first on the basis of partisan loyalties and second on the need for the governor to have the support of loyal assistants whose policy priorities and personal convictions are compatible with his own. Even with such appointments, top-level administrators complain that the civil service system extends so far up the organizational hierarchy that it is impossible to appoint trusted and personally loyal individuals to key policy positions.

The civil service system in New Jersey, as in most states, was instituted in response to the widespread corruption, high cost, and inefficiency of the spoils system. Today, however, New Jersey's civil service is widely regarded as among the most archaic systems in the country; it is cumbersome and awkward in its operational dimensions and contradictory in the values and ends it appears to represent. The current system has many critics and few real defenders, but nonetheless it manages to withstand virtually every onslaught. Legislative efforts aimed at even the most modest reforms have failed, challenges in the courts have been turned back, even efforts by the Department of Civil Service itself to streamline its operations have been challenged and deflected.

One of the most peculiar and frequently criticized aspects of the system is a concept known as absolute veterans' preference. This means that any military veteran who receives a passing score of seventy on any civil service examination automatically moves to the top of the list of eligibles, even if some nonveteran taking the test scored far higher. Although many state civil service systems, and the federal system, will add points to a veteran's or a veteran's spouse's score, only in New Jersey are all passing veterans preferred over all others.

Absolute veterans' preference has been attacked by women's groups, who view the law as discriminatory. The courts, however, have ruled that since the intent of the law was not discriminatory, and since women presumably have an equal opportunity to become veterans, it does not violate constitutional guarantees. Others have pointed out that veterans' preference, especially in so total a form, violates the merit premise of the civil service, which dictates that selection should be based on demonstrated capacity to do the job not extraneous qualities. Nevertheless, the provision remains and, after several legislative rebuffs, has become one of the great sacred cows of state politics. It stands as a tribute to the political power of both veterans' and labor organizations, which have successfully fought off all reform efforts.

New Jersey's civil service system has also been subject to many other criticisms over the years. Unlike a number of systems, which have attempted to consolidate testing for many positions within one broad examination, the New Jersey Civil Service continues to require a different examination for virtually every type of job. The justification is that the examination, to be valid, must test for the specific needs of each position. Consequently many jobs are filled on a provisional basis, awaiting development and administration of an appropriate examination. Months, sometimes years, go by before the test can be given. If provisional appointees are not veterans or not good test-takers they may eventually lose their jobs, regardless of the quality of work actually performed. Partly to avert this possibility, and sometimes for less laudable purposes, a kind of gamesmanship has developed within state agencies. An agency with a vacancy may write a position description so detailed and narrow that only the incumbent has the necessary qualifications to sit for the examination. Ironically, despite the effort to tailor-make each test, managers still complain that the paper-and-pencil approach to assessing ability simply does not and cannot gauge such personal and intangible qualities as judgment, motivation, commitment, and cooperation. These qualities frequently are critical for effectively dealing with both clients and co-workers.

Although problems of hiring civil servants may be aggravating, one of the greatest sources of frustration for managers—as well as of public disenchantment with the system—is the difficulty of firing civil servants. Once an individual has survived the probation period, usually three to six months, efforts at removal are subject to a complex series of procedural constraints. Designed to protect workers against arbitrary firing for personal or partisan motives, these procedures require substantial documentation and considerable time and effort by the supervisor to justify removal. Adding to the difficulty is an overlay of additional protections established through collective bargaining agreements.

As a consequence, a certain mythology has developed among managers and supervisors in state government that removing a state employee is virtually impossible. That opinion is certainly exaggerated. Incompetent and ineffective employees have been and will continue to be terminated in ways completely consistent with civil service protections. Nevertheless, guidelines require written documentation of the failings of the employee, substantiation of the supervisor's prior attempts to inform the employee of the problem, and evidence of previous efforts to improve performance. In all but the most extreme cases, the cure often seems worse than the disease. Mediocre performance is tolerated in the absence either of tangible rewards to promote higher achievement or of a credible threat of termination.

Providing Money

Access to the material resources needed by state government is controlled by the Treasury Department, which operates as a central management agency. Within the treasury, the Office of Management and Budget is responsible for planning, preparing, and implementing the state's annual multi-billion dollar budget, as well as for oversight of all financial operations in state agencies. The OMB was formed in part to integrate ongoing performance evaluations and management improvement activities into the budget process. The hope was that increased attention would be given to how effectively state programs operated, not simply to whether or not appropriate accounting and financial controls were in place.

The effort to use the budget process as a tool for management has a long history in this state's government. The fact that so many different approaches have been tried provides some testimony that none has proven an unqualified success. Getting control of state government in order to evaluate performance or to slow the growth in expenditures is an exceptionally elusive goal.

Since the early 1960s, virtually every budgetary innovation tried at the federal level has had a counterpart in New Jersey. During the Cahill years, New Jersey experimented with the Program Planning Budgeting System, a complex budget format that attempted to integrate long-range planning, program evaluation, and funding requests, all within one document. The system, which demanded reams of paper and a level of analytical skill foreign to most government managers, was quickly abandoned at the federal level. In New Jersey PPBS was phased out during the Byrne administration to be replaced by another new budget format then attracting national attention—zero-based budgeting. ZBB was an attempt to undermine the basis for most growth in government budgets, the fact that, once established, few programs are ever funded below the prior year's level; budget requests, therefore, are always increasing. By requiring budgetary justification from scratch for both new and established programs each year ZBB aimed to identify and eliminate obsolete or marginally useful programs, as well as to cut funding in areas with a low gubernatorial priority.

Despite the hoopla that accompanied its inauguration, New Jersey soon learned that ZBB in practice was far different from ZBB in principle. Excessive paperwork and cumbersome procedures soon led to abandonment of a pure ZBB concept in favor of one that required justification only for funding requests above 75 percent of the previous year's budget. Even this relatively modest reform failed to create either an appreciable diminution of funding or a noticeable slowing in the growth of the state budget. Understandably, state managers developed something of a ho-hum attitude toward the budget process and a this-too-will-pass response to each new set of budget instructions. Use of the budget as either a tool for rational planning or an effective instrument for executive policy has remained aspiration rather than reality.

The Kean administration devised a new strategy in the budget wars. Rather than adopting a new format for managers to use when submitting their budget requests, the Kean people stood the budget process on its head. The traditional plan of budgeting in government is from the bottom of the organizational hierarchy upward. Managers submit requests to the cabinet officer, who trims and adjusts in accordance with various priorities and judgments. The departmental request is then forwarded to the budget bureau and the Office of the Governor for further paring. Historically, requested funds exceeded available funds by 10 to 15 percent. Critics argued that the cutting process created after-the-fact policy decisions based on budget reductions rather than on rational planning and priority setting.

The state budget for 1984–1985 was the product of a process very new to New Jersey. Known as target budgeting, the process both begins and ends in the governor's office. Initially, the treasury budget officers and the governor establish targets for each department's budget, based on prior funding, projected growth in mandated programs, gubernatorial policy priorities, and projected revenues. Departments are expected to design base budgets that do not exceed these targets, and they must also submit three-year projections. Additional funds beyond the target figure may be requested only for programs that fit within one of the governor's stated priorities. In the 1984–1985 budget, these were confined mostly to economic development, data processing and computer initiatives in state government, and strengthening of the state's infrastructure.

For the fiscal year beginning July, 1984, the new process did appear to have produced a noticeable slowing in the growth of state spending. Growth in direct state spending was 4 percent compared with 7.5 percent, 12.1 percent, and 16.3 percent, respectively, for the three previous years. Actual decreases in existing programs, however, were minimal. Critics of the new process take a more jaundiced view. Some argue that the difference is more in style than in substance: budget negotiations now simply precede the determination of targets rather than follow the submission of requests. Others argue that the self-discipline required to confine budgetary requests to predetermined targets prevents the governor's office from seeing the consequences of lost services. In an effort to meet their predetermined targets, departments and agencies delete from budgetary requests program proposals that may, in fact, be desirable to retain or support. The process, therefore, while encouraging priority-setting at the department level, limits the governor's capacity to review the full range of prospective state services in any given budget year.

The long-range effect of the new budget process is difficult to predict. Bureaucrats generally develop an adaptive quality, which in the long run can survive virtually any attempt to impose control. They have seen budgetary reforms come and go with little long-term impact on state operations. Their capacity for gamesmanship has been virtually limitless, and every executive effort to impose control has been met with a bureaucratic counterthrust. Without a very firm and consistent commitment by the Office of the Governor and by cabinet members, politics and not procedure will continue to dominate the budget process.

In addition to control of budget preparation, the Office of Management and Budget has also assumed a greatly expanded role in general managerial oversight of the state bureaucracy. In 1982 Governor Kean announced the creation of the Governor's Management Improvement Plan. This program included both short-term and long-term components. The short-term program involved a comprehensive organizational and program review of the executive branch. The long-term program was intended to establish a strategic planning framework for state government.

Fueled by anticipated shortfalls in the 1983–1984 budget, the initial plan was designed to streamline organizational structures, eliminate unnecessary or duplicative functions, identify cost reduction opportunities, and find ways to make state government more cost efficient. Using as resources teams of corporate executives on loan from their companies, over $3 million contributed by the business community, and the services of a Massachusetts-based management consultant firm, the governor's staff undertook an intensive analysis of all major state agencies. Their major goal was the elimination of excess layers of management and consequent reduction in personnel costs. In a series of meetings, agency heads, consultants, business executives and OMB staff reviewed the reams of data produced by the study and identified positions to be eliminated or downgraded, as well as organizational processes that could be streamlined.

After expenditure of considerable time and money, GMIP received only mixed reviews. Most agency managers found that the exercise had made them more aware of the structure and operation of their agencies and more sensitive to impediments to productivity. Most agreed that the GMIP had been the most significant and most substantial managerial intervention in state history. Few, however, expect it to have a long-term effect on state government operations. If one of the objectives was to reduce substantially the size of the state work force, little seems to have changed: the total number of state employees even showed small increases from 1982 to 1983 and from 1983 to 1984. Skeptical state managers have been less than completely won over to the cause of management improvement under which GMIP was inaugurated, for many saw cost-cutting, not management improvement, as the primary aim.[5]

THE POLITICS OF BUREAUCRACY

The bureaucracy, like every other facet of state government, is part of an essentially political process. Agencies compete with each other for power, influence, and budget. A complex network of shifting alliances with state legislators, lobbyists, other agencies, and members of the governor's staff supports efforts to acquire new programs and enlarge old ones, to resist encroachments by other state departments and to reduce controls or constraints that the governor, his staff, and the cabinet officers are struggling to impose on an entity at once amorphous and impenetrable.

THE STRUGGLE FOR INFLUENCE

One agency's search for legitimacy, credibility, and power provides a microcosm of the dynamics played out on a daily basis at many levels of government. Although the creation of a new department may provide a visible and newsworthy symbol of commitment to a critical public need, the reality of minimal authority, small staff, and tight budgets may present a very different picture.

The New Jersey Department of Energy was created in 1977, in the aftermath of the serious gasoline and heating oil shortages of 1973–1975. The department was established ostensibly to assure the state an adequate supply of energy from all sources and for all anticipated purposes. The department's powers, however, were limited to planning, not implementation. In most cases, regulatory power still rested with the Board of Public Utilities, which was uneasily housed within the DOE, and with other departments, such as the Department of Environmental Protection. Consequently, despite its broad mandate, the new DOE exercized only minimal power and influence and was greatly overshadowed by older, more established agencies. Critics predicted a rapid demise.

In the bureaucratic wars over power and influence, however, DOE has scored some recent victories. Most importantly, it has taken away from the Board of Public Utilities jurisdiction over certificates of need, the first permission required for construction of electricity–generating plants. As is generally the case in state government, however, the DOE's new authority is constrained by the powers of other departments and agencies. For example, the Department of Environmental Protection still can halt construction deemed environmentally unsound and the Board of Public Utilities can refuse rate increases to pay for new construction.

In a system in which budget and staff size as well as substantive authority are indicators of status and power, the relatively tiny DOE may never rank close to the top. Still, its struggle to assume more substantial power illustrates a continuing process in state government—the contest between agencies for expanded influence and authority.

MANAGEMENT OF THE BUREAUCRACY

One of the greatest challenges facing new cabinet members, most of whom have had little or no experience in government, is to gain some understanding of and control over departmental employees. They, the bureaucrats, will be the primary means to achieve departmental goals for the next four years. Most cabinet members find that process an eye-opener and soon realize that the governmental arena is far different from any other they have known.

For one thing, most of the bureaucrats have been in place a long time and are likely to remain long after the tenure of any commissioner. Longevity and experience with departmental operations have several implications. After years of interaction, bureaucrats come to know each other well and so form something of a fraternity among themselves. Relationships cross departmental lines and are particularly useful for dealing with outsiders like new political appointees. Breaking into this tight circle, particularly to get thorough and accurate information on agency operations, is difficult if not impossible. Generally a new department head has only a small staff of personal appointees, whose knowledge and experience may be as limited as the new head's own. Without substantial hiring authority and removal power, a new department head's capacity to generate either fear or loyalty is reduced.

Top-level government managers, particularly those drawn from the private sector, may find this kind of management itself exceptionally difficult. Those who want to gain some sense of control or oversight in their departments find that the task requires a great deal of attention to operational details, a capacity to detect flaws or contradictions in analyses presented by subordinates, and a constant cross-checking of information using a variety of sources at different functional and organizational levels.

A case in point is the New Jersey Department of Motor Vehicles. Long a source of citizens' anger, frustration, and bad jokes, the operations of the DMV became the target of a long and bitter confrontation with the public advocate in a suit brought on behalf of the citizens and the state against the division. In response to pressure from both within and without state government, and in an effort spanning several administrations, directors of the division have attempted to streamline operations, increase efficiency, and improve the demeanor of DMV employees. Using a combination of staff training, computerization, and other approaches, several successive directors of the DMV made a concerted effort to gain increased control over the direction and operation of the agency. Although the success of the program may not always be apparent to every visitor to every inspection station or DMV office, the agency has made some tangible improvements. Waiting times have been reduced; courtesy and responsiveness of employees has increased. The struggle continues, however. As the one state agency with which virtually every citizen over the age of seventeen has direct contact, DMV bears the brunt of most complaints about the operations of state government, and symbolizes the difficulty of controlling an entrenched bureaucracy.

Those who labor at other management levels within the bureaucratic structure also experience difficulties and frustrations. Problems most commonly articulated relate to the morass of procedural constraints within which bureaucratic managers must operate. Policy directives emanating from the upper level of the department, combined with those produced by other divisions, such as civil service, the treasury, and the public advocate, combine to produce an exceptionally complex administrative environment. Efforts to produce even modest changes require clearance at multiple levels, and this greatly restricts risk-taking, change, or innovation. The bureaucratic system is perceived by these middle managers as fragmented, divided, and without a clear sense of overall goal or purpose. Individual departments, as well as divisions within departments, protect their own turf, budgets, and staff from outside incursions. With some exceptions, the gubernatorial appointees who head the departments appear at best as administrative amateurs with little genuine understanding of management within the context of governmental bureaucracy.

State managers are frustrated also by what they perceive as a widespread negative image of bureaucrats: a problem exacerbated by extensive media coverage of bureaucracy's worst failings as well as frequent pot shots aimed by electioneering politicians. The negative portrayal of public servants, and of public service in general, creates difficulty in recruiting qualified individuals and in keeping those whose skills and experience make them attractive to private-sector employers. For those who do remain, morale is constantly low. Some, the more committed and optimistic, continue to press for change and improvement, chipping away at what often appears a vast, ponderous, and immovable entity. Others grow tired and frustrated and retreat to a mechanical repetition of tasks accepting the job security and modest living provided by government service.

Future of the Bureaucracy

The growth of the state bureaucracy undoubtedly will continue. The expansion of the state's regulatory functions, particularly into the conditions and affairs of local government, shows no evidence of decline. An aging population coupled with an increasingly archaic and obsolete industrial base can only generate new service demands at the corporate and individual levels.

The increasing sensitivity of citizens in the state to environmental hazards, to the fragile nature of the state's ecology, and to the quality of life in the Garden State in general inevitably will increase pressures for a more active and aggressive role for the state as protector of its most essential resources. Nor can the crumbling infrastructure of the cities or the decay of the network of bridges and highways long remain unattended without courting disaster. Finally, the complex and seemingly intractable issues of solid waste disposal, of resource recovery and recycling, long left to local prerogatives, will require the continued involvement and oversight of state authority if the state is to avoid eventual suffocation in its own garbage. The ultimate success or failure of current efforts to streamline, professionalize, and control the growth of bureaucratic functions remains to be seen. Meanwhile, the wheels do turn, albeit in sometimes perverse and peculiar ways, and the work of government continues.

And so we come full circle—back to "Susan" and "Jim" and "Walter" as they begin another workday. Like thousands of their counterparts in hundreds of state divisions and agencies, they truly are responsible for keeping those wheels of state government turning. Despite the frustrations, the impediments, and the general lack of recognition, these are the people who maintain the state of New Jersey.

Notes

1. *Budget Message and Taxpayer Guide, Fiscal Year 1984–1985* (Trenton: N.J. Department of the Treasury, 1984), 1a–11a.

2. For historical and other data concerning each department see, Edward J. Mullin, ed., *Manual of the Legislature of New Jersey*, (sometimes *Fitzgerald's Legislative Manual*) (Trenton, N.J.: Edward J. Mullin, 1984), 526–784.

3. *Book of the States*, 24 (Lexington, Kentucky: Council of State Governments, 1984): 335–344.

4. Richard W. Roper, et al., "The Effects of Federal Grant-in-Aid Changes in New Jersey, 1981–1984" (unpublished paper prepared for the Program for New Jersey Affairs, Princeton Urban and Regional Research Center, Princeton University; May 1984).

5. Matthew Kauffman, "From the Top to the Bottom Line," *New Jersey Reporter* (April 1984): 6–11.

8

JOHN C. PITTENGER

The Courts

The courts of New Jersey, especially the supreme court, have become major sources of public policy since World War II. Increasingly, they have shared center stage with the governor and the legislature, sometimes to the discomfiture of both. In the process, the supreme court has acquired a reputation as one of the most aggressive and innovative state supreme courts in the nation. Its opinions are widely cited and followed, both by federal and other state courts. In addition to settling controverted questions of law and public policy, these decisions have contributed to the emergence of a sharper sense of state identity. They have also lessened the discretion of many other actors on the political stage.

AN ILLUMINATING EPISODE

The character and prestige of the New Jersey Supreme Court was highlighted dramatically in a 1983 controversy concerning the proposed reappointment of Judge Sylvia Pessler to the appellate division of the superior court.

The appellate division is New Jersey's intermediate court of appeals. It hears appeals from the trial courts and various specialized courts and agencies. Sometimes its decisions are reviewed by the supreme court, but most actions of the appellate division are final.

Judge Pressler was originally appointed to the superior court in 1976 by the governor, with the advice and consent of the state senate, for a probationary period of seven years. Renominated by Governor Kean at the end of the probationary period, she would have enjoyed tenure for life, or until the age of seventy, if again confirmed by the senate.[1] During her seven years on the bench, she had become known as an energetic, forceful, and opinionated member of the judiciary. The tenor of her opinions is perhaps best captured in a speech she delivered to the graduating class of the Rutgers/Newark School of Law in 1983:

> It is apparent to me that people seek judicial redress and judicial resolution because of their justifiable confidence that the courts provide a remedy which is not available from the other branches of the government, the business community, the social structure, or any other forum. We will not solve our individual and social problems by withholding the availability of the favored, if not the exclusive, remedy, or by diverting those who seek it away from the judicial system or by ridiculing or attacking lawyers. . . . I think my point is clear. *The legal system is the only show in town.* [emphasis supplied][2]

Upon Judge Pressler's renomination, a major controversy erupted. Senator Gerald Cardinale (R-Bergen), in whose district Judge Pressler resided, let it be known that he would seek to block her renomination through the use of senatorial courtesy, a custom of long standing that permits a legislator to block the appointment of persons from the legislator's home district who are for some reason deemed unacceptable.

Governor Kean did not budge from his support of Judge Pressler. Newspaper editorials around the state strongly denounced Senator Cardinale (who was discovered to have been the losing party before Judge Pressler in two recent cases and demanded an end to senatorial courtesy. The *New Jersey Law Journal*, editorializing on page one for the first time in its history, deplored the exercise of senatorial courtesy.[3] The president of the New Jersey Bar Association endorsed Judge Pressler's nomination and urged that the full senate be permitted to vote on it. Chief Justice Wilentz made a much publicized (and, in some quarters at least, much criticized) trip to the senate chambers to enlist support for Judge Pressler.

These groups united to emphasize the importance to the state as a whole of a strong and independent judiciary. In so doing, they attacked the established but parochial institution of senatorial courtesy. Legislative leaders, intent on preserving their privilege, sought to al-

low the senate to vote on the nomination. Their way out was to define
the issue as one of a conflict-of-interest. If Senator Cardinale was opposed to Judge Pressler's nomination for reasons connected with his
appearances before her—a fact the senator staunchly denied—then
the senate might be justified in refusing to honor a claim of senatorial
privilege *in this case only*, leaving the privilege itself intact (if somewhat sullied). They did just that, and the nomination sailed through
on a vote of 35 to 2.

The Pressler affair illustrates several prominent features of judicial
politics in New Jersey. First and foremost, the episode demonstrates
the triumph of a statewide principle—the independence of the judiciary—over a local principle—senatorial courtesy. In this respect it
is typical of many of the issues resolved by the court itself.

Secondly, the issue of Judge Pressler's renomination was *not* a partisan one. Judge Pressler, a Democrat, was nominated by Governor
Kean, a Republican. While her chief critic was a Republican, the leadership on both sides of the aisle ultimately came to her support. The
controversy galvanized a good government brigade in defense of
Judge Pressler and the independence of the judiciary. In this instance
the brigade included regiments from the press, the bar association,
the law schools, and civic organizations such as the League of Women
Voters. The issue was quickly framed in moral terms. It focused not
on whether Judge Pressler was entitled to a life term on the bench,
but on whether Senator Cardinale had behaved properly in invoking
senatorial courtesy. Lost in the general commotion was any attempt to
address an issue which Senator Cardinale had attempted, however
clumsily, to raise: the issue, that is, of whether or not Judge Pressler's
record merited a life-time appointment to the bench.

Finally, the legislators seem to have accurately gauged public opinion in the matter. Senator Cardinale, who had been elected with
a margin of 10,981 votes in 1981, found that his majority had dwin-
dled to 1,257 in 1983, an outcome ascribed chiefly to his role in the
Pressler Affair. It thus appears that public opinion, or at least the voters in the thirty-ninth district, endorsed the central importance of a
strong and independent judiciary.

COURT DECISIONS AND PUBLIC POLICY

This strong and independent judiciary, especially the supreme
court, has contributed to the emergence of a new political consciousness in New Jersey. Decisions in four areas of public law—school
finance, exclusionary zoning, criminal law, and intragovernmental

relations—exemplify how the court has defined the obligations of public institutions toward the citizenry and toward one another, thereby educating the voters of New Jersey in their rights and responsibilities.

PUBLIC EDUCATION

In *Robinson v. Cahill*, decided in 1973, the New Jersey Supreme Court attempted to exert a major influence on public education.[4] Applying the New Jersey Constitution, it declared unconstitutional a system of financing public schools that relied heavily on local property taxes. At the same time, it contributed to the diminution of local control over schools and school finance and focused more authority in the commissioner and state board of education.

The complaint had been that urban school children were being discriminated against because they lived in districts that were tax poor, that is, where the value of taxable real estate supporting each child was far lower then the value of taxable real estate supporting each child in wealthy suburban districts. Chief Justice Weintraub, speaking for a unanimous court, struck down the New Jersey system of financing public education. The basis for the decision was the state constitutional requirement that the legislature make a "thorough and efficient" education available to all the school age children of the state.[5] The decision specified no remedy. Rather, it urged the governor and the legislature to get on with the task of devising an appropriate solution.

The 1973 *Robinson* decision turned out to be the beginning, rather than the end, of the school finance drama. Act II involved money. The court put its stamp of approval on a new school subsidy formula, but appeared to condition its endorsement on a real decrease in the disparities between property-rich and property-poor districts.[6] But no revenues were forthcoming to fund the new formula. The climax came in the summer of 1976, when the court prohibited further spending on public education until *Robinson* had been implemented.[7] A constitutional crisis loomed, but wiser heads prevailed, and the legislature ultimately enacted a personal income tax to help fund the new system.

Act III began in 1982, with the filing of a complaint on behalf of another group of urban school children. Essentially, said the complaint, nothing has changed; children in tax-poor districts are still being shortchanged.

A trial judge held, late in 1983, that the plaintiffs should be thrown out of court because they had not tried to solve the problem through the commissioner and the state board of education.[8] In May, 1984, a panel of the appellate division reversed that decision. Finding that the plaintiffs had made a case of constitutional magnitude, the court sent the case back to the trial judge for a plenary hearing.[9] Then the supreme court agreed in July 1984, to hear the case, so we are not yet close to a definitive supreme court pronouncement in this second round of school finance litigation. The guess among scholars is that the court will not give the legislature the same benefit of the doubt that was accorded it in the first round. The court is likely to insist that any legislation adopted to carry out its decision have the effect of lessening, if not removing, disparities in interdistrict wealth. And, if the legislature balks, the court that decided *Mt. Laurel II* (see below) might well decide to frame its own school subsidy formula.

Although Act III of the drama of school finance has not yet come to a close, and the script for Act IV does not even exist, several conclusions emerge. In *Robinson* the court essayed a bold new interpretation of the New Jersey Constitution, putting New Jersey squarely in the ranks of those states seeking to narrow the spending gap between rich and poor school districts. In so doing, it came close—and may yet come closer—to a major confrontation with the legislative branch of government. Still uncertain, however, is the effectiveness of the court's intervention in this politically sensitive area of public policy. The court has revolutionized the law; it has not yet revolutionized patterns of spending for public education.

LAND USE

Just as the supreme court in *Robinson* began to alter the historic balance of power between the state and local school districts for the funding of public education, so in the *Mount Laurel* decisions, it has undermined the historic power of municipalities to restrict the use of local land.

Municipalities have come, through zoning and other ordinances, to exert a wide authority over the use of privately-owned land. Typically, these ordinances divide a municipality into certain zones—residential, commercial, and industrial—regulate the uses of land within each zone, and limit the type of structures that may be built there.

New Jersey, resembling most other states in this respect, confers broad authority on its municipalities to regulate the use of land. Some suburban communities in exercising that authority have sought to preserve their "exclusive" character by means of zoning ordinances that require, among other things, minimum lot sizes and place limitations on use that appear designed to keep out the poor (the disallowing of mobile homes, for example).

Mount Laurel, in Burlington County, was one municipality employing such devices. In 1972 the local NAACP took Mount Laurel to court, urging that its "exclusionary zoning" practices violated New Jersey law and public policy.

In a sweeping decision in 1975, the New Jersey Supreme Court unanimously agreed, making perhaps even more creative use of the state constitution than it had in the school finance cases. Chief Justice Hughes agreed that municipalities have the power to zone in order to promote the general welfare, but, he argued, if the general welfare is the source of that power, it is also the source of limitations on its exercise. That is to say, any exercise of the power to zone that is not in the general welfare is void, and specifically, the attempt to restrict home ownership in a particular community to people with higher incomes is unconstitutional.[10]

The original decision in *Mount Laurel* was both widely praised and condemned. It had, however, no immediate effect. The court—perhaps deliberately—included no enforcement mechanisms in its decree. The legislature, though clearly invited to do so by the court, studiously avoided any effort to remedy the underlying housing shortage either by restricting the zoning powers of municipalities or by other means.

In effect, it was left to local courts (and ultimately to the supreme court itself) to carry out the unclear mandates implicit in *Mt. Laurel I*. Many municipalities used delaying tactics: by making minor adjustments in their zoning ordinances, they sought to put off the day of reckoning. Others, in effect, defied the supreme court's effort to bring them into line. In fairness to the municipalities, the decision was in some respects opaque; it did not make clear which communities were covered by *Mt. Laurel* nor what was the exact nature of their responsibility.

By the early 1980's *Mt. Laurel I* was in danger of becoming a dead letter. But in the spring of 1983 Chief Justice Wilentz, again speaking for a unanimous court, issued a 216-page opinion that has come to be known as *Mt. Laurel II*.[11] After reaffirming the earlier doctrine, the court took steps to ensure that its second *Mt. Laurel* opinion would have more practical effect than the first. It decreed the use of a land-use map of the state developed (for other purposes) by the state's Department of Community Affairs as a basis for determining which particular municipalities would be covered by the new decision. It then ordered those communities to make provision for low and moderate-income housing by revising their zoning ordinances. It required them to take other steps—such as applying for federal and state funds, for example—that might help meet their obligations. Finally, the court appointed three full-time superior court judges for the northern, central, and southern counties, respectively, to oversee implementation of all phases of the *Mt. Laurel* decrees and vested them with wide authority, including the imposition of the so-called builder's remedy, which would allow development even when contrary to provisions of local zoning ordinances if a developer agreed to include in his plan a certain percentage of low and moderate cost housing.

Galvanized perhaps by the supreme court's opinion in *Mt. Laurel II*, the legislature finally bestirred itself, passing in the summer of 1985 a bill creating a Council on Affordable Housing, halting the imposition of builders' remedies, authorizing the transfer of *Mt. Laurel* obligations from one municipality to another, and making many other changes in existing law.[12] It is not unfair to characterize the new statute as one that transforms a mandate into an option; instead of meeting court-imposed tests, municipalities are now given legal and fiscal incentives to provide their fair share of low and middle-income housing. How the statute will fare in the inevitable court challenge is anybody's guess. The outcome of that challenge will say a good deal, however, about how far the New Jersey Supreme Court is prepared to go in defending its right and duty to extract public policy from the sometimes opaque language of the New Jersey Constitution.

CRIMINAL LAW

Decisions of the New Jersey Supreme Court have fettered school boards in *Robinson* and town councils in *Mt. Laurel* and required that major policy issues be settled by uniform rules imposed at the state level. Similarly, decisions in criminal law have limited the discretion of local law enforcement officials by invoking protections guaranteed by both the federal and state constitutions.

It would not, however, be entirely accurate to characterize the New Jersey Supreme Court as a liberal court, i.e., as a court zealous to ensure the rights of criminal defendants at all costs. Rather, two imperatives seem to be at work in the court's recent opinions in this area. The court first asks itself, are vital interests, protected by either the federal or state constitution, at stake? In answering that question, the court has tended to give a broad reading to the protections afforded criminal defendants. If these rights are not involved, however, the court has been equally zealous—in implementing sentencing statutes, for example—to give full force and effect to legislative policies aimed at dealing harshly with criminal defendants. The court reaches this result even when it believes those policies to be unwise.

The court's approach to constitutional guarantees is best illustrated by two recent decisions that attempted to resolve the conflict between a student's protection from unreasonable search and seizure (a right guaranteed by the Fourth Amendment) and the duty of school officials to ensure an atmosphere in which learning can take place. One case involved a junior high school girl (identified as T.L.O.), suspected of smoking in the lavatory. Ordered by the principal to open her purse, she disclosed not only a pack of cigarettes but drug paraphernalia. Convicted of the possession of unlawful substances, she appealed, arguing that it was wrong to use the contents of her purse as evidence. The companion case involved the search of a high school boy's locker. Acting on information provided by the police, school officials, who had heard rumors, searched his locker and found speed. The student appealed his subsequent conviction.

A divided court reversed both convictions. The majority declared that the Fourth Amendment's stricture against unreasonable searches and seizures applies in school settings. Evidence from such searches could be used in a trial only if school officials had reasonable grounds to suspect "illegal activity or activity that would interfere with school discipline and order." The court concluded that such grounds were not present in either case. The United States Supreme Court reversed the decision of the New Jersey Supreme Court in *T.L.O.*, holding that while the New Jersey court had applied the proper standards, it had come to the wrong conclusion, since the search of T.L.O.'s pocketbook was reasonable under the circumstances.[13]

The court has recently shown concern for criminal rights in a wide variety of other settings. It has thrown out a prosecution based on the unauthorized scrutiny of a defendant's telephone billing records. It has laid down strict standards for searches authorized by judges in telephone conversations with the police. And a trial judge's admonition to defense counsel not to discuss the case with his client during an overnight recess was held to violate the Sixth Amendment.[14]

But this is not the full story. Consider, for example, the case of an eighteen-year-old boy with no previous record who committed two burglaries, carrying off two unloaded handguns among his other loot. He was prosecuted under the Graves Act, which makes it a crime to be in the possession of a gun while committing certain crimes, and which carries a mandatory three year minimum sentence. The defense argued that the legislature only wanted to impose a minimum sentence where the gun was crucial to the crime. Wrong, said Chief Justice Wilentz, perhaps that is what they ought to have said, but they didn't. He added,

We do not pass on the wisdom of this legislation's mandatory three year imprisonment term or the wisdom of its imposition on the offenses covered. That is a matter solely for the Legislature to decide. Once the Legislature has made that decision, and has made it within constitutional bounds, our sole function is to carry it out. . . . Our clear obligation is to give full effect to the legislative intent, whether we agree or not. We have endeavored to do so here.[15]

Another example of the court's deference to legislative judgments about sentencing can be found in two recent cases of aggravated sexual assault. Both defendants pleaded guilty and were given relatively light sentences—five years' probation in one case, five years' probation plus sixty-three days in jail in the other. Both trial judges focused more on the circumstances of the individual defendant than on the nature of the crime.

The supreme court unanimously upset both sentences.[16] It found that in drafting the new penal code the legislature intended to promote more uniform sentences, reducing the wide latitude previously given to trial judges. The legislature, said the court, wanted trial judges to pay more attention to the nature of the crime and less attention to the circumstances of the individual defendant. Judges should use aggravating and mitigating factors only to increase or decrease the penalties above or below a certain norm. Finding that the trial judges had not been guided by these considerations, the court remanded both cases for resentencing in the light of its discussion of legislative purpose. Once again, we see the court imposing a uniform statewide policy (albeit one laid down by the legislature), diminishing in this instance the discretion of trial judges.

ABORTION FINANCING

One other recent decision of the court is worth noting, in part because of its intrinsic importance, and in part because it shows the court once again making creative use of the New Jersey Constitution to shape public policy.

The legislature, which formerly had been willing for the state to fund all Medicaid abortions, voted in 1980 to limit state funding to situations in which the life of the mother was at stake. A 1980 decision of the U.S. Supreme Court, dealing with a similar Illinois statute, made it clear that this was an acceptable outcome in terms of federal constitutional doctrine.[17] Justice Pollock, speaking for himself and four others, reached the opposite conclusion under New Jersey law.[18] He reasoned that Article I, Section I—New Jersey's equivalent to the equal protection clause—prevented the legislature from distinguishing between situations where the health of the mother, as opposed to her very life, was at stake; but the same clause did not, as he saw it, require the state to fund nontherapeutic Medicaid abortions, as a dissent would have required.

THE COURT AS STATE UMPIRE

From time to time the New Jersey Supreme Court finds itself having to umpire disputes involving the three branches of state government. These decisions do not involve the exaltation of state over local power. Rather, they involve a balancing act not unlike that involved in the resolution of criminal cases. On the one hand, the court is zealous to ensure that neither the executive nor the legislative branch transgresses clear constitutional limits. Once that point has been established, however, the court is equally zealous to ensure that the other branches are able to carry out their responsibilities vigorously and efficiently.

The court's solicitude for gubernatorial power is especially noteworthy. Two kinds of cases illustrate this point.

New Jersey, like most industrial states, permits public employees to organize and bargain collectively with state and local governments, but not to strike.[19] The bargaining concerns "wages, hours, and other terms and conditions of employment"—language borrowed from the National Labor Relations Act. The question then arises, how broadly should this language be construed? Should courts allow public employee unions to force public employers to negotiate over a wide range of issues? Or should they preserve management prerogatives by limiting bargaining to a relatively narrow range of topics?

The New Jersey Supreme Court has given a loud and clear answer: it favors a narrow range of bargaining between public authorities and their employee unions.[20] The court has come close to limiting the scope of bargaining to no more than "wages, hours and fringe benefits." And it has steadily refused to sanction the creation of a middle ground covering a range of topics such as class size and teacher transfers about which bargaining is permissible but not mandatory. This is a relatively conservative result from a court whose jurisprudence is more often thought of as liberal or progressive. Philosophically, the court seems to be saying to managers in state and local government, "We will look closely at any exercise of your authority that may conflict with constitutional norms. Once we have ruled out any conflict, however, we will avoid doing anything to inhibit the vigor with which you exercise your powers."

On a different level, the outcome may be explained in political, but not partisan, terms. Four present members of the court have played key roles in the executive branch of state government, either as members of the cabinet or counsel to the governor. (The chief justice has also served in the legislature). These experiences perhaps convinced the justices that the governor and other public executives need enhanced capacity to provide vigorous leadership. Being forced to bargain with public employee unions about a wide range of issues, many of them involving important fiscal and administrative restraints, might weaken this capacity.

A different slant on the court's solicitude for the executive branch can be obtained from its resolution of a recent case involving a direct clash between executive and legislative power. The New Jersey legislature, like Congress and the lawmakers of many states, became increasingly disturbed during the 1970s by the voluminous rules and regulations issuing from the executive branch. The New Jersey lawmakers responded in 1980 by passing a bill that delayed the effect of executive regulations until they had been presented to the legislature for sixty days; moreover, if either house, by majority vote, struck the regulations down during that time, they would be nullified.

A unanimous court struck down this New Jersey version of the legislative veto, and so revealed its strong convictions about the role of a vigorous executive in the New Jersey scheme of government.[21] The court described vividly the evils that might be expected to flow from the statute:

> Even where the Legislature is not using its veto power to effectively change the law, the veto can legitimately interfere with executive attempts to enforce the law. The chief function of executive agencies is to implement statutes through the adoption of coherent regulatory schemes. The legislative veto undermines performance of that duty by allowing the Legislature to nullify virtually every existing and future scheme of regulation or any portion of it. . . . Moreover, the Legislature need not explain its reasons for any veto decision. Its action therefore leaves the agency with no guidance on how to enforce the law.[22]

A very recent case reinforces this picture of a court eager to sustain the governor's authority. In this case, it was the line item veto. When Governor Kean signed the 1983 appropriations bill on June 30, 1982, he exercised his line item veto power to delete or reduce certain items of appropriation and to delete certain general provisions that were conditions on the governor's power to spend the money appropriated.

Instead of trying to override the veto, the presiding officers of the two houses filed suit alleging an unconstitutional abuse of the line item veto. But the court, in a 6 to 0 decision, sustained each exercise of the line item veto, holding in effect that if the language was properly a part of the appropriations bill, then it was properly subject to the line item veto.[23]

The court's solicitude is not merely for the governor but for all those who wield his authority. Absent constitutional considerations, the court will sustain rules and regulations of administrative agencies even when the results are harsh. For example, the New Jersey Department of Human Services, in drafting Medicaid regulations, prohibited reimbursement for "environmental control equipment." The mother of a young boy suffering from asthma sought reimbursement for the cost ($264) of an air filter that had improved his condition. The court denied her request, deferring to the administrative agency notwithstanding the severity of the results.[24]

EXPLAINING THE COURT

The New Jersey Supreme Court is clearly not some run-of-the-mill tribunal, content merely to build upon precedent and to construe literally or narrowly the provisions of constitution and statute. On the contrary, its decisions are characterized by broad readings of constitutional guarantees of individual liberty, by a willingness to use the state constitution in novel and far-reaching ways, by zeal in shoring up the powers of the other branches of state government, and by creativity in shaping remedies for asserted deprivations of constitutional or statutory rights. In all of this the court has tended to exalt state authority at the expense of local control and home rule, and in so doing, it has educated the political consciences of the rising generation of New Jerseyans.

POLITICAL FORCES

The usual explanation for this judicial energy and creativity points to the events of 1947–1948—to the approval of a new judicial article in the state constitution and the appointment of Arthur T. Vanderbilt, law reformer and dean of the New York University Law School, as first chief justice of the new system. These events are a necessary but not a sufficient explanation. A more complete understanding comes from an inspection of the political forces that have sustained and strengthened the reforms of 1947 and given them a life of their own.

Back to 1947. That year's constitutional convention replaced a hodge-podge of courts and jurisdictions with a relatively unified system and concentrated enormous authority in the supreme court and in the chief justice. The justices (as well as all judges of the lower state courts) were to be appointed by the governor, with the advice and consent of the senate.[25] Judges were forbidden, while in office, to "engage in the practice of law or other gainful pursuit."[26] The supreme court was given general supervisory authority over the entire state court system,[27] and the chief justice was empowered to appoint an administrative officer for the courts and to assign and transfer judges of the superior court.[28]

Not surprisingly, one result of these reforms has been a bold and self-confident supreme court. The contrast with Pennsylvania, where the justices are elected, is instructive. There is no doubt, for example, that the method of selection is one reason why two state supreme courts construing similar language about public employee collective bargaining have come to quite different conclusions. Quite simply, the courts of Pennsylvania need to worry about organized public opinion in the form of employee unions, which contribute both money and labor to their campaigns; the courts of New Jersey do not, but are perhaps more sensitive to the needs of the governor, who both appoints and reappoints them.

Not content, however, with the relative independence conferred upon it by the new constitution, the supreme court has adopted a number of strategies that, intentionally or not, have had the effect of reinforcing its independence.

The court has taken a strict view of the limits imposed upon its members' abilities to augment their incomes by moonlighting. For example, New Jersey judges may not be paid for teaching at New Jersey law schools, although federal judges regularly are paid for such work and Pennsylvania judges encounter no similar bar. This result is hardly mandated by the language of Article VI, but it implements the court's desire to remain, like Caesar's wife, above suspicion.

The court polices with equal vigor all judges who are part of the system. The case of Judge Peter Coruzzi is illustrative. While serving on the superior court bench in Camden County, he was apprehended on the steps of the Camden County Courthouse with $12,000 in his pockets, allegedly the fruits of a successful attempt to influence the outcome of particular cases. Within twenty-four hours, he had been relieved of all duties and suspended without pay. Within six months he had been arrested, indicted, convicted, and sentenced to five years in prison. His appeals having been rejected, the supreme court affirmed a recommendation from a three-judge panel that he be removed from office.[29] The court noted that this was only the second time since 1947 that a judge had been indicted.

It is also worth noting how often the court has managed to reach a consensus, even in cases like *Mt. Laurel* that might be expected to produce deep divisions. The contrast with the oft-divided U.S. Supreme Court is striking. To some extent the difference is obviously a product of the greater diversity of the nation and the greater complexity of the issues reaching its highest court. To some extent it can be accounted for by the fact that the justices of the New Jersey court have tended to share a common philosophy to a greater extent than their counterparts in Washington. But, as one reads the opinions of the New Jersey court and studies what slender evidence exists outside those volumes, one cannot escape the impression that the court— goaded perhaps by a succession of strong-minded chief justices—has worked overtime to achieve consensus. Paradoxically, this is most apparent when there are dissents. Those dissents are invariably respectful of the majority point of view and display none of the asperity people have come to expect from Washington.

Finally, the court has not been shy to exercise the authority conferred on it by Article VI and various statutes to hire staff, make studies, issue reports, and generally monitor the health of the rule of law in New Jersey. From humble beginnings, the Administrative Office of the Courts has grown to a substantial bureaucracy, employing more than three hundred people and overseeing the expenditure of a judicial budget that now amounts to $57 million per year. By contrast, the comparable office in Pennsylvania (a state half again the size of New Jersey) has a staff of only forty-eight.

Thus, the New Jersey Supreme Court has taken a number of steps to protect and strengthen the independence conferred upon it in 1947. But the high prestige of the court has other sources as well.

Gubernatorial support has been critical. The vigorous program of Chief Justice Vanderbilt, for example, was sustained by Governor Driscoll. New Jersey has elected six governors since the reforms of 1947—three Republicans and three Democrats. All appear to have been supportive of an independent judiciary willing to use the New Jersey constitution as an instrument for social and political reform. Five of the six were themselves lawyers—a fact that perhaps explains their acquiescence.

The best measure of gubernatorial support, however, is the caliber of people appointed to the state courts, and especially to the supreme court. Neutral observers tend to rate the current court, in terms of experience and ability, as at least the equal of any other state supreme court in the country.[30] Moreover, it would not be stretching matters to suggest that a climate of opinion has been created that would make it difficult, if not impossible, for a governor to nominate to the supreme court anyone less than first-rate.

Alongside the tradition of competence has grown up a tradition of bipartisanship. It is now widely assumed, though nowhere required, either by constitution or statute, that every other appointment to the supreme court will be from the opposite party, so that the partisan balance on the court will never be more than 4 to 3 either way. A similar understanding applies to appointments to the superior court. (It should be noted, however, that the ties of some judicial appointees to one of the two major parties are more nominal than real.)

In regard to legislation, recent governors have been generally supportive of bills endorsed by the court. Thus, Governor Hughes supported legislation incorporating the county courts into the state court system; Governor Kean was equally supportive of legislation creating a unified family court. Governor Byrne used the court's decisions in *Robinson* to urge an income tax and a revised school subsidy system upon a reluctant legislature; Governor Kean endorsed the court's call for a thoroughgoing revision of the jury system, including the elimination of most exemptions from jury duty. Only in the area of housing and land-use planning have governors hung back: neither Byrne nor Kean could apparently muster much enthusiasm for *Mt. Laurel*, leaving the court to carry out its own mandate, at least until the passage of the bill setting up the Council on Affordable Housing in the summer of 1985.

The legislature, too, has generally fortified the independence of the New Jersey courts. In some ways, this support is surprising. Some recent decisions—for example, the one nullifying the legislative veto —have undermined the powers of the legislature itself. Others—for example, the decision on abortion funding—have angered large majorities in both houses. The anger, however, has always dissipated rather quickly, and New Jersey has experienced few attempts to trim the jurisdiction, the powers, or the staff of the courts, certainly nothing of the sort that have become a staple of the congressional diet since the early days of the Warren court.

One potential conflict with the legislature involves the court's rule-making power, which Chief Justice Vanderbilt defined expansively in an early case under the new constitution.[31] Even here, however, the court has displayed sensitivity to the reach of its rule-making power. Recently the court dealt with a 1980 statute limiting contacts between state officials (including judges) and the new casinos opening up in At-

lantic City.[32] The precise issue was whether or not part-time municipal judges were covered by the limitation and, if so, whether or not
the rule as applied to them was constitutional. The court steered
deftly between judicial and political rocks, holding the rule both applicable to judges and constitutional.[33] It thus vindicated legislative
authority and avoided a collision between the two branches of government. The opinion also hinted, however, at a reservoir of judicial authority, and to make sure that everyone got the point, the court used
that authority to extend the legislative rule to judges who had been
specifically exempted by statute in 1981! The opinion suggests a willingness to take account of political realities while preserving the
court's leadership role.

The eminence of the New Jersey Supreme Court is not, then, simply the product of constitutional arrangements put in place in 1947.
The court itself has worked hard to preserve and even expand its role
on the political stage; and governors and legislators have generally
been supportive, notwithstanding their occasional discomfort with the
court's decisions.

THE IMPACT OF PUBLIC OPINION

The final step towards a complete explanation is an exploration of
the impact of public opinion on the court—and the court's role in
shaping that opinion. Public opinion consists of an inner and an outer
layer. The inner one—the one with the most immediate impact
on the court—is professional opinion, in this case, the opinion of
practising lawyers operating through the New Jersey State Bar Association. The outer layer—perhaps more influential over the long haul
—is lay opinion, expressed in and shaped by the daily press, television, and journals of opinion.

The relationship between the court and the bar has not been without its strains. Increases in minimum fees have been criticized as too
little or too late, and a cap on contingent fees aroused widespread opposition.[34] A move to centralize authority for attorney discipline was
widely criticized; in the wake of this criticism the court relented
somewhat and returned a greater measure of responsibility to the District Ethics Committee. Increases in the amount that each attorney
must pay annually into the Client Security Fund, which protects clients against attorney fraud, are not popular.

These are, however, essentially intramural squabbles. At the first
sign of attack from outside, the bar association comes to the defense of
the court and the present system of justice, as in its spirited defense of
Judge Pressler's nomination.

In fact, the bar association's central criticism of the present system is that it does not go far enough in the direction of merit selection. The bar is uneasy about the extent to which senatorial courtesy, operating behind the scenes in ways that are not only hard to see but also hard to measure, may have eliminated highly qualified people from appointment to the bench. From time to time the bar agitates for a constitutional amendment confining governors to choosing appointees from a list submitted by an expert commission,[35] but the very satisfaction with the present system, which the bar association has helped nurture, generally militates against further change.

Press coverage of New Jersey court decisions suffers from the failings of such coverage nationwide: it often misses the real issues at stake. Of the ten largest dailies in New Jersey, few have full-time court reporters in Trenton. Coverage is sporadic in the New Jersey editions of the *New York Times* and the *Philadelphia Inquirer*, in the monthly *New Jersey Reporter*, and even on public television, the New Jersey Network.

Nonetheless, the courts have relatively good standing in public opinion—usually higher than the legislature (see Chapter 1). This reputation quite possibly results less from press coverage than from the extraordinary lengths to which the court itself has gone in promoting citizen involvement in the affairs of the judicial branch. For example, lay persons have been appointed to many of the committees established by the court, including those that advise the court about the discipline of judges and attorneys. In addition, a substantial number of lay persons are among those participating in the court's annual judicial conferences, each of which focuses on a separate aspect of the administration of justice. By persuading the legislature to eliminate most exemptions from jury duty, the court also enlarged the pool of citizens from which the state's jurors are chosen.

The widespread use of television in the courtroom, in which New Jersey has been a pioneer, has made the courts more familiar to the state's citizens. And a series of court decisions—the most recent narrowly limiting the circumstances under which pre-trial hearings may be closed to the press[36]—have given the media wide access to judicial proceedings.

No doubt each of these initiatives has played a role, however small, in propelling the court to center stage. But in the last analysis, it is the decisions themselves that best explain the central role that the court has come to play in shaping not only the issues, but also how New Jerseyans think about the issues.

The Courts and New Jersey Democracy

For thirty-eight years now the Supreme Court of New Jersey has been construing constitutions and statutes in a series of momentous decisions involving major issues of public policy — school finance, exclusionary zoning, crime and punishment, and the powers of governors and legislatures. These decisions have not only *made* policy, they have begun to shape the way citizens of the state *think* about policy. In the process, they have made citizens of the state more self-conscious. If New Jerseyans are less inclined today than they were in 1947 to think of the state as merely suburban New York connected to suburban Philadelphia by means of a turnpike, they owe some of this transformation to their courts, and particularly to the supreme court.

Those courts present a paradox. They are at once elitist and democratic. Nothing can alter the fundamentally elitist character of the court, consisting as it does of members of a single profession, chosen for life and insulated by that fact and by their own self-denying ordinances from the rough and tumble of political life. In another sense the courts are democratic, because the ends they seek and the values they promote by their forays into public policy are basically democratic values. In its public law decisions the supreme court seems to have had in mind, not simply fairness in the narrow, or procedural sense — due process — but also fairness in a broader sense — equal access to schools and housing and medical services and other goods and services. The court has been especially concerned to protect those not well situated to defend their own interests, whether in the market place or the polling booth. For such as these, the Supreme Court of New Jersey has been an eloquent champion.

Has the activism of the New Jersey courts been a good thing? Not easily answered. The pluses are clear, the minuses less obvious. Two qualms are worth a mention.

The strength of the courts both reflects and reinforces the weakness of the legislature; but the legislature, as a representative body, ought to be central in a democracy. This is something of a vicious circle. First, a problem, lying clearly within the legislative realm — school finance, low and moderate-income housing — becomes acute, but the legislature does nothing. So the courts finally intervene. In some cases — *Robinson*, for example — the court elicits a legislative response; in others — *Mt. Laurel* — the legislature remains mute. Then after an interval, because it deems the legislative response to be inadequate, the court intervenes again more massively than before. Meanwhile, the legislature occupies itself with trivial and largely symbolic issues—for example, prayer in the schools.

The other qualm arises from the increasing bureaucratization of the courts. The supreme court, controlling to a large extent the number and nature of cases coming before it, has been least affected, but the appellate division (and it is important to remember here that most litigants never get beyond the appellate division) appears to be groaning under the burdens imposed by increasing caseloads, committee assignments, and reports to the Administrative Office of the Courts. It seems likely that the quality of deliberations, and hence the quality of justice, may suffer over the long haul.

What is clear, however, is that no immediate change in the composition or philosophy of the court is on the horizon. No current member of the court is over sixty. Absent death, early retirement, or radical philosophic change, the court in 1995 is likely to resemble closely the present court—that is, it will continue to exalt state power over local considerations and to insist that all citizens of the state share in the advantages created or protected by public policy.

Notes

1. Constitution of New Jersey, Article VI, Section VI, Par. 3.

2. "Pressler Delivers Rutger/Newark Commencement Address," *New Jersey Law Journal*, 111 (June 30, 1983): 1.

3. "Senatorial Courtesy: A Public Outrage," *New Jersey Law Journal*, 113 (Sept. 22, 1983): 1.

4. 62 N.J. 473, 303 A.2d 273 (1973).

5. Constitution of New Jersey, Article VIII, Section 4, Par. 1.

6. Robinson v. Cahill, 69 N.J. 449, 335 A.2d 129 (1976).

7. Robinson, 70 N.J. 465, 360 A.2d 400 (1976).

8. Abbott v. Burke, unpublished opinion by Hon. Virginia Long, J.S.C., (Nov. 28, 1964).

9. Abbott v. Burke, 195 N.J. Super. 59, 477 A.2d 1278 (App. Div., 1984).

10. South Burlington County N.A.A.C.P. v. Township of Mt. Laurel, 67 N.J. 151, 336 A.2d 713 (1975).

11. South Burlington County N.A.A.C.P. v. Township of Mt. Laurel, 92 N.J. 158, 456 A.2d 390 (1983).

12. Fair Housing Act, N.J.S.A. 52:27D-301 *et seq.* (1985).

13. State in Interest of T.L.O., 94 N.J. 331, 463 A.2d 934 (1983), rev'd. U.S., 83 L.Ed. 2d 720, 105/S. Ct. 733 (1985).

14. State v. Hunt, 91 N.J. 338, 450 A.2d 952 (1982); State v. Valencia, 93 N.J. 126, 459 A.2d 1149 (1983); State v. Fusco, 93 N.J. 578, 461 A.2d 1169 (1983).

15. State v. Des Marets, 92 N.J. 62, 455 A.2d 1074 (1983), 65–66.

16. State v. Roth, 95 N.J. 334, 471 A.2d 370 (1984); State v. Hodge, 95 N.J. 369, 471 A.2d (1984).

17. Williams v. Zbaraz, 448 U.S. 358 (1980).

18. Right to Choose v. Byrne, 91 N.J. 287, 450 A.2d 925 (1982).

19. N.J.S.A. 34:B A-1 *et seq.* (West Supp., 1983).

20. *See* Dunellen Board of Education v. Dunellen Education Association, 64 N.J. 17, 311 A.2d 737 (1973); Ridgefield Park Education Association v. Ridgefield Park Board of Education, 78 N.J. 144, 393 A.2d 278 (1978); Bethlehem Township Board of Education v. Bethlehem Township Education Association, 91 N.J. 38, 449 A.2d 1254 (1982).

21. General Assembly of New Jersey v. Byrne, 90 N.J. 376, 448 A.2d 438 (1982).

22. *Ibid.*, 386–387.

23. In Re Karcher, 190 N.J. Super. 197, 162 A.2d 1273 (App. Div. 1983), rev. in part 97 N.J. 483, 479 A.2d 403 (1984).

24. Dougherty v. Human Services Department, 91 N.J. 1, 449 A.2d 1235 (1982).

25. Constitution of New Jersey, Article VI, Section VI, Par. 1.

26. *Ibid.*, Par. 6.

27. *Ibid.*, Section II, Par 2.

28. *Ibid.*, Section VII, Par. 1.

29. See Matter of Coruzzi, 95 N.J. 557, 472 A.2d 546 (1984).

30. Mary Cornelia Porter and G. Alan Tarr, eds., *State Supreme Courts: Policymakers in the Federal System* (Westport, Conn.: Greenwood Press, 1982).

31. Winberry v. Salisbury, 5 N.J. 240, 74 A.2d 406 (1950).

32. N.J.S.A. 52:13D-17.2 (West Supp. 1984).

33. Knight v. Margate, 86 N.J. 374, 431 A.2d 833 (1981).

34. See American Trial Lawyers Association v. New Jersey Supreme Court, 66 N.J. 258, 330 A.2d 350 (1974).

35. *New York Times*, Jan. 3, 1984, Section VI, 11.

36. See State v. Williams, 93 N.J. 39, 459 A.2d 641 (1983).

THREE
PUBLIC
POLICY

9

SUSAN S. LEDERMAN

Financing the State

In the waning days of the summer of 1984 an unusual issue dominated New Jersey politics—too much surplus in the state treasury! How should the excess money be spent? Reduce the sales tax? Rebate some income taxes? Increase state aid to schools? Assume county costs for the judiciary? Clean up the hazardous waste sites? Rebuild the state's roads, bridges, and sewers? These competing solutions to the pleasant problem of excess cash could have a variety of impacts—not just on government expenditures or individual taxes, but also on the relationship between the state and on local government. And this is the basic point of this chapter—financial decisions are policy decisions.

By setting the budget, the governor and legislature also set program priorities, determine what level of government will provide public services, and which citizens will pay these costs of government. The budget determines the scope of direct state services: hiring prison guards, controlling air pollution, subsidizing bus transportation, training doctors and dentists, or rehabilitating the handicapped. Spending money on a program shows precisely its value and priority for the state. Although expenditures may change only marginally from year to year, the state's agenda can be redirected, new programs emphasized, and established programs maintained or curtailed.

Funding decisions bring heated partisan debate, interdepartmental squabbles, and bitter quarrels between the governor and the legislature. The outcome of the budgetary process offers clues to political power distribution among political parties, cabinet departments, interest groups, and local governments. The outcome of the budget battle also has great significance for local officials, state employees, potential beneficiaries of state programs, and, of course, for all the state's taxpayers. Moreover, the process itself can reveal much about the character of New Jersey politics in general and about the relationship between the state and its local governments in particular.

FISCAL TRADITIONS

In New Jersey the annual battle of the budget takes place in a context of political, cultural, and legal traditions that define the arena of combat and establish the rules of the fight.

New Jersey has traditionally been a fiscally conservative state, late to enact broad-based taxes, very reluctant to introduce new taxes or even to raise the rates of existing taxes. New Jersey's fiscal prudence —some might say fiscal prudery—can be seen not only in its resistance to broad-based taxation, but also in the state's low tax effort and in its concern over preservation of sound fiscal policies. Home rule has also been a cherished tradition, and New Jersey's extraordinary reliance on the locally raised property tax has been yet another aspect of the boundaries within which state leaders have had to operate.

Once taxes have been adopted, raising their rates, albeit not easy, has proven less difficult than passing new taxes. Taxing out-of-staters or finding seemingly voluntary revenue sources have also been popular remedies, and whenever possible, the state's politicians have sought to dedicate new tax sources for purposes with wide and powerful constituencies.

The recurrent themes of fiscal conservatism echo in the state's history of taxation. New Jersey's reliance on property taxes assessed and spent by local governments dates back to colonial times.[1] Well into the twentieth century, most services such as public education have been financed locally with property tax revenues.

AVOIDANCE OF BROAD-BASED TAXES

Another persistent motif is the attempt to avoid any direct taxation of New Jersey citizens by clever maneuvers to raise revenues from hapless individuals and goods in transit through the state. New Jersey's fortunate position within the northeastern transportation corridor for a time made it possible to collect sufficient indirect revenues to run the state. At first, the monies came from an unsavory deal made in 1830 when the state granted the Camden and Amboy Railroad a monopoly on rail traffic across New Jersey. In return, the railroad imposed a duty on passengers and freight traveling through the state and these funds flowed into state coffers.[2] This monopoly and funding arrangement did not last long; however, as other railroads were established in New Jersey, the taxes they generated generally covered the state's need for revenues. Because of this rich revenue source, there was little need for broad-based state taxes during the nineteenth century.

Although the traditional avoidance of broad-based taxes continued into the second half of the twentieth century, conflicts between the complex needs of a modern economy and the fundamental political rule of no new taxes began to develop.[3] A strong anti-tax sentiment persisted during the 1930s, even in the face of acute demands to meet growing welfare burdens. But in 1935 Republican Governor Harold Hoffman appealed to the legislature to enact a modest sales and income tax to pay for state relief programs. The opposition to both forms of taxation was widespread and vocal. Little support could be found on either side of the aisle. Democratic and Republican legislators, mindful of organized anti-tax groups that included labor, manufacturers, retailers, and civic groups, refused support. Finally, Governor Hoffman struck a deal with Mayor Frank Hague of Jersey City, the power broker of the Democratic party. Reportedly, the mayor was promised hundreds of patronage jobs, and in return, he delivered sufficient Democratic votes to insure enactment of the sales tax.[4] The tax had only a brief and stormy four-month life, for both the tax and its political origins had antagonized the public, and forced Governor Hoffman to call a special session of the legislature to repeal the revenue law.[5]

The specter of the Hoffman tax repeal cast a long shadow on the state's tax politics. For over three decades, no broad-based taxes were enacted, even with pressing, unmet state needs. Finally, in 1966, after failing to get senatorial acceptance of an income tax, Democratic Governor Richard Hughes succeeded in the enactment of a 3 percent sales tax. Today it is harder to adopt a new tax than to raise the rates of an existing tax. At Republican Governor William Cahill's initiative, the state in 1970 increased the sales tax to 5 percent. Given the previously bloody legislative tax battles, the increase in sales tax passed with astonishing ease.[6]

Another attractive means to avoid broad-based taxation has been to develop revenue sources that either reach into the pockets of out-of-staters or that don't feel like taxes because they are voluntary. The state lottery enacted in 1969 is a growing source of non-tax revenue. By 1984, games of chance added almost $360 million to the state's coffers.[7] The search for painless non-tax revenues then led in 1977 to the approval of casino gambling in Atlantic City, which has become the most rapidly growing source of state revenue. In fiscal 1979, $26 million of the state budget came from casino revenues; in fiscal 1984 gambling produced $182 million.[8]

Casino revenues are dedicated for aid to senior and disabled citizens and for enforcement of casino regulations. Lottery yields are dedicated to aid education and state institutions. This earmarking of funds is another favorite gambit in state finance. It is not only politically prudent to find nontax revenue sources, but also politically necessary to dedicate these yields to worthwhile programs with large constituencies. Thus gambling revenues are made palatable by promising to limit their use to a noble cause.

THE INCOME TAX

Enactment of New Jersey's gross income tax came after years of gestation and struggle and under extraordinary circumstances. Three decades after hapless Governor Hoffman broke ground with his income tax proposal, governors Hughes and Cahill each tried and failed to get legislative acceptance. Democratic Governor Brendan Byrne, in response to the state supreme court edict of *Robinson v. Cahill*, first proposed a graduated income tax in 1974, his first year in office. The levy was reluctantly adopted by the legislature only after the supreme court had closed the state's public schools. But the legislature felt it necessary to placate voters in several ways. For one, it provided a sunset provision: barring legislative readoption, this new tax would expire in 1978.[9] For another, revenue from the tax would be dedicated to property tax relief: aid to school districts and local governments and rebates to homeowners would come largely from this source. In order to reassure voters that these new funds would truly help hold the line on property taxes, the legislature also enacted caps, or limits, on school, municipal, and state expenditures and on county taxes.

BALANCING THE BUDGET

Political constraints on the search for new revenue sources did not end with adoption of the gross income tax. The state constitution requires a balanced budget and the governor must insure that expenditures do not, at any time, exceed anticipated income.[10] At the same time, the legislature must approve taxes and spending. Both branches, therefore, are politically compelled to exercise fiscal restraint. When a budget deficit threatens, a struggle follows inevitably. Illustrative is the resolution of the budget crisis brought on by the 1982 recession. As worsening economic conditions reduced state revenues from income and sales taxes, Governor Kean proposed a 5 percent sales tax on gasoline as a way to bridge the budget gap. By dedicating revenues for transportation, the governor enlisted backing from a coalition of construction firms, corporations, and mass transit riders; however most labor unions attacked the tax as regressive, and truckers vehemently opposed a tax on their essential raw material, gasoline. Some citizen groups like the New Jersey Taxpayers Association and the League of Women Voters backed the tax but not its dedication to a single purpose. Responding to these pressures, the Democratic legislature resisted the governor's proposals and passed a streamlined budget with most of the governor's transportation agenda omitted.[11]

The executive and legislative branches were locked in uncompromising positions and no tax plan received sufficient support for passage.[12] By late 1982 it was clear that the revenue projections for the budget adopted in June had been overly rosy. Governor Kean yet again proposed a gasoline sales tax and the Democrats countered with proposed amendments to the income tax that would raise rates for high-income earners. The governor then parried by proposing to lay off state workers, reduce the salaries of those who remained, and cut back or eliminate state funds for local school districts.

Competing tax plans included a two-cent sales tax increase and a sharp progression in income taxes for those earning over $40,000. During a marathon, all-night session straddling New Year's Eve of 1983 the compromise of a penny increase in the sales tax and a 3.5 percent tax rate on incomes over $50,000 won narrow legislative approval. In the senate each tax plan garnered but 21 votes—the minimum needed for passage. The governor signed both bills but with mixed feelings. "It is not what I wanted or what anybody wanted," said Governor Kean. "It's basically a compromise."[13] Yet another New Jersey fiscal disaster was averted, but with sufficient drama to long color the budgetary process.

Since tax increases are so difficult to enact, tax cuts in a period of budgetary surplus are less appealing. The prospect of midnight tax battles should the economy falter are more frightening than explaining excess revenues to voters, or better yet, than spending the surplus. And the 1982 tax increase, coupled with an unexpectedly robust economic recovery in 1984, produced this happy dilemma for the state's politicians.

The history of New Jersey finance, then, evidences reluctance to impose or raise taxes and the use of various strategies to disguise the growth of state revenue. However difficult it has been to increase revenue yields, the state, in the last two decades, generally has succeeded in finding the necessary revenue sources to fund its growing activities. The result is, paradoxically, that New Jersey's conservative tradition now allows it to spend liberally—at least for the present. A similar trend is evident when we compare the Garden State with the rest of the nation.

FINANCE IN NEW JERSEY AND THE NATION

In the 1982 fiscal year New Jersey's state and local governments spent more than $14.5 billion—certainly, a vast amount of money. Still, in order to understand the significance of these expenses, it is useful to compare New Jersey with its sister states. These states vary in population size, density, level of urbanization and industrialization, as well as in their political and cultural traditions of government finances, all factors that affect taxing and spending patterns of the state.

EXPENDITURES

New Jersey early depended on locally raised property taxes to fund most public programs. The state funded its limited services through corporate and nuisance taxes and was a reluctant latecomer to broad-based taxation. These broad-based revenues have provided the state with increased resources not only to spend more on state services but also to pay for a larger share of total government services.

Until the past decade or two, New Jersey was indeed modest in supporting public programs (see Table 9.1). In the 1962–1970 period, New Jersey's average per capita spending for state and local government was considerably lower than the average in other states. After 1972 the pattern changed. New Jersey's recent expenditures have equalled or slightly exceeded per capita spending averages throughout the United States. In 1982, for example, New Jersey governments spent $1,950 per person, compared with the national average of $1,868. New Jersey now ranks twentieth among the states in overall spending. Broken down into categories, New Jersey's spending ranks higher than average for local schools, police, libraries, and sewage; lower for higher education, highways, health, and hospitals; and close to average for housing and urban development and public welfare.[14] Clearly, in New Jersey the levels and patterns of expenditures have changed over the years. In the last decade alone, public spending in

TABLE 9.1   AVERAGE PER CAPITA EXPENDITURES BY STATE AND
LOCAL GOVERNMENTS, 1962-1982

Year	United States	New Jersey	New Jersey (as a percentage of U.S. Average)
1962	$321	$302	94
1968	512	452	88
1972	801	802	100
1978	1,355	1,402	103
1982	1,868	1,950	104

SOURCE: ACIR, *Significant Features of Fiscal Federalism*, appropriate years.

New Jersey rose over 20 percent, after inflation.[15] This rise in expenditure is due to the positive response by governments to demands for increased services and new programs.

REVENUES

Another change has come in the sources of government spending. In the past, New Jersey differed from most states in its heavy dependence upon local funds (see Table 9.2). Sixty-three percent of the money for government programs in New Jersey was locally raised in 1962 (only 28 percent came from the state). Almost all of this local revenue came from property taxes. New Jersey's local focus sharply contrasted with the rest of the nation, where on average less than half of program costs were paid by local governments. By 1972, however, there was a significant change in New Jersey. In that year less than half of government expenditures in the state were financed at the local level, with the state assuming better than a third of the fiscal burden. During the last decade this balance of responsibility has continued to shift from local governments to the state government. With the adoption of the income tax in 1976 and consequent influx of monies to the state coffers, New Jersey used more statewide revenues to pay for elementary and secondary education, public health and hospitals, and public welfare. By 1982 the state of New Jersey was paying for close to half (49 percent) of all public services, outdistancing the 46 percent paid by the average state government. New Jersey's local governments carried 34 percent of the burden, equalling their sister states in the proportion of the burden they assumed.

Gaming revenues—monies from the state lottery and taxes on casino gambling—also lined the state's treasury. These growing reve-

TABLE 9.2   SOURCES OF STATE AND LOCAL REVENUES, 1962-1982
(as a percentage of total revenues)

Year	United States (Average)			New Jersey		
	Federal	State	Local	Federal	State	Local
1962	14	41	46	9	28	63
1968	17	43	40	12	35	53
1972	19	42	39	16	36	48
1978	23	43	34	20	41	39
1982	20	46	34	17	49	34

SOURCE: ACIR, *Significant Features of Fiscal Federalism*, appropriate years.

nue sources reinforced the shift in intergovernmental responsibility
for funding public services and made possible the expansion of novel
programs, such as state payment for large portions of senior citizen
pharmaceutical costs.

Although New Jersey in many ways has become more like the
average state, its revenue sources still show a distinctive pattern (see
Table 9.3). The contrast between New Jersey and other states was
vivid in 1962, when revenues came primarily from the locally raised
property tax. With the advent of the sales tax, New Jersey's reliance
on the property tax dropped somewhat. By 1978, as income tax revenues also became available, only 40 percent of the state and local "own
source" revenues (not including federal funds) came from the property

TABLE 9.3   SOURCES OF GENERAL STATE AND LOCAL REVENUES,
1962–1982 (as a percentage of nonfederal revenues)

	Property Tax		General Sales Tax		Individual Income Tax		Other Taxes		Charges, Fees, Misc.	
	NJ	US	NJ	US	NJ	US	NJ	US	NJ	US
1962	55	38	-	12	<1	6	30	26	15	18
1968	48	33	8	14	<1	9	28	25	16	20
1972	47	31	12	15	1	11	24	23	17	20
1978	40	27	12	17	13	18	18	17	17	21
1982	34	22	11	16	10	14	23	20	22	28

SOURCE: ACIR, *Significant Features of Fiscal Federalism*, appropriate years.

tax. By 1982, the property tax yielded a third of the revenues raised throughout the state. Though this represented a significant change for New Jersey over the previous two decades, the state still stood high in its dependence on this traditional tax source. Nationally, property taxes account for less than a fourth of state and local revenue.

TAX EFFORT

A different way to compare fiscal patterns is to measure the states' tax efforts. States differ both in their wealth and in their fiscal traditions. Low taxes may result simply because there are few taxable resources in a state, or a state with low taxes may not have the political will to raise revenues, or it may be bound by conservative fiscal traditions. Tax effort measures the level of revenues in relation to the available wealth, the potential for taxes.

Poverty is not New Jersey's problem, for it is a wealthy state. In 1983 its per capita personal income averaged $14,057, ranking the state third in the nation. This personal wealth is but one measure of the ability of New Jersey to tax itself. A comparison between New Jersey's state and local tax revenues and personal income shows that the state traditionally has been conservative in its tax effort, but has changed considerably in recent years (see Table 9.4). New Jersey in the 1960s ranked among the states with lowest levels of taxes as a percentage of personal income. The adoption of state broad-based taxes has made it possible for New Jersey to improve its tax effort considerably.

Finances in New Jersey appear to have altered even more strikingly, if a different measure called tax capacity is used. A state's wealth

TABLE 9.4   NEW JERSEY TAX EFFORT IN RELATION TO STATE PERSONAL INCOME (as indexed on a scale where 100 = U.S. average)

	1965	1975	1978	1980	1982
Tax Effort (NJ)	86.5	94.3	97.4	101.3	100.2
NJ effort as ranked against other states	40	29	23	18	21

SOURCE: ACIR, *Significant Features of Fiscal Federalism*, appropriate years.
NOTE: An index of tax effort as a factor of state personal income is based on the state's actual state and local taxes, divided by state personal income and then indexed to the average of all states. The national average is computed by adding the state and local taxes of all states and dividing this result by average national personal income.

TABLE 9.5   NEW JERSEY TAX EFFORT IN RELATION TO TAX
CAPACITY (as indexed on a scale where 100 = U.S. average)

	1967	1975	1977	1979	1981
New Jersey	97	103	113	118	112
NJ as ranked against other states	25	13	9	8	10

SOURCE: ACIR, *Significant Features of Fiscal Federalism*, appropriate years.

does not consist entirely of its citizens' personal income; state and local revenues also come from a variety of other sources—property,
corporate income, sales, and excise taxes; services; and, more recently, gaming. Tax capacity takes into account all of these sources of
wealth and revenue and provides a more reliable basis for comparison
with other states.[16] (See Table 9.5.)

Although New Jersey's conservative fiscal traditions had made it
difficult for the state to institute broad-based taxes, together the state
and the local governments have been energetic in imposing taxes in
recent years. New Jersey now ranks among the five top states in overall tax charges. In tax effort, when state and local governments are
both considered, New Jersey ranks among the top ten states.

Overall, these national comparisons show a clear trend—New Jersey is responding to modern life by increasing the state's fiscal capacity, contrary to its historic conservatism. Relative to other states and
to its own past, New Jersey is spending more, particularly at the state
level, while reducing its reliance on the property tax. A wealthy state,
New Jersey is increasingly willing to use this wealth for public expenditure, for developing new programs as new revenues are found. Political effort has now made tax revenues out of tax capabilities.

STATE-LOCAL RELATIONSHIPS

The state's tradition of fiscal conservatism remains alive in relationships between Trenton and local, county, and school governments. It
is reflected in two ways: fiscal oversight and budgetary limitations,
or caps.

FISCAL OVERSIGHT

Although in New Jersey, local governments still account for significant aspects of the tax and spending efforts, municipalities, counties,

and school districts tax and spend under the watchful eyes of the state. New Jersey, in keeping with its tradition of fiscal prudence, maintains a long-standing tradition of good fiscal management. The state, through its Division of Local Government Services, the policy-making Local Finance Board, and the commissioner of education, exercises tight supervision over local budgetary practices.[17]

The division's oversight role includes issuance of standard budget forms, examination and certification of all budgets, and provisions of technical assistance to local officials. Local governments must balance their budgets, which have to follow a prescribed format and must adhere to a strict timetable in adopting the budget. Counties and municipalities retain the freedom to allocate resources. If, for example, Montclair wishes to pay for sidewalk snow removal with public funds, it may do so, provided that the authorization was properly made within the local budget law. If, however, a local government approaches insolvency, more extensive state intervention can occur.[18]

The state regulates the issuance of debt by local governments, because it assumes that there is a strong interrelationship between the fiscal health of the state and its localities. An unfavorable credit rating of one level of government can damage the borrowing capacity and raise borrowing rates of other units. In effect, if Newark sneezes, or Camden catches a fiscal flu, the State of New Jersey's health is imperiled. Members of the legislature and governors of both parties have acted on this premise of the fiscal interdependence of local governments and the state government. Republican Governor Cahill provided needed funds for Newark in 1970 to meet a critical budget shortfall despite the resistance of Democratic members of the state legislature. The beneficiary was Democratic Mayor Kenneth Gibson, who inherited a nearly bankrupt city from his predecessor.[19] In 1981, Democratic Governor Brendan Byrne ensured the fiscal bailout of the City of Camden and the legislature authorized the temporary state takeover of that city's finances. The state's Local Finance Board required Camden to nearly double its property taxes and institute door-to-door tax collections to achieve a higher rate of payments.[20]

This close scrutiny of local government finance is coupled with an insistence on sound budgetary and fiscal management policies on the state level. Revenue estimates tend to be cautiously low, and surpluses, when available, are distributed with an eye to a possible rainy day. These practices have preserved for the state a coveted AAA credit rating from bond rating services. No other urban northeastern state can claim such a distinction.

CAPS

The close scrutiny of finances is a long-standing New Jersey tradition. Of more recent vintage are tax and expenditure limitations, which place considerable constraints on these subordinate governments. The caps were born as part of the political compromise that produced the state's first income tax. The legislators had mixed motives for insisting on caps, but at least one purpose was to "insure a reduced dependency on the property tax to finance government services,"[21] while trying to permit local government to provide necessary services to its residents."[22] Initially, caps were placed on *all* levels of governments, but the nature of those limits differed. New Jersey's caps, predating California's famous Proposition 13 limits, are complex and their consequences far-reaching.

Under the original cap provisions, municipalities could spend but 5 percent more each year, while counties were limited to a 5 percent raise on their levy. (Capital investments and debt service were exempt from restraints.) Local governments found these limits particularly onerous when inflation hit double digits. Local officials clamored for added exemptions to caps, and when the local government caps were reenacted in 1983, the law was revised to permit counties and municipalities a more flexible limit, based on an inflation index.

The impact of these limits has varied by municipality and county. Local governments whose finances had been tightly managed found that they had no fat to cut. When they faced huge increases in utility and other uncontrollable costs, these governments could no longer provide expected services. Towns cut back school-crossing guards, reduced garbage pickups, reduced or eliminated recreation programs, instituted fees for previously free services, and, in some cases, turned off street lights.[23] For others, the caps merely served as incentives to "streamline operations and eliminate waste without significant reduction in services."[24] Some local officials at first welcomed caps as screens behind which they could hide from unions whose demands for wage increases seemed excessive, or from interest groups whose program or service needs were bothersome. "Sorry," they could say, "our cap is restrictive—we cannot meet your demands."

The average annual increase in county and municipal purpose property tax levies was significantly lower after the adoption of caps, as was the average annual increase in expenditures. Thus the cap law could be termed successful in meeting the goal of restraining taxing and spending. This was accomplished, however, at the cost of service reduction for at least a number of local governments, and at the expense of sharply curtailing the decision-making authority of local officials. This loss of local discretion was particularly resented by local officials. They complained that they were, after all, subject to public scrutiny and citizens could vote them out of office if they were profligate spenders. Why subject them to rigid spending limits? The legislature, in effect, set itself up as the protector of citizens from the profligate habits of their local elected officials; the mayors and county freeholders deeply resented this implied superiority of the legislators in matters of fiscal prudence and chafed under the reduction of home rule.

The cap laws extended even further the state's oversight over local government finance. The budget document, due to cap law calculations, became less of a vehicle for setting local priorities and a means of communication with citizens. Instead, it resembled a maze of technical tricks to gain every possible cap exception and add-on. Imprudent budgeting was encouraged by basing a current year's taxing or spending growth on the previous year's level—it became a "use it or lose it" system.[25]

Caps also were applied to school districts, with expenditure limits determined by a complicated formula. Besides aiding in control of property tax rates, the school district caps were meant to promote greater equalization of school spending. They would presumably limit the growth of expenditures in high spending districts, but permit low spending districts to approach the state average.

As with municipalities and counties, the impact of school caps has not been uniform. Because of the way the caps are calculated, school districts with declining enrollments have benefited; they have had greater leeway to increase their per pupil expenditures. Moreover since the wealthy, high-spending districts have tended also to have declining enrollments, these districts have been able to spend more in spite of caps. Low-spending districts have not been able to bridge the gap, and disparities in per pupil expenditures between rich and poor districts have actually increased since 1976.[26] School officials also resented the constraints of caps even if at times these limits made it possible to make the politically difficult but fiscally prudent decisions to close schools in the face of declining enrollments.

On the state level, budget growth was linked to rate of growth in New Jersey's per capita income. As inflation increased, per capita income also tended to rise, so that state's cap proved to be a flexible limitation. The state cap did not prove to be a significant barrier to raising state expenditures, however; rather, the level of revenues generated by taxes was seen to be a far more effective limit on state spending. When the State Expenditure Limitations Act expired in 1983, it was quietly buried. The legislature reenacted limits on local government expenditures but left no cap barriers to its own spending.

CONCLUSIONS

New Jersey finances in the last two decades mirror the emergence of the state government as a strong institution and reflect the decline of the power of local governments. This shift in institutional power is documented in the change in the revenue sources for state and local services. The state continues to provide an ever increasing share of support for public services. New Jersey today more closely resembles its sister states than it once did.

New Jersey, though retaining its conservative traditions in managing its finances, has also increased its level of taxation. The rise in revenues from broad-based sales and income taxes has enabled the state to institute new programs, provide additional direct aid to counties, municipalities, and school districts, decrease its dependence on the property tax, and still maintain its cherished AAA bond rating as a symbol of prudent fiscal management.

Yet, significant problems remain. Increasing percentages of the state budget are eaten up by mandated expenditures such as pensions, social security, pharmaceutical assistance to the aged, Medicaid and debt service, thus limiting discretionary spending for new programs. Though surpluses abound in fiscal 1985, the clamor for increased spending—for transportation, infrastructure repair, environmental protection and cleanup, social services, and hosts of other unmet needs—places ever greater demands on existing revenues. Although the rate of increase in property taxes has slowed, New Jersey still relies heavily on the property tax to finance locally delivered services. The property tax burden is unequally distributed: cities, with declining property values and decaying industries must tax their citizens more heavily for fewer services than residents of affluent communities with expanding property tax bases. These inequities lead to differences in school spending and the provision of other services, differences in the ability to attract new businesses and keep old ones, and thus to differences in job opportunities.

Poor communities, unable to maintain their infrastructure and needing to tax at higher rates, tend to be uninviting places for private investment. The gap between rich and poor localities increases. The state has made strong attempts to reduce these disparities by increasing direct aid to localities and enlarging direct state services. Nevertheless, the disparities remain and continue to provide a localist counterpoint to a generally strong state fiscal role. The remedy is radical;

to reduce interlocal fiscal disparities the state would have to pay for more services, force consolidation among some of the state's 567 municipalities, and institute tax-base sharing, which allows each locality to benefit from the increased value of property within a region. New Jersey's finances will continue to be a political battleground, the scene for the clash between old traditions and new demands.

Notes

1. League of Women Voters of New Jersey, *New Jersey Spotlight on Government*, 3rd ed. (New Brunswick: Rutgers University Press, 1978), 100–101.

2. *Ibid.*, 201.

3. *Ibid.*, 101.

4. Governor Hoffman's tax troubles are vividly described in Dayton McKean, *Pressures on the Legislature of New Jersey* (New York: Columbia University Press, 1938), Ch. 6.

5. *Idem.*

6. Richard Lehne, "Revenue and Expenditure Policies" in *Politics in New Jersey*, Alan Rosenthal and John Blydenburgh, eds., (New Brunswick: Eagleton Institute, Rutgers University, 1975).

7. *New Jersey Budget, 1984–1985* (Trenton: Department of the Treasury, 1984).

8. *New Jersey Budget, 1979–1980* and *1984–1985* (Trenton: Department of the Treasury).

9. For a full account see Richard Lehne, *The Quest for Justice: The Politics of School Finance Reform* (New York: Longman, 1978). The effects of the tax battle on the 1977 gubernatorial election are discussed in Gerald M. Pomper and Susan S. Lederman, *Elections in America: Control and Influence in Democratic Politics*, 2nd ed. (New York: Longman, 1980), Ch. 6.

10. *Official Statement, $150,000,000 State of New Jersey General Obligation Bonds* (Trenton: Department of the Treasury, May 15, 1983).

11. This account is derived from articles by Joseph F. Sullivan: "Jersey Assembly Votes to Impose Gasoline Surtax," *New York Times*, June 18, 1982, Section 11, 2; "Jersey Legislature Votes Scaled Down Budget," *New York Times*, June 29, 1982, Section 11, 1; "Kean Signs Budget, But He Criticizes It as Not Responsible," *New York Times*, July 1, 1982, Section 11, 7; and "Jersey's Budget, Act II," *New York Times*, July 26, 1982, Section 11, 2.

12. *Idem.*; also discussions with legislative staff. The interbranch crossfire bruised and maimed several legislative and executive programs. For example, Governor Kean revoked *all* the appropriations for the County and Municipal Government Study Commission, a respected legislative agency. The monies

were partially restored after the year-end tax increases, but for six months the commission was, in effect, wiped out.

13. Joseph F. Sullivan, "Kean Signs Bills Raising Two Taxes to Cut Budget Gap," *New York Times*, January 1, 1983, Section II, 1.

14. *New Jersey Tax Facts* (Newark: Regional Plan Association, New Jersey Committee, 1983), 10–11.

15. *Idem*.

16. The Advisory Commission on Intergovernmental Relations defines tax capacity as "an estimate of a government's relative ability to raise revenue from a full array of tax bases (income, property, sales, natural resource extraction, etc.). It is calculated by estimating the amount of revenue that each state (including state and local governments) would raise if an identical set of rates were used." Tax capacity estimates are not affected by *actual* individual state practices or even the absence of a certain tax. ACIR, *Significant Features of Fiscal Federalism*, 1981–1983 edition (Washington, D.C.: Advisory Commission on Intergovernmental Relations, 1983), 84.

17. James A. Alexander, Jr., *The Municipal Budget Process*, 3rd ed. (New Brunswick: Rutgers University, Division of Continuing Education, 1982), 1–9.

18. Idem.

19. This account was based on reporting by Ronald Sullivan: "Tax on Employers Looms in Newark," *New York Times*, December, 1, 1970, Section II, 53; and "Jersey Assembly Votes $50 Million Newark Tax Aid," *New York Times*, December 13, 1970, Section II, 51.

20. The Camden fiscal crisis was reported by Carlo M. Sardella, "Troubled Camden Seeks Revival," *New York Times*, November 14, 1982, Section XI, 1; and Donald Janson, "Camden Makes House Calls for Taxes," *New York Times*, November 15, 1983, Section II, 6.

21. *Report of the Joint Committee on Tax Policy, pursuant to Senate Concurrent Resolution #64 of 1978* (Trenton: New Jersey Legislature, 1979), 22.

22. NJSA 40A. 45.1.

23. The *Report of the Local Expenditure Limitations Technical Review Commission, pursuant to Joint Resolution #5 of 1982* (Trenton: New Jersey Legislature, 1982) documents some of the service cutbacks reported by local officials.

24. *Ibid.*, 66.

25. *Ibid.*, 75.

26. For a full discussion of the disparity in school district expenditures see: Helen Lindsay, *New Jersey Issues: T & E Revisited* (Trenton: League of Women Voters of New Jersey Education Fund, 1984) and *School Budget Caps in New Jersey, 1976–80: Four Years of Experience with Schools*, a report prepared for the New Jersey Legislature Joint Committee on Public Schools (New Brunswick: Rutgers University, Bureau of Government Research, 1980).

10

ALBERT BURSTEIN

Educational Policy

"Improving public education is one of the most important tasks we face as a state . . . during the remainder of this century." Governor Thomas H. Kean emphasized this theme in his State of the State message of 1985. With but slight alterations in wording, the same ideas without exception can be found in similar addresses of past governors.

No one can doubt the importance of education as a state supported enterprise. There are about 1.1 million students attending public schools in New Jersey, divided among more than six hundred school districts. Education is a significant undertaking, traditionally consuming approximately 25 percent of the annual state budget and, depending on location, between 15 and 90 percent of locally raised taxes. In fiscal 1986 the state will provide aid to school districts in excess of $2 billion.

This chapter examines the schools, the state's most important concern, by looking at the people and the processes that create and implement education policy. The impact of the federal government and interest groups as well as present and future policy problems also provide matters of interest.

The State Role

The state constitution obliges the legislature to "provide for the maintenance and support of a thorough and efficient system of free public schools." These deceptively simple words have provoked intense judicial scrutiny and political activity.

Judicial interpretation of that section of the constitution gained national attention. The case of *Robinson v. Cahill* had important implications. It represented major intervention by the courts in public education and led to the statewide closing of all public schools in 1976. It also provoked a massive change in the way school districts were financed and a long-range shift in power relationships. (See Chapter 8.)

In the 1980s the name of the case has changed—it is now *Abbott v. Burke*—but the issues remain nearly the same—the uneven distribution of resources and the generally lower quality of education in poorer school systems. The outcome of this case cannot be foreseen, for its ultimate determination will take a long time. What is clear is that the state's role will continue to be important and that the state's influence on policy creation and implementation will predominate.

It is said that the law of life is change; certainly that law applies to education too. After the second World War, the demography and landscape of New Jersey were transformed. Suburbs grew with dramatic explosiveness. Where no schools had existed, entire sytems were created. In these areas growth was the order of the day. Concurrently came the gradual decline of the cities, and with it, the decline of their schools as well. The flight of commercial, industrial, and individual wealth from the cities reduced urban tax bases and curtailed cities' abilities to meet municipal needs, including education.

The 1950s and 1960s witnessed the rise of teacher unionism. Although teachers' unions had long existed, there now grew demands for a legal right to bargain collectively, along with a new militancy among educators.[1] These pressures culminated in enactment of the Public Employees Relations Act in 1969 (over Governor Richard Hughes' veto). Organizations previously considered solely professional in scope took on the more traditional vestments of trade unionism—demanding better pay scales, working conditions, and fringe benefits.

Another major trend in education has been the increased concentration of power in the state, or what one leading writer called the "hyperrationalization" of learning.[2] But the state's power is not an abstraction. It is made manifest and is wielded by individuals, both elected and nonelected, governmental and nongovernmental. They include the governor and his immediate staff, the commissioner of education and a substantial education bureaucracy including county superintendents and local school boards, as well as the two houses of the legislature, and particularly their respective education committees. In the aggregate, these bodies represent state interests. Nongovernmen-

tal interests include unions and citizens. The policy successes and failures of each of these groups determine their impact upon current and
future problems in education.

EXECUTIVE BRANCH

Educational policy-making—its tone, content, and funding—centers in the governor's office. The legislature, despite its constitutional
obligation, has traditionally permitted the chief executive to take the
lead in matters of policy. Further, the governor's power to appoint
both members of the state board of education and the commissioner of
education enables even the most passive of executives to advance major educational initiatives.

Centralized authority over education did not always exist in New
Jersey, however. Prior to adoption of the modernized constitution
in 1947, the chief executive was that in name only. The governor's
authority was severely circumscribed by the 1875 constitution and
power was exceptionally diffuse. The advent of the new charter stimulated a slow shift of authority. At first, local control was the ritualistic
utterance of all political figures, and was intended to ensure that district boards of education maintained full control over their districts,
relatively unrestricted by outside (state) interference.

The swirling currents of change, however, compelled successive
governors to devote increasing time and attention to education. Early
during Governor Hughes' administration the emphasis was on the improvement of higher education. This focus led to the creation of a separate Department of Higher Education, under the administration of a
chancellor, to govern the system of four-year, state-funded liberal arts
colleges. Attention then was turned to public elementary and secondary schools, which lagged behind in responding to new needs; in 1967
Hughes selected Carl Marburger to be his commissioner of education.

In a clear demonstration of the power of the executive department
to effect change, Marburger, under Hughes' direction, altered the
agenda of public education. In order to increase public involvement,
he implemented, throughout the state, the Our Schools program of
citizen meetings for the purpose of formulating local educational
goals. This initiative unsettled the establishment, which had an un-
alterable belief in the inability of the lay public to understand problems of the profession. Marburger further proposed a system of school
assessment and remediation for slow learners. At the time, this initiative was seen as a revolutionary state intrusion into local affairs. Although it preceded the 1975 education law, it now has become a fixed
part of the school structure.

William T. Cahill provides another example of a governor's ability to set the agenda and direct public and legislative attention to particular problems. The framework for debate, the nature of issues to be addressed, the emphasis and ordering of priorities, were all executive initiatives during his term. Advised by Commissioner Marburger, Cahill convened the legislature in 1970 in a special session devoted solely to education. He requested legislation to change the formula for state financial aid to local districts, to establish a needs assessment program including a pupil testing program, and to institute a system of merit pay for teachers.

By the time Brendan T. Byrne was shown into office as governor in 1974, he knew he would have to deal with judicial mandates requiring changes in tax policy as well as in education law. Not only did he need an educational funding law that would pass constitutional scrutiny by the New Jersey Supreme Court, but also an income tax to raise the required revenues. At that time there was a widespread belief, raised to the level of conventional wisdom, that anyone proposing or voting for such a tax was doomed to political oblivion. Given past virulent opposition by vocal interest groups to any tax increase, only the governor could provide leadership. Further complicating his role was the absence when he took office of a replacement for Carl Marburger as commissioner: for a time there was no lightning rod to deflect criticism from the governor.

Nonetheless, Byrne recognized his responsibility. In a conscious effort to avoid a constitutional confrontation with the supreme court, he made available the potent resources of the executive office to crafting a solution. By strength of his leadership he forced a reluctant legislature to face up to the compelling requirement for new revenues to fund a revised state-aid distribution program. The success of these efforts culminated in adoption of a new education law (1975) and the income tax (1976).

After the turmoil of the mid-1970s everyone needed a period of contemplation and quiet. Despite problems in implementing the 1975 law, executive attention was, with relief, directed to other matters. During the late 1970s there was decreasing interest in education policy, not only in New Jersey but nationwide. Without gubernatorial initiative, state legislatures too avoided education issues as if they carried disease.

As the nation moved into the 1980s, and with a suddenness that was startling in its impact, education again took center stage in New Jersey and elsewhere. This was caused by publication by a presidential commission of *A Nation at Risk* in April 1983.[3] Its jaundiced view of the state of education, in conjunction with a series of additional critical analyses, spurred action by New Jersey's new governor, Thomas H. Kean.

Imitating Cahill's 1970 move, Governor Kean convened a special session of the legislature in 1983 to advocate a set of changes in the schools.[4] The issue came naturally to the governor, himself a former teacher. Among the proposals were a statewide graduation test, an alternative route to teachers' certification, significant increases in starting teacher salaries, establishment of an academy for the advancement of teaching and management, and a master-teacher program.

In one stroke, a field barren of ideas worthy of public discussion had gained a new definition of goals. Whether good or bad, whether ultimately adopted in whole or in part, the program set forth by Governor Kean established the dimensions of the debate. It was a striking reiteration of a political truth: the chief executive and his appointees have the unsurpassed ability to delimit the subjects of discussion.

The Commissioner of Education

The commissioner of education also significantly affects policy formulation in education. The commissioner is appointed by the governor and is a cabinet member. The commissioner's five-year term overlaps that of the governor's, a situation deliberately created by the framers of the 1947 constitution in an attempt to make the office independent and apolitical. In fact, commissioners are only effective in establishing and pursuing policies when they have political support.

Carl Marburger was highly respected when appointed by Governor Hughes, a Democrat. He also won the confidence of Governor Cahill, a Republican. The educational establishment, however, viewed him as a controversial opponent. He took office at a time when school integration and desegregation were causing conflict among citizens and when urban frustrations were leading to street rioting. His desegregation orders, when combined with the unhappiness of established education groups over his other innovations, led to the refusal by the senate to confirm his reappointment to a second term.

After a fifteen-month hiatus (during which the department was headed by an acting commissioner) Fred Burke, formerly commissioner of education in Rhode Island, was appointed by Governor Byrne. Burke took office in the midst of the turmoil created by the decision in *Robinson v. Cahill*. That contentious setting foreshadowed the ensuing difficulties faced by the gentleman from Rhode Island. Whatever he touched in educational policy became controversial. Though a political scientist by training and aware of the political currents coursing through his department, he never seemed able to cope with contending interest groups and elected officials. Yet he was doing what the new 1975 law and the regulations adopted by the state board seemed to require. Burke continued as the administration's spokesman in education, and, with the sufficient confidence of Governor Byrne, he earned reappointment to a second term.

His successor, Saul Cooperman, came from a relatively insulated suburban school district in New Jersey. Initially he had difficulty in adjusting to the strident special interest voices competing for attention, but after acclimating himself to a scene substantially different from his past environment, he began to address current problems and exercise primary influence on Governor Kean's 1983 proposals. Cooperman has benefited from consistent media support, which has enabled him to mobilize public opinion behind many of his more controversial proposals. Ironically, Cooperman, coming to the commissioner's office with far less statewide experience than Marburger or Burke, has achieved greater political success than either of his predecessors in fashioning the supportive coalitions that lead to programmatic achievement.

The State Board of Education

The state board of education often plays a central role in the establishment of policy. It promulgates regulations that implement the laws and, in so doing, frequently breeds dispute. Establishing procedures for reporting on goals, standards, and objectives in compliance with the 1975 law, for example, evoked protests from local districts, as did the new state system of evaluating school performance and the creation of the minimum basic skills testing program. Recently the mandating of family life, or sex education, courses has caused outcries at public hearings that have almost succeeded in defeating the proposals.

The family life education course, now required in every school district and through all grade levels, is an instructive example of the use of state board powers. In 1967, because of an increase in teenage pregnancies, the board recommended to school districts that they offer sex education. As a result of a legislative resolution, implementation of the policy was temporarily suspended for one year, until 1970. Thereafter, the moratorium was lifted, but fewer than half the state's school districts implemented any program. Further, even in those districts with programs, the classes were ordinarily taught by physical education teachers with little relevant training. During the following decade the number of teenage pregnancies continued to increase greatly. Acting upon a request from the health commissioner a special committee again recommended mandating the family life curriculum. The board agreed again. Though every opinion poll revealed a substantial majority in favor of the program, opposition, at times violent, erupted at the board's public hearing. But the willingness of that body to persist in the face of controversy, with the considerable outside help of the New Jersey Catholic Conference, demonstrated the policy role the board can and does play. All indications are that the programs are now working well and have been accepted by parents and the general public.

In summary, the governor, commissioners, state board, and all their allied personnel predominate in education policy-making. Executive pre-eminence stems from the fiscal resources and skilled people available to it. Nonetheless, it would be erroneous to conclude that this branch of government can act in an unfettered, uninhibited manner; other actors, both on-stage and off, play significant roles.

THE LEGISLATIVE ROLE IN EDUCATION

In contrast to the central policy-making role of the governor, the legislature has traditionally been passive, enacting laws only after executive proposal. Initial stirrings of a legislative policy-making role came during Governor Cahill's administration, with passage of the Bateman-Tanzman Education Act to equalize educational tax burdens. Despite a later finding by the supreme court that the law was inadequate and unconstitutional, it was the precursor to the basic educational statute adopted in 1975.[5]

After *Robinson v. Cahill*, new legislative leadership recognized the need for greater staff resources and a pooling of skills to achieve effective participation in educational planning. In 1974 these improvements came through the creation of a joint education committee and the hiring of staff. Thus began an unparalleled collaborative effort between the legislature and the executive that resulted in enactment of the education law that continues to be the fundamental policy of the state.

The legislature made a unique contribution by balancing the acknowledged power of the commissioner with the desire to retain local citizen involvement and control of education. Some argue that local control may now be more myth than reality,[6] but the law did make an effort to institutionalize citizen participation in setting district goals and objectives. This provision would never have received the emphasis found in the law without the legislature's insistence. Similarly, insertion of an annual cap on local education expenditures was the legislature's device to assure that increased state aid would result in fewer local taxes for school purposes.

This experience in policy development reverberated in subsequent years. The legislature has continued to be aggressively involved in making educational policy, though not with uniform success. For example, it pushed for adoption of a law extending special education services to three- to five-year-olds before an official position on the issue was announced by the Department of Education. It compelled the state board to modify the proposed regulations that mandated a family life planning curriculum. It caused a change in the regulations proposed by the commissioner to evaluate individual school performances. It has taken the lead in proposing improvement in the salary levels of starting teachers.

The increasing legislative capacity to gather information and formulate judgments is a clear indication that it now has the ability and the willingness to play a significant role, although overall the legislature will probably continue as junior partner to the executive in future educational policy-making.

JUDICIAL INTERVENTION IN EDUCATION

Controversy over the role of the courts in setting policy through judicial decision has been part of the political scene for many decades. In New Jersey this issue was elevated to a heightened intensity by *Robinson v. Cahill* (see Chapter 8). Nevertheless judicial intervention has occurred only after legislative inaction, and the court's role has been that of the educational arbiter of last resort.

Striking evidence of its restraint may be found in the seven separate decisions by the supreme court regarding *Robinson v. Cahill.* Indeed, more than three years passed after the original trial court's decision before the issue was finally resolved. Throughout the case the court demonstrated its sensitivity to legislative prerogatives. The court's draconian closing of the schools in 1976 finally produced the legislative response, but this tool was only reluctantly employed. There were politically inspired charges that the court wanted to impose an income tax, or other additional tax, to fund education, but no fair reading of the decisions can justify that allegation.

The court in its function as interpreter of statutes or constitutions may leave an impact on policy, as in *Robinson*, but this is a rare event. With the growing strength of the legislative will, moreover, it may be reasonably anticipated that the judicial role as a policy-creating institution will in the future be minor.

INTEREST GROUPS

Education policy is also influenced inevitably by those outside of
state government or the courts—by teachers, administrators, and
local school boards. By sheer force of numbers, the alliances these
groups form and the positions they assume have impact. The major organizations through which these interests advance their ideas are the
New Jersey Education Association and the American Federation of
Teachers, the New Jersey Association of School Administrators, and
the New Jersey School Board Association.

Of these, NJEA is the major force. Its large state headquarters is located across the street from the State House. That proximity, together
with a skilled staff of lobbyists and a large annual budget, make it a
union to be reckoned with. It is politically active and perceives politics and education as inseparable.[7] For each legislative session it prepares lists of desired bills and holds regional meetings with legislators
to promote them. Its representatives attend every meeting of the senate and assembly education committees and discuss matters of interest with individual legislators on session days. Governors usually consult with the NJEA before appointing or reappointing a commissioner
of education. At campaign time it endorses legislative and gubernatorial candidates and supplies tangible reinforcements, money and manpower. One might expect that the group is reasonably successful in at-
tainment of its goals; yet, given the effort that NJEA expends, the
return is relatively meager.

Illustratively, though successful in having a public employees' bargaining law enacted in 1969, the NJEA has not succeeded in blunting
the impact of limiting court decisions. The question of appropriate pa-
rameters for public sector collective bargaining has been festering unsettled since adoption of the basic law. A decision by the New Jersey
Supreme Court limited the subjects that are negotiable, specifying
that school boards' managerial functions, such as teacher assignments
or class size, could not be the subject of collective bargaining.[8] The
decision pleased the school boards but drew attacks from the NJEA.
Ever since, the teachers union has given first priority to legislation to
broaden the scope of negotiations. The most recent version was in
fact passed by the assembly but defeated in a dramatic senate vote in
June 1983.[9]

After passage by the assembly and in anticipation of the senate's deliberations, a major lobbying effort was made by the NJEA and the
School Boards Association. Legislators were alternately cajoled and
threatened with retaliation at the polls. School board lobbyists, having

been caught unaware by the assembly vote, enlisted the aid of business groups and individuals not usually involved in education matters. It was a tough contest on a major issue, and the NJEA loss was reflective of the limitations on its presumed influence. Despite the setback, however, it remains an important force in policy-making.

While much smaller in size, the influence of the New Jersey School Boards Association can, as illustrated, be effective. Composed of all boards throughout the state with an inherently varied membership, consensus views on many substantive issues are often hard to come by. As a result its potential for power-wielding is diffused, making it a less potent force than its teacher counterpart. Nonetheless, as a citizen organization, when a matter does enable it to take a unified stand, its representatives are listened to both by the executive and the legislature.

The New Jersey Association of School Administrators is the smallest of the three principal educational lobbies. It holds periodic regional meetings to present its views to legislators, and it can have an impact. Illustratively, after adoption of the public education law in 1975 requiring many local reports to the state Department of Education, these educational managers were highly disturbed. Their position, that the paper work was overwhelming and often unneeded, was ultimately accepted and remedies were instituted.

Since publication of the national critique of education, a new type of group has emerged, with broader membership. Among others there is Public Responsibility for Educational Success, a group of citizens from all walks of life whose purpose is to generate cooperation between the private sector and local school systems and to produce ideas for usable programs within the schools. More recently Governor Kean announced formation of New Jersey Citizens for Better Schools, whose objective is the creation of a grassroots citizen organization to work for excellence in the schools. Underlying the formation of both these groups is the common desire to draw private sector interests into finding a solution for continuing problems: low student achievement, high dropout rates, a corps of teachers who feel unappreciated and poorly paid—the usual litany of school difficulties does not seem susceptible to quick remedies. It is still uncertain whether or not these new organizations will help or even whether they will remain in existence long enough to resolve fundamental problems.

THE FEDERAL ROLE

On average, the federal monetary contribution for all education programs to the State of New Jersey has been between 5 and 7 percent of total expenditures. Yet dollars alone are not a true indicator of Washington's influence. Most of the money is for compensatory education programs particularly needed in urban areas. Thus Newark relies on federal funding for approximately 12 percent of its total school budget. Special education is another example. When the Congress adopted the Education for All Handicapped Children Act in 1975, the amount of money sent to the state was relatively nominal, yet the standards set forth in the new law became the framework for providing educational resources to the handicapped.

Even the tone of the debate has been substantially influenced by the federal government. Although a number of initiatives sponsored by Governor Kean were already under way when national critiques were issued, there is little doubt that his address to the legislature on education in 1983 was, at least partially, the result of the attention given to the national reports.

Current trends foretell a lessening federal presence. Assuredly no new programs are on the horizon. Fiscal constraints are having a harmful impact on existing programs, and the national political leadership has made clear that future policy initiatives must come from and be established at the state or local level. Certain laws already in place, however, such as the Elementary and Secondary Education Act of 1965 and the law concerning the handicapped, will require a continuing, albeit not expanding, federal concern.

FORMULATION AND IMPLEMENTATION OF POLICY

An oft-repeated aphorism goes, "Never watch laws or sausages being made." This particularly applies to the formulation of public policy in education. The average citizen probably envisions people engaged in deep discussion on the merits of issues, based on the best available research and creative thinking. Before ideas surface for public consideration, the idealist supposes that all implications to be derived from policy adoption and implementation have been thought through. Unfortunately all evidence points to the conclusion that, at least for the creation of public policy, the process falls far short of this ideal. The reality can be demonstrated by many examples.

For instance, much of Governor Kean's program for education was set out in his speech of September, 1983. Yet, one learns that ideas were being advanced and discarded up to the last moment before delivery. Further, in view of the importance assigned by the administration to the address, it was surprising that the speech was unaccompanied by a legislative package. Instead there followed a piecemeal approach that has, at minimum, delayed implementation of those proposals requiring new law.

The key problem for Governor Kean was the adequacy of the teaching corps. He wanted a new minimum salary for starting teachers, to be partially state funded on a declining basis over five years; an alternative route to teacher certification; a master teacher program; and a teacher's academy. Except for the alternative teacher certification aspect, the program was comparatively noncontroversial. Yet the entire plan was delayed and the certification proposal in particular opposed by NJEA, partially because that organization had not been consulted in advance. Experience has demonstrated that for innovative education programs to succeed, teachers must be actively involved.

In the matter of equitable distribution of state aid, court cases continue. Despite the innovative 1975 law, studies conclude that significant inequities in distributions remain.[10] Policymakers seem oblivious to these continuing problems, apparently hoping that a new court will take a more benign view of state aid efforts than previous justices. Despite this calming hope, there is little reason for that belief Legislators find it unpleasant to devote thought to another formula change and, almost inevitably, different funding provisions. Accordingly, the people and institutions making policy have frozen into immobility, until there is new court intercession.

Not all policy formulation is chaotic, however. While the governor may have waited until the last minute to propose new teacher certification methods, much previous spade work had been done on the idea within the Department of Education, and since its proposal, it has been elaborated upon by a commission of highly qualified professionals. Their suggestions have helped gain it wider acceptance.

Polling data seem to reveal general public satisfaction with school performance.[11] Characteristically, people are even more pleased with their local schools than with education as a whole. They tend to support Governor Kean's initiatives to increase starting salaries (though less than a majority want a general tax increase to fund them), to institute merit pay, to establish master teacher programs, and to allow an alternate teacher certification system. These verbal attitudes change remarkably, however, if substantial price tags become linked with policies. The resulting pressures generated by ad hoc taxpayer groups have an impact that elected representatives find difficult to withstand. Assuredly, this was the reason it took so long to resolve the school aid issue. While inattentive to detail and slow to evolve an opinion, the public is always in the back of the minds of policymakers. It acts as a subtle restraint that wisely and providently militates against revolutionary change.

Local—defined as school board—influence over policy-making is on a downward trend, which is probably irreversible. Board activities have been circumscribed and focused largely on budget preparations and salary negotiations with teachers. Boards play a significant role in school policy by providing the care and enthusiasm needed to carry out state and federal mandates. Refinement of such functions will encourage citizens to serve on boards.

FUTURE POLICY

The rising state role in education during the past decade is evident. Increased funding to local districts, uniform state tests of pupil performance, evaluation of school performance, teacher training mandates —all witness centralization of power in state hands. While not unique among states, New Jersey has been a leader in this trend.

These reforms have narrowed the scope of local control. To offset this apparently inevitable trend, some educational theorists argue for adoption of a voucher system that would allow a direct state payment of a prescribed amount to the parents of a student, who could then make a free choice of any school for their child.[12] Critics contend this would prove the death knell of urban schools—and so the debate continues.

Still unresolved is whether or not existing state-directed reforms (or the voucher system) will actually result in improved educational opportunity for New Jersey's students. One can only predict with confidence that the state's involvement in educational policy formulation will continue to grow and be increasingly intrusive.

Notes

1. For a good discussion on the rise of unionism see Robert E. Doherty, "The Impact of Collective Negotiations on Policy Making in New Jersey Schools," June, 1972.

2. Arthur E. Wise, *Legislated Learning* (Berkeley: University of California Press, 1979).

3. National Commission on Excellence in Education, *A Nation at Risk* (Washington, D.C.: U.S. Department of Education, 1983).

4. *Newark Star-Ledger*, September 6, 1958.

5. Details on the Bateman-Tanzman Act are examined in Robinson v. Cahill, 118 N.J. Super. 223 (1972).

6. See, for example, Denis P. Doyle and Chester E. Finn, Jr., "American Schools and the Future of Local Control, *The Public Interest*, Fall 1984.

7. Victor J. W. Christie, "State School Finance: The Historical Development of the N.J.E.A. as a Political Action Group" (Ann Arbor, Mich.: University Microfilms, 1968).

8. Ridgefield Park Education Ass'n. v. Ridgefield Park Board of Education, 78 N.J. 144 (1978).

9. *Newark Star-Ledger*, June 22, 1983.

10. See, for example, Margaret Goertz's "Analysis of Ch. 212, L1975" (Princeton: Educational Testing Service).

11. Star-Ledger/Eagleton Poll, November 20, 1983; see also Chapter 1.

12. Doyle and Finn, "American Schools."

11

RICHARD J. SULLIVAN

Environmental Policy

The environmental revolution was well under way in New Jersey by the first Earth Day in 1970. For years an uneasy, vaguely defined feeling had been growing that the quality of the state's environment was deteriorating. New Jersey's physical scene was changing very quickly. The state's population had grown 25 percent in the 1950s and 17 percent in the 1960s. Its motor vehicle population had grown more. In the mid-1960s, energy consumption was doubling every eight years. Demands on metropolitan water supplies had exceeded their safe yields. Dirty air and water became a problem. Land development was frenetic and often mindless of environmental consequences.

Old-fashioned conservationists had always argued that people must husband their resources in order to meet the demands of the future. The concerns that surfaced in the late 1960s and early 1970s caused many to ask whether these demands were themselves ethical. Should we burn our coal now? Or should we save it for later production of pharmaceuticals and for other, higher uses? Should we build an oil pipeline across the Alaskan tundra so we can tear up the winter landscape with our snowmobiles? Are we building another nuclear power plant only to light up more billboards? These questions suggest the apprehensions felt and expressed during this time: the environment was closing in; there weren't enough resources; and what was left was getting dirty.

Reflecting these anxieties, many individuals and organizations pushed for a no growth policy, opposing all development—housing subdivisions, shopping centers, interstate highways, sewer lines in undeveloped areas, and power plants. Special fury was directed at power plants; and among those, the most furiously regarded were nuclear power plants. Apart from legitimate safety questions, many simply rejected the new growth that this electrical power would accommodate. Of course those who objected could go home afterward, flick on the switches in their houses, and become part of the problem.

If there were a man who lived in a tent, surviving on muskrat and cabbage heads, he would have the credentials to protest that we don't need any more! Testimony from the rest of us is tainted. Earth Day spoke to this moral ambiguity.

The Earth Day sermon, given in many forums throughout the nation, was that the environment is an entity. It is a closed system. Pollution is matter in the wrong place. Man may be the highest form of creation, but he does not have his own private ecology.

In New Jersey, the Earth Day sermon had already been preached. Indeed, the state has been a leader in environmental protection. Well before Earth Day water quality standards were established. New Jersey was the first state government to enforce air pollution control, and it was the first to raise bond revenues for the preservation of open land. These efforts to protect the environment have won support from both parties, a broad coalition of interest groups, a series of governors, and the courts. While New Jersey has not always been a leader in other areas of state public policy, it has earned high marks for its environmental programs.

AIR POLLUTION CONTROL

New Jersey's official environmental management activity really began with the adoption of the Air Pollution Control Act of 1954. This bill was enacted in response to public apprehension, heightened by an air pollution episode that had occurred in Donora, Pennsylvania, in 1949. In the Donora Valley temporary air stagnation had permitted a phenomenal accumulation of air contaminants causing many residents to become acutely sick. Later studies showed that there was a marked increase in the death rate during and shortly after the episode, especially among the aged and those suffering from chronic respiratory illnesses.

New Jersey was the first state in the nation to enact a statewide air pollution control law (P.L. 1954, c. 212). There had been early regulatory activity in Los Angeles in an attempt to deal with its notorious smog. There were control efforts in Allegheny County (Pittsburgh), in the city of Detroit, and in other localities, mostly in pursuit of old-fashioned smoke abatement. But no state had assumed regulatory responsibility for comprehensive air pollution control. In New Jersey itself, polluted air had been considered only a local problem of environmental sanitation, a neighborhood nuisance. The little official attention it did receive was through mostly desultory enforcement of the sanitary code by local health departments. Even in the late 1940s, however, some people were coming to believe that air pollution was dangerous to their health. Donora only convinced them.

The new statute was full of elaborate due process provisions, designed to protect the chimney owners from hasty enforcement. Performance rules and standards were promulgated by a commission established by the statute to represent major, but sometimes conflicting, community interests. The law encouraged "conference, conciliation and persuasion."

Thirty years later it is easy for us to dismiss this law as hopelessly ineffectual. It was, in fact, a tentative enactment: the state had only put its big toe in to test the temperature. Yet, at the same time, its adoption was a pioneering achievement for these reasons:

It established an essentially political—not technical—definition of air pollution, calling it an unreasonable interference with the enjoyment of life.

It determined that the then current levels of air pollution were a menace and not just a public nuisance.

It recognized the regional character of environmental pollution by raising enforcement from the local to the state level.

As the years passed, public interest advanced but progress under the statute did not. It became apparent to clean air proponents and to state officials that the act was essentially unenforceable.

In 1961 the environment became a campaign subject for the first time in a New Jersey gubernatorial election. The Democratic candidate, Judge Richard J. Hughes, promised reform of the Air Pollution Control Act. He kept that promise in 1962, when his administration secured passage of a streamlined version of the statute. But it was not enough.

During the years that followed, editorial writers, cartoonists, and much of the public waggled fingers at the villains—at the pollution atrocities visible to everyone. If only the bureaucrats would straighten them out, they argued, our air would be clean again.

But the air did not get that dirty simply from a few conspicuous chimneys. The real cause was more general—automobiles, trucks, incinerators, factories, power stations, space heating—thousands of sources each individually unobjectionable, but which together had spread a gray pall over the state. The real culprit was total community growth without compensating pollution controls.

Government's response to this endemic pollution first showed itself in 1966 with adoption of legislation on motor vehicle pollution. The original version of the bill regulated the construction and maintenance of new and used cars. The proposal provided an interesting lesson in the politics of state-federal relationships. Car manufacturers came from Detroit to Trenton to protest legislation under which one state would regulate products manufactured for national sales. They then traveled to Washington to oppose national legislation, claiming that air pollution was a problem only in certain states. But these arguments could be turned around, and the industry later acquiesced to federal legislation that imposed national manufacturing standards as well as to legislation in New Jersey providing for performance standards, measured by annual vehicle inspections.

The New Jersey legislation was a significant policy initiative. For the first time the law treated the public as the cause and not just the victim of environmental pollution. Furthermore, it recognized that it is the totality of pollution sources that causes ambient pollution. New Jersey, with more motor vehicles registered per square mile than any other state, was first to adopt statewide regulation of this pollution source.

Despite such innovations, this effort was clearly not enough. In New Jersey, the real environmental uprising began in the late 1960s. In 1967, three years before the celebration of Earth Day, dirty air hit the fan. One of the political consequences of the uproar was that the senate and assembly held joint public hearings throughout the state on proposed legislation to control air pollution.

The initial problem was defining the concept of control. Smoke from individual fuel-burning operations had been limited on the basis of its visibility. One might conclude that this was simply reducing the visual offensiveness of air-borne waste disposal. Actually, the visual standard was related to what was achieveable if the equipment were properly operated with the right fuel. It was a *practicable* performance standard. Yet, reducing visual offensiveness might still leave the air dirty, because of the large number of stacks. Even if everybody met the individual standard, the total pollution would still not be acceptable.

On the other hand, the concept of *general* air quality standards— that is, the acceptable degree of air cleanliness—is reassuring. It gives an easily understood and measurable objective. It seems to free the system from arbitrariness. There are five steps in the process of enforcing general air quality: 1) for a given contaminant, set a protective standard; 2) then measure the average atmospheric concentration; 3) then conduct an inventory of all sources producing this pollutant; 4) next calculate how much pollution reduction is needed to achieve the standard; and 5) impose this reduction in the form of an enforceable regulation.

This approach, however, has its problems. It assumes that all existing sources are equally correctable. Even more fundamentally, it presumes that for each commonplace pollutant, a standard defining the threshold of harm can be established. But a search of the literature then—or even now—would be disappointing. There was not then and there is not now scientifically valid proof of the harmfulness of many air contaminants at the levels commonly encountered.

This ignorance of thresholds of harm, in a way, was considered by some to support a policy of the less the merrier, i.e., of reducing pollution at the source without prior proof of harm. "Why should anyone be allowed to put his garbage into the air (or water) just because it can't be proved with exactitude that it is causing specific harm?" the argument goes. Chemicals are no substitute for oxygen for breathing purposes. If a company wishes to continue its manufacturing operations, it should provide the maximum achievable degree of waste removal. To do less is physically and socially offensive.

The 1967 legislation reflected these notions. It required that all new sources of air contamination must be equipped with state-of-the-art controls. Additionally, the new laws abolished the commission; all rule-making was given to an executive agency. Simplified enforcement proceedings were established.

Under the provisions of these new statutes, a regulation was adopted in 1968 that, as in the control of motor vehicle emissions, recognized the importance of the cumulative pollution coming from certain widespread sources. The regulations governed the sulfur content of coal and oil used in all space heating and power generation facilities in the state. Their purpose was to reduce community pollution by sulfur dioxide.

A court challenge of the regulation raised a basic policy question— without proof of harm to health, can air pollution from fuel-burning be

considered such a threat as to justify the enormous economic disloca-
tions resulting from this regulation? The courts answered affirmatively
and laid the foundation for future regulations. They supported a pollution control policy of the less the merrier.

This case, however, did not dispose of the argument of economic
hardship. The chimney owners continued to protest that stern regulation would cause marginal industries to fail. Perhaps even worse, it
would cause New Jersey to be uncompetitive with other states where
regulations were more lenient or nonexistent. New statutes and regulations were adopted despite these objections, but the arguments re-
appeared later in support of national legislation that would provide
better equalization among the states.

Ideally, such federal legislation would do three things:

Set ambient air quality standards.

Regulate air pollution sources that are truly national (like the automobile)

Enforce controls to meet the standards in states that are shamelessly
inactive.

The federal government, through the agency of the Public Health
Service, had already moved toward the control of air pollution with
the 1963 Clean Air Act. This statute acknowledged the primacy of
state responsibility for control; it provided funds for the states to
operate their programs and offered them technical assistance. It regulated nothing.

In 1970, however, Congress acted decisively in response to growing
public impatience. Amendments to the Clean Air Act abandoned
vague notions of the less the merrier and provided for the establishment of a specific air quality standard for each major contaminant. On
paper, the states were mandated to adopt approved programs to
meet, on a specified timetable, the standards established for outdoor
air quality.

Real life required much more. In those states that were just getting
started—and there were many of them—the new federal law provided an inflexible specification. Many state officials resented, even as
most of the public welcomed, the new federal intrusion.

The debate continued over who should do what to best make up for
the neglect of past decades. Some argued that the whole attempt to
set enforceable performance standards and then police their compliance was inefficient and out of character for Americans. They said that

free market forces would provide the incentives and the form for public environmental policy.

These critics suggested a pollution fee—a tax on effluents or emissions—as a promising capitalist approach. It was an intellectually satisfying concept, applicable both to polluted air and water. The proposed policy would have required those who disposed of waste in the environment, which belongs to everyone, to pay into the public coffers in proportion to that use. This cost would then become an expense of the manufacturing process, ultimately causing a higher price for the product. In theory the added cost should cause those processes that produce the most waste to have the least competitive products. Market forces would then tend to favor products that damaged our environment the least. Such mechanisms were thought by some to be far superior to the expenditure of public funds to police the wide variety of operations, in order to cause them to meet arbitrary performance standards.

The market approach never really worked, however. A considerable inspection establishment would have been needed, first, to determine the amount of pollution being caused in order to set the fee, and, second, to make sure that companies were not putting out more pollution than they paid for. Another and perhaps more important deterrent to adoption of this policy was the offensiveness of the idea that the right to dump waste with impunity into the environment could be bought.

WATER POLLUTION CONTROL

During the 1960s and into the 1970s, the public had the same anxiety about dirty water as it did about dirty air. The people felt that corrective measures were slow and ineffective, and that instead of improving, pollution conditions were getting worse. Essentially, they were correct.

In 1899 there were statutes in effect in New Jersey that prohibited the pollution of waterways that might be used for drinking water. Intended as public health measures to combat the spread of cholera, typhoid fever, and other infectious disease, these laws were written with a magnificent simplicity that could have permitted their use forever. They were not written, however, to provide for environmental protection as it is understood today.

New Jersey began to move away from this public health approach and into modern water quality management in the mid-1960s, when it adopted regulations limiting the amount of pollution entering streams, rivers, bays, and coastal waters. The new regulatory program was designed to cause each waterway to meet standards of water quality based upon its particular nature and its intended uses.

In 1967, Governor Hughes, in an effort to emphasize the need for more effective programs, administratively created the Division of Clean Air and Water within the state Department of Health. And, in fact, for the three years of its life, this division made New Jersey the plaintiff in more pollution enforcement litigation than was moved in any other state in the nation. For the bureaucracy to act in this focused way and to engage in such an agressive enforcement offensive provided a hopeful suggestion that at last the government was taking the pollution problem seriously.

On the federal level the Clean Water Act offered helpful guidelines and technical assistance to states while leaving them primarily responsible for maintaining their own water quality. More important, it provided a funding mechanism for the construction of public sewage disposal facilities. In 1969, New Jersey, in advance of similar commitments by other states, confidently adopted a $271 million clean water bond issue. It provided state funds to match federal grants to underwrite an enormous capital program for new sewage treatment systems. (This grants program continued until federal funds dried up in the early 1980s.)

The great division of responsibility for water quality management between state and federal governments occurred in 1972 with the adoption of the federal Clean Water Act Amendments. This detailed statute provided for the establishment of local water quality standards and an elaborate, federally-supervised program for their achievement. While the act continued to maintain that the state has primary responsibility, the fact is that the federal government composed the music and the states played the tune, some well, some off-key.

PROGRESS TOWARD AIR AND WATER QUALITY

Over the last twenty years, progress toward higher air and water quality has been slow, painful, and fitful. Air and water quality each have their own special constituency, but both have had the support of an apprehensive public.

In general, during this period, the air has gotten cleaner faster than has the water. Indeed air quality control has been an environmental success story, so evident has been the progress. Of course, some air problems are still to be solved, like acid rain and low-level toxic contamination.

The disparity between air and water programs comes from differences in the manageability of the two problems. Most air pollution sources are privately owned. Enforcement procedures in the form of cash penalties and court injunctions can be made to work. Many of the worst water pollution sources, however, are publicly owned sewage plants that do not provide effective treatment. Enforcement by one public entity against another is awkward at best. Fines against local governments are state aid in reverse; they are no more than an embarrassing shift of taxes and do not work as a sanction.

Unlike the sky, which is rapidly cleaned, rivers and streams can remain dirty long after the amount of pollution entering them has been reduced, because of contaminated sediment at the bottom. Proper liquid waste disposal requires the construction of regional public waste water treatment systems. These are very expensive, long-term undertakings, usually involving political agreements among municipalities. Moreover, many of the engineering methods for waste water treatment have not changed much and so have not kept up with the changing character of the waste stream. This is in direct contrast to the development of innovative, privately financed air pollution control techniques that have advanced rapidly.

LAND AND RESOURCE MANAGEMENT

Clean air and water are fundamental to environmental protection. But the Earth Day message was also one of environmental integrity. It called for the management of all natural resources—air, water, and land. Many administrative actions were responsive to this concept of environmental completeness.

At the federal level, Congress in 1970 created the Environmental Protection Agency, whose responsibilities included not only those of the Clean Air Act but also the administration of all environmental legislation passed during the decade, including the clean water legislation, controls on pesticides and other toxic chemicals, and ultimately hazardous waste.

In January, 1970, New Jersey initiated its own concerted environmental management, when Governor William T. Cahill, shortly after taking office, proposed the creation of a state Department of Environmental Protection. The new agency would allow consolidation of pollution control with the state's conservation responsibilities, including fish and wildlife protection, the maintenance of parks and forests, and coastal protection. Without public hearings, the bill establishing DEP was adopted by the legislature one vote short of unanimity. It was signed into law by Governor Cahill in celebration of the first Earth Day.

The new DEP was given extensive authority to enforce environmental standards and the power to approve or disapprove many projects having environmental consequences. In defining DEP's role, some argued that in many cases legitimate environmental objectives were in conflict with legitimate economic objectives; therefore the department should define the proper balance. Others claimed that the language of the enabling statute clearly made DEP the public's environmental advocate. In fact, the agency has defined itself as an advocate, but with a reasonable appreciation of all affected interests. In any case, when the Department of the Public Advocate was created in 1974, it too was given the power to serve as ombudsman in environmental matters as well as in other areas of governmental regulation. In some cases the public advocate has challenged DEP decisions as insufficiently protective.

The new DEP was dedicated to the Earth Day message that the land is a resource and not a commodity. In spite of pollution controls, unless land use is managed properly, the environment will ultimately suffer. Actually, without enunciating it in just that way, the New Jersey public had understood for years the necessity for prudent land management. And the public has voted to support that goal whenever it has had the chance.

In 1961, for example, the first Green Acres Bond Issue was adopted by a comfortable plurality. This was the first bond issue in the nation to provide for the public acquisition of lands with natural characteristics deserving of preservation, and the voters have since renewed that bond issue four times. Along the same lines, in 1963, a state referendum was approved giving preferential tax status to farmland. The public hoped this action would slow the rapid loss of farms through development.

These two unique referenda were precursors to New Jersey's broadest environmental effort—the revision of the state's regulation of land use. This effort began in 1969 when, in the midst of great controversy, the legislature created the Hackensack Meadowlands Development Commission and gave to the commission land-use control over a twenty-thousand-acre district comprising substantial parts of fourteen municipalities.

As the name of the commission suggests, however, this statute was not designated solely for protection of the environment; rather the commission was charged with providing a mix of development and preservation. The statute recognized that the district comprised the estuary of the Hackensack River as well as some of the most valuable real estate in the country. The great significance of the statute lay in its conveyance to a regional state agency of the power to determine the uses of land—a power that had previously been jealously guarded by New Jersey municipalities as their right to home rule.

In 1970, the Wetlands Act was adopted to safeguard the marshlands. The law did not explicitly prevent the filling of these ecologically valuable lands, but, for the most part, it did have that net effect. It was an attempt, later upheld in the courts as constitutional, to achieve preservation without confiscation. This trend may continue with the possible adoption of proposed legislation providing for a mixture of state and municipal regulation of inland freshwater wetlands, as well as attempts to provide for the retention of agricultural lands.

Another statute, enacted in 1973, recognized the special environmental characteristics of New Jersey's shore. It gave to the Department of Environmental Protection review authority over development decisions that were previously in the exclusive domain of municipalities. Again, the act was in conflict with the honored tradition of home rule, and again environmental protection won the argument.

Later in the decade legislation with a similar objective was adopted for the protection of the Pinelands, a one-million-acre section of land (about one-fifth of the area of the state) with a unique ecology. Supervision over development decisions was given to a Pinelands commission appointed by the governor and representing local, state, and federal interests.

This collection of statutes changed remarkably land-use policy in New Jersey. In many areas, it took authority away from municipalities and assigned it to state agencies. Probably none of these laws would have been approved in the name of good regional land-use planning, because of the strength of home rule. They *were* approved, however, because they were presented as environmental protection measures.

THE POLITICS OF ENVIRONMENTAL POLICY

Bipartisanship marked the passage of these environmental laws and of others dealing with noise, pesticide control, regulation of ocean dumping, solid waste management, and protection of the riverine flood plains. Although some of this legislation was strongly contested, the battle lines were not usually drawn along party lines. Environmental protection has had the support of a series of strong governors. In 1967 the Democratic Hughes administration easily moved stringent new air pollution control laws through a Democratic legislature.

During 1970 to 1974, a Republican controlled legislature adopted more than one hundred environmental bills. Some of them were trivial, others were quite substantial. The majority of them were moved on the initiative of Republican Governor Cahill, but the most controversial of them, the coastal protection law, was approved only with help from Democratic legislators. During the term of Democratic Governor Brendan Byrne, bills were adopted concerning solid waste management, water supply, and the Pinelands. A Democratic controlled legislature did not mean there were no controversies, however, although in the end Governor Byrne was able to overcome them and obtain passage of the desired bills. Since 1982, strong environmental protection laws, particularly concerning the management of hazardous chemicals, have been adopted by a Democratic legislature and signed by a Republican Governor Thomas Kean. Thus, bipartisan legislative and gubernatorial support have combined to strengthen New Jersey's environmental program.

Impetus for all of New Jersey's environmental activism came from the apprehension and impatience of the general public (see Chapter 1). Those who articulated this uneasiness and lobbied for the cause included some unusual coalitions. Forceful and enthusiastic, these coalitions were also fragile and of uncertain duration. Citizens from the lush countryside, owners of land and money and, for the most part, holders of politically conservative views, manned the environmental barricades alongside working class union members. Conservative Republicans, who cherished their tradition of home rule, joined with the shore preservationists to support the coastal area bill, even though it conveyed land-use decisions to the state. Conservationists, who for years had preached prudent management of resources without an audience, now lined up with populists who were demanding that industry stop polluting their air and water resources.

In the early 1970s there was a short-lived and fascinating alliance between environmental organizations and the social protestors on the left. This coalition, however, did not last. Those who protested the Vietnam War and fought for civil rights and a better life for the urban poor came to regard environmental efforts as an elite distraction which they could not afford. "Who wants to breathe clean air in a racist society?" they asked. To respond that it beats breathing dirty air in a racist society was not permitted. The left's disdain for the environmental cause was based on resentment at the human and financial resources that it commanded. The urban poor did not worry much about the need to preserve green acres or the fate of any endangered species other than themselves. These critics said that environment is for people, not for wildlife. New development in the precious, open, natural countryside is not cancerous growth, but human settlement. It allows a rising generation to participate in a life the environmentalists already enjoy and don't want to share.

The argument of elitism is still heard from time to time, but it has not deflected environmental efforts. More influential have been arguments from the opposite ideological direction. The criticism of greatest force and consistency maintains that extreme and unnecessary environmental protection measures by legislatures and regulatory agencies are destructive of the economy. In individual cases, of course, the argument may be either specious or legitimate depending upon the facts and one's judgment. As a general criticism, however, it must be appraised in terms of a fundamental policy question: is the state's first priority to protect the environment without undue harm to productive industry, or is it to promote industry without undue harm to the environment? New Jersey has opted for protection of the environment, other states have chosen promotion of industry.

The public here has shown no affection for cost-benefit analyses of environmental protections, nor for the federal Office of Management and Budget's cost-effectiveness analyses of new EPA regulations. In environmental and health matters in New Jersey, cost has not been the controlling factor.

Yet, in New Jersey and elsewhere, the impact of the argument of economic harm varies with the times. In the prosperity of the early 1970s, concern about restrictions on industry were suppressed by the political force of a public worried about the environment. As the oil embargo and a variety of economic factors brought us into the mid-decade recession, that argument won more spokesmen. An example of this counter-revolution in New Jersey was The Society for Environmental and Economic Development, which was formed late in 1973. SEED was an unusual alliance among industrial and labor leaders who were concerned that environmental regulation would stifle economic progress. A more dramatic presentation of the argument was made in September, 1975, when ten thousand construction workers walked, or rode on flatbed trucks, into downtown Trenton to ask Governor Byrne, what's more important—habitat for birds or food for our families?

Although in the early 1980s the national recession and an administration scornful of environmental protection produced some retreats, that administration has since discovered that the public has its own notions about environmental policy and will reprimand officials who seem too easy on polluters. The complaints and fears of economic harm have not brought any serious reversal of environmental improvement programs in New Jersey, however. In the 1980s DEP has not retreated at all, but has moved into new areas of environmental protection, such as dealing with gigantic amounts of garbage and hazardous wastes. Consistent with the notion that pollution is matter in the wrong place, the state must now seek the right place for these unwanted materials.

In part, this newly perceived problem of hazardous waste is a tribute to past progress in other areas. Hazardous chemicals have been excluded from the ocean, from our rivers, from lawful landfills, and in many cases, even from the sewer systems. Garbage has been excluded from landfills, closed because of their environmental destructiveness. The system has been more effective in eliminating hazardous disposal methods than it has been in devising acceptable replacements. As one North Jersey collection contractor complained, "Everybody wants me to pick up his garbage, but nobody wants to let me put it down."

THE FUTURE OF ENVIRONMENTAL PROTECTION

In New Jersey environmental protection efforts for the rest of this decade will concentrate on two issues: 1) the construction of solid waste disposal facilities to replace the offensive landfill, and 2) the control of the threat to our ground water created by the creeping presence of low levels of toxic chemical contamination. The technical, financial, and legal remedies are available. The procedural arrangements are coming into place.

New Jersey has more civilization per square mile than any other state. Such density brings with it both opportunities and problems. For the last twenty years the state has had enlightened environmental protection leadership from a succession of governors. Strong laws and regulations are in place. The public's demand for improvement is an insistent as ever. The state's environmental protection programs are more rigorous than those of many other states in the nation. The prospects are very good for continued progress.

12

CARL E. VAN HORN

Economic Development Policy

Economic development is a central concern of state government in New Jersey and throughout the nation. Governors, legislatures, party leaders, and interest groups seek effective public and private strategies that will promote economic prosperity and produce job opportunities for their states' residents. Economic development has always been an important feature of state government policy and politics, but recently it has leapt to the top of the political agenda. In the mid-1980s, economic development has become an obsession.

Why is economic development so important to state officials? Changing economic and political conditions have given new urgency to state economic development. The nation's economy suffered a series of setbacks during the last two decades. Unemployment, inflation, energy prices, and trade imbalances have all soared, sometimes simultaneously. Recently, the U.S. experienced the highest levels of unemployment since the 1940s. Recessions have come with increasing frequency. Sustained and seemingly limitless economic growth seems to have vanished, at least for some states and communities.

Given this new economic environment, it is not surprising that state officials are compelled to try to insulate their states from economic crisis. Shocks to the national economy reverberate at the state level. When economic activity slows and unemployment rises, state revenues decline, yet demands for state services increase. State governments must figure out how to cover increased costs for unemployment insurance, social services, and public welfare with diminished revenues. Even in prosperous times, economic development strategies remain important as a means to provide the services that citizens demand from state government and to guard against the problems of future economic downturns.

Greater attention to economic development strategies is also fueled by rising interstate competition. In recent years, the states have become locked in a struggle for economic growth. States increasingly view one another as contestants in a game of economic survival. Conflicts deepened during the 1970s as many businesses and industries migrated to the south and southwest in search of lower living costs and cheaper land, labor, and energy. The Frostbelt states of the northeast and midwest initiated new economic development strategies hoping to stem the flow of jobs to the Sunbelt and to rehabilitate their reputations with the business community. In the 1980s, cross-state and cross-regional economic "border wars" are commonplace, as states try to outdo one another in offering financial inducements and encouragement to new and existing businesses.

Following a general overview of state strategies and their limitations, this chapter describes various approaches to stimulating economic growth. The objectives and accomplishments of Governors Brendan Byrne and Thomas Kean will receive special attention.

The State's Role in Economic Development

While recent economic problems have fostered greater interest in economic development strategies, state government involvement is hardly new. Since the beginning of the Republic, and increasingly since the industrial revolution, state governments have facilitated business activity. State governments built transportation networks, funded public education, supported public colleges and universities, and, in conjunction with local governments, provided for other essential facilities such as water and sewer lines. Citizens and businesses alike depend on state financial resources and public servants.

State governments have also been deeply involved in business regulation for decades. Banking and insurance laws, environmental and public health policies, land and public water usage, and work place and labor standards are all governed by state policies and have been since the nineteenth century.

Additionally, tax policy has always been an important element of state economic development. The cost of doing business is affected in dozens of obvious and subtle ways by the state's tax structure. The state raises revenue to compensate workers who are injured on the job and to sustain those who are laid off. The state taxes businesses on the energy they consume and for the inventories they maintain. Since every state does not levy the same amount or type of taxes on business, tax policy often influences how businesses view a state as a place to locate.

During the last decade, state policymakers have become more sensitive to the influence of state government on economic growth. They are now determined to use state policies strategically to foster economic prosperity. Debates over how state taxes, regulation, and infrastructure affect business location decisions are relatively recent. Moreover, state governments have expanded their arsenal of economic development weapons. States are now using public policies to aid selective industries and communities to boost overall business activity. States have established financing mechanisms and tax abatement programs to induce firms into their state. States have shifted from merely facilitating activity to aggressively stimulating and channeling economic growth.

Consider a recent example from New Jersey. Although public and private leaders have always known that mass transportation can create opportunities for economic expansion, state officials are now becoming more concerned about the connection between transportation policy and the economy. A few years ago, the Johnson and Johnson Corporation announced that it would spend over $250 million in New Brunswick on a new headquarters, a new hotel, and other revitalization plans, but only if the state would upgrade and relocate the city's principal highway. Faced with this ultimatum, Governor Brendan Byrne channeled $63 million in state and federal highway funds to the New Brunswick project. Without state action, Johnson and Johnson might have invested elsewhere, perhaps outside of the Garden State.

States have also created agencies whose sole purpose is to encourage economic development. In New Jersey, an Economic Development Authority was established in 1974. It provides low-cost financing to businesses for the purchase of land and new equipment or for construction of new facilities. The EDA also guarantees loans for commercial and industrial firms and operates several industrial parks. By 1983, the EDA had supplied $4.3 billion to 2,800 businesses and claimed to have generated over 84,000 permanent jobs.[1]

The other government entity that promotes the Garden State's economy is the Department of Commerce and Economic Development. Created in 1981 with a modest budget of $5.4 million (in a $7 billion state budget), the department's budget had grown 35 percent to $7.3 million by 1984. The department's staff of one hundred promotes international trade, provides technical assistance to new and small firms, and helps employers who are locating or expanding in New Jersey. The department's most visible and expensive undertaking is the promotion of travel and tourism, with radio and television advertisements featuring Governor Thomas Kean, comedian Bill Cosby, and actress and Princeton undergraduate Brooke Shields.

THE LIMITS OF STATE ECONOMIC DEVELOPMENT POLICY

Even though state government actions are important to economic development, they are overshadowed by national and international economic conditions and by decisions made in the private sector. No matter how ambitious and expensive state strategies become, they pale in significance to policies and events that are shaped beyond the state's borders. Federal spending and taxing policies, the cost of borrowing money, international trade conditions, energy prices, and corporate business decisions are beyond the authority of state policymakers.

State economic development policies may influence the pace and location of economic growth, but they will not determine the overall vitality of a state, because it is part of a national and international economic system. Years of hard work in the State House can be obliterated by one decision in the White House or a corporate boardroom.

Consequently, state economic development strategies have only modest impacts on overall economic health. Recent declines and recoveries in New Jersey's economy are illustrative. In 1976 New Jersey's unemployment rate was 10.4 percent—well above the national average of 7.7 percent. By 1985 the state's unemployment rate had dropped to less than 5 percent, more than two points below the national average. Yet no politician or economist could credibly assert that state government policies in 1976 caused New Jersey's high unemployment rate or that state policies in 1984 and 1985 brought about a strong recovery. In fact, New Jersey's position in the national economy has been governed primarily by changes in the state's economic base: for example, the change from a reliance on traditional manufacturing firms such as automobiles to a service and high-technology economy made the state less vulnerable to the economic problems experienced in the recession of 1982 and 1983.

To some extent, therefore, debates over state economic development policies may seem like much ado about nothing. If overall state economic trends are determined by federal policymakers and multinational corporations, then the impact of state policies will be of minor significance. Nevertheless, state officials feel justified in constructing economic development strategies precisely because they may make a difference in some instances. With a state economy of over 3 million jobholders, if state policies affect only 1 percent of the work force, that still represents 30,000 jobs—something that no politician could afford to ignore. As a result, most state economic development strategies either attempt to compensate for national and international economic trends or to take advantage of them.

COMMON ENDS, DIFFERENT MEANS

The central question in contemporary economic development debate is not whether states should do something, but what something states should do. Political leaders of all stripes agree that economic development is vital, but sharp disagreement remains about the particular role state government can or should play. From the Civil War through the early 1960s, a bipartisan consensus existed on some economic policy objectives. At the very least it was agreed that state governments should facilitate economic growth by financing an infrastructure for business and commerce. During the Great Depression of the 1930s federal and state governments also funded public works projects that provided temporary jobs for millions of unemployed workers. Following World War II, state governments were content to provide minimal support and encouragement to the private sector. Relatively unambitious state policies were suited to a time when the nation's economy was rapidly expanding. The optimism of the post-war period was captured by the slogan on a bridge in New Jersey—"Trenton Makes, The World Takes." During this era, New Jersey's economy grew along with the rest of the nation's.

Since the late 1960s, however, the national economy has not followed a steady upward path. Instead, there have been five major recessions, urban riots, rising unemployment, and a huge decrease in the number of manufacturing jobs. The post-war consensus about economic development policies has unraveled. Overall economic growth has continued, especially along suburban highways (see Chapter 2), but pockets of urban and rural poverty are now evident. Moreover, wide fluctuations in the economy have led many policymakers to conclude that the policies of the past are no longer adequate.

These new economic concerns, coinciding with the expansion of state power, have spurred a new and more contentious debate over state economic development strategies. While policymakers generally agree about ultimate ends, they disagree over specific objectives and how to achieve them. Should the state promote existing smokestack industries or search for nonpolluting replacements? Should the state steer development into the urban areas or encourage businesses to locate in the suburbs? Should the state create jobs through public works projects or offer tax incentives to private firms thereby creating jobs through expansion?

Partisan politics and interest group conflicts also influence economic development policies. Both major political parties and virtually all interest groups favor economic growth, but they often disagree over which approaches should be followed and who should benefit from state investments. On many economic development issues, conflict can be mitigated by ensuring that traditional Republican and Democratic constituencies receive a share of the benefits. For example, public works projects are popular with elected officials because benefits are enjoyed by business and labor, city and suburb.

Policymakers are sometimes forced to chose between conflicting interests, however. Big city mayors, labor organizations, and civil rights activists want to see state economic development strategies directed toward their constituents. Business organizations oppose attaching strings to government economic aid. A recent economic development policy dispute occurred during the debate over New Jersey's right-to-know law. Labor organizations pushed for this legislation because it required private firms to inform workers about potential chemical hazards in the work place, but business organizations claimed that such regulations would have a chilling effect on the business climate. The legislature and the governor enacted the law after an intense and sometimes bitter debate.

During the last two decades divergent strategies have been advanced to promote economic growth. These strategies can be arrayed along a continuum. At one end, state government aspires to manage economic expansion: state spending can create jobs and regulatory policies may encourage businesses to locate in targeted communities. At the other end of the continuum are policies that follow existing economic trends: government policy tries to improve the overall business environment and bolster strong sectors of the economy. State economic management strategies rely on government spending and state regulation; state strategies that follow economic trends lean heavily on tax incentives and tax reductions to stimulate economic growth. Both of these alternative strategies have been pursued in New Jersey.

ECONOMIC DEVELOPMENT STRATEGIES IN NEW JERSEY

New Jersey's recent governors made economic development a top state priority, but their approaches differed sharply. Economic development was emphasized throughout Governor Byrne's two terms. In his 1978 State of the State message he declared, "There is no more urgent need facing New Jersey than to provide meaningful employment for every man and woman who is willing and able to work."[2] Economic development was also a central priority of the Kean administration. During the 1983 State of the State message, the governor observed, "There is no greater responsibility for government than to create conditions in which people . . . can work and prosper. Thus as government, we should always strive to measure our actions against the yardstick of jobs—productive and meaningful jobs."[3]

Governor Byrne used state spending and regulatory policies to channel public works projects and private investments to distressed areas of the state. His underlying objective was to reverse prevailing negative economic trends in the cities and to revitalize them with government assistance.

Governor Kean's policies were intended to support and supplement contemporary economic trends. During his administration, government spending and tax policies were designed to aid robust sectors of the economy. Jobs were created by stimulating investment in private firms through state spending and tax incentives. Like Byrne, Kean endorsed public works projects; however, his transportation improvement projects were not targeted exclusively to urban communities but spread throughout the state.

The Byrne and Kean strategies were as much a product of current state economic conditions as they were a reflection of different governmental philosophies. When Byrne took office, New Jersey and the nation were in a deep recession and the governor was forced on the defensive. He was expected by business, labor, and the public to help get people back to work. When Kean was inaugurated the economy was also in bad shape, but New Jersey was not faring as poorly as the rest of the nation and, within a year, New Jersey experienced an unusually strong recovery. For this reason it was possible politically for Kean to encourage existing trends rather than to buck them.

THE BYRNE STRATEGY

When the Byrne administration entered office in 1974, the state's jobless rate had risen above 10 percent. Job creation through economic development became an immediate priority. In his first State of the State message the governor outlined his goals: "Any effort to improve the quality of life in New Jersey must begin with . . . our cities. If we—the Administration and the legislature—fail in our promises to those who live in urban centers, we have broken our pledge to make the future as just as it can be."[4] State assistance would be targeted to distressed communities: the power of government would be marshalled on behalf of disadvantaged citizens.

The Byrne administration accomplished much of its economic development agenda. The state's crippling and uncertain financial conditions were stabilized with the adoption of a state income tax in 1976. The concern that businesses would be forced to pay for increasing educational costs and other state services was thus eliminated. Workmen's compensation laws were made less burdensome and arbitrary. And, new state agencies were established to promote international trade and high-technology firms and to help businesses navigate through government red tape.

Three economic development acheivements stand out as hallmarks of the Byrne era: the Meadowlands Sports Complex, Atlantic City Casino Gambling, and the Governor's Urban Strategy. In each instance, the governor aided urban and distressed communities either by spending state money or by stimulating private investment.

The Meadowlands

A swampy wasteland adjacent to the New Jersey Turnpike known as the Meadowlands was transformed into a vibrant center of economic activity during the Byrne years. By enacting several regulatory changes and pushing through a $435 million bond issue, the state created one of the world's largest sports complexes—the Meadowlands Racetrack, Giants' Stadium, and the Byrne Arena. During its eight years of operation, the complex has created 4,500 full and part-time jobs, generated $107 million in state tax revenues, and attracted over half a billion dollars in private investment. Without the allocation of any state revenues, except for initial seed money that was subsequently repaid, the Meadowlands Sports Complex has become a major economic success story and an important public amenity.[5]

Atlantic City

Another landmark of Byrne's economic development strategy was the establishment of casino gambling in Atlantic City. By the late 1960s and early 1970s, Atlantic City had deteriorated to a point that seemed beyond renewal. With the governor providing strong support, a state referendum authorizing casino gambling was approved by the voters in 1976. The casino industry was not viewed primarily as a source of state tax revenues but as a unique urban development tool.

According to Governor Byrne, "The most significant consideration . . . was the role of casinos in stimulating convention income, resort, and entertainment industries in Atlantic City."[6]

Since 1978 nine casinos have been built at a cost of over $1 billion in private investment. Over 30,000 permanent jobs have been created for New Jerseyans. By January 1983, the casinos had raked in nearly $4 billion in gross revenues. In one year, 1982, the state received over $150 million in taxes, of which $120 million went to aid senior citizens.[7]

Despite these positive signs, Atlantic City's revitalization has not been an unequivocal success. Critics charge that Atlantic City's residents have not benefited from the casinos. A major study concluded: "There has been amazingly little spillover growth into noncasino employment within Atlantic City. The absolute number of unemployed has not changed appreciably."[8] The goal of rebuilding the city's convention and resort industry and revitalizing an entire region has not yet been fulfilled.

Targeted Urban Investments

In addition to the Meadowlands and Atlantic City projects, the governor pursued an urban strategy designed to create permanent jobs for city residents. He did this by steering investments made by the Economic Development Authority and Housing Finance Authority to urban communities with high unemployment and low income. State assistance was forbidden for commercial and retail facilities planning to move outside of large cities. The governor also pushed through a Community Development Bond Act that provided funds for capital projects in urban areas. Finally, the Byrne administration substantially increased the utilization of federal sewer and water construction grants—a tactic that generated over $1 billion in public investment and thousands of construction jobs.

Notwithstanding the strong urban commitment of Governor Byrne, he was wary of overpromising. The governor believed that state government could influence patterns of economic growth by targeting public and private investments to certain distressed areas, but he also recognized the profound nature of the problems in the cities: "The causes of urban decay . . . result from longstanding federal policies and demographic changes over which our control is limited. [This administration's proposals] . . . do not suggest a major influx of new state dollars; rather they entail the use of current resources on a more rational basis."[9] Given the state's fiscal problems (which were exacerbated by a national recession), new, large-scale spending programs were simply not feasible. Nevertheless, strong efforts were under-

taken to focus public and private investments in communities suffering most severely from economic decline.

THE KEAN STRATEGY

The election of Thomas Kean in 1981 ushered in new state economic development policies. Kean's strategy was intended to bolster
growth sectors of the state's economy rather than to bail out blighted
communities or declining manufacturing firms. His objectives were
announced during the gubernatorial campaign: "The major challenge
facing our state is to restore a sound business environment, to keep
business here and attract new firms to New Jersey in the future. This
infusion of economic growth will provide job opportunities lost by this
state in the last decade because of rising, oppressive taxes."[10] Economic growth would be stimulated principally by lightening the burden for taxpayers.

The governor's desire to reduce sales and income taxes was thwarted
in the early months of his administration. Facing the possibility of
huge budget deficits and a state fiscal crisis, the governor and the legislature were obliged to increase both sales and income taxes. Businesses benefited from the elimination of the net worth tax and by
changes in unemployment compensation taxes, but the state's overall
tax bite was larger.

Governor Kean's abandonment of tax reduction proposals demonstrates that states are captives of national economic conditions. It is
virtually impossible for New Jersey or other states to lower taxes during a national recession. With service demands increasing, due to
higher unemployment and poverty, and tax revenues declining,
all but a handful of states raised taxes during 1982–1983. These tax
increases did not prove to be a major obstacle to economic
growth, however.

Despite setbacks on the tax front, Governor Kean pursued his strategy of promoting overall economic growth through public and private
investments. Three components of the governor's record are especially noteworthy—the high-technology strategy, the Transportation
Trust Fund, and efforts to improve the state's image. Each of these
programs reflects the Kean administration's approach to state government intervention in the economy.

High Technology

Governor Kean singled out high-technology industries for special
state assistance. A commission on science and technology recommended increased public and private investment in high technology

firms.[11] By adopting the high-technology strategy, Governor Kean was following trends in the state's economy and responding to the pressures of interstate competition. New Jersey's political leaders were concerned that thirty-seven other states had already developed high technology programs during the preceding decade. High-technology firms are already an important part of the state economy, employing nearly 10 percent of the work force. The high-technology program complements and augments this growing sector, although most of these firms would prosper even without state aid. The hope is that state investments in high-technology research centers, for example, will convince private firms to expand or locate in New Jersey. Substantial job creation will occur only if private firms take the bait.

Transportation

Governor Kean also tried to enhance the overall business environment by improving highways and mass transportation in New Jersey. In 1984, the legislature established a $3.3 billion trust fund to resurface roads, repair bridges, and upgrade mass transit services. The fund was created by increasing truck user fees, dedicating a portion of the gasoline tax, and reallocating toll money from the turnpike and parkway authorities. According to the governor, the fund will enhance "travelling convenience, economic development opportunities, safety, and jobs for New Jerseyans."[12]

This approach to economic development provides a public investment on behalf of the private sector. Government is upgrading transportation facilities so that goods and people can be more efficiently transported. Benefits from the transportation projects are likely to be spread around the state, not concentrated exclusively in distressed communities. In fact, such investments may encourage businesses to locate outside central cities because workers and materials will now have better access to suburban communities.

The State's Image

Promoting New Jersey as a place to visit and to locate a business has been another important economic development objective of the Kean era. In 1983 Kean unveiled New Jersey's answer to "I Love New York"—a new state slogan—"New Jersey and You: Perfect Together." Media messages describing the state's advantages to new firms and tourists were produced and distributed on radio and television at a cost of more than $3.4 million during 1984.

New Jersey is again following in the footsteps of its neighbors. Other states in the Northeast have been tooting their horns for years. For example, New York State spends $14 million annually on its advertisements. There is more than state bragging rights at stake. Reporting on a recent battle between New York and New Jersey over the development of the Hudson River waterfront, the *New York Times* noted: "Behind the barbs and bombast, the states are vying for some important prizes: billions of dollars in redevelopment, thousands of jobs, and that illusive, but all important commodity: image."[13] The struggle for slices of the economic pie is escalating and shows no sign of abating.

The governor enjoyed bipartisan support for his high-technology and transportation initiatives, but his campaign to enhance New Jersey's image generated some grousing from Democratic lawmakers. They charged that the governor was merely using the tourism commercials to promote his reelection. Furthermore, they argued that promotional campaigns have only marginal impact because there are other more important factors that affect business location decisions and vacation plans.

Governor Kean's economic development strategy casts the state as cheerleader and bankroller for private investment. Kean's public encouragement of new businesses was matched by a financial commitment to high technology centers and by expenditures to improve the state's infrastructure. The governor's strategy was designed to promote strong sectors of the economy. New Jersey's Sunbelt may become even more prosperous. Although cities have not been ignored entirely—the governor and the legislature created urban enterprise zones and authorized a Community Development Bond Act to stimulate private investment in urban areas—substantial state resources have not been devoted to declining urban centers.

CONCLUSION

"Economic development" has become a modern day shibboleth of state government. Every political candidate, legislator, and governor comes equipped with recommendations for how government can stimulate economic growth. Less than two decades ago most state officials would not have given economic development matters a second thought. Today economic development is a major political issue. The prevailing concern that has pushed economic development to the forefront is the perception that New Jersey and the Northeast will suffer prolonged economic decline unless steps are taken to counter the advantages offered by other states and foreign nations.

Talk of economic revitalization and job creation may be on every politician's lips, but the state's elected leaders are uncertain and divided about how state government can most effectively promote economic prosperity. It is difficult to assess the efficacy of economic development strategies because it is usually impossible to know what would have happened if the state had taken no action or had acted differently. In the absence of proven government strategies, economic development policies are forged by political beliefs, interstate competition, national economic conditions, and interest group politics.

Increased government attention to economic development goals has raised public expectations that state action can offset the negative consequences of a slack national economy or take advantage of growth in the national economy. As state governments are drawn into the economic development game, many state elected officials have tied their political fortunes to the state's prosperity. Yet their attempts to influence the economy may be undone by national policies, international events, and the decisions of private firms. Politicians have shouldered a major burden.

State economic development strategies may have been oversold. Governors and other lawmakers are exerting leadership, and state governments can obviously influence some aspects of the economy, but the states are not the principal determinants of economic growth. Politicians are poised to claim credit for success, but they may also be held responsible when the economy falters.

There are political risks involved when a governor becomes identified with an issue he can't control. With the Garden State's economy outpacing the national economy in 1984 and 1985, Governor Kean was in an enviable position. Economic development had been a key priority of his administration and the economy had been healthy. If the economy slides into another recession during his time in office, however, the governor may rue that day that economic development became so important. The public may hold the governor accountable, yet he would be no more responsible for the state's general economic problems than he was for its economic recovery.

Notes

1. New Jersey Economic Development Authority, *1983 Annual Report.*

2. Brendan T. Byrne, "Annual Message to the New Jersey Legislature," January 10, 1978.

3. Thomas H. Kean, "Annual Message to the New Jersey Legislature," January 11, 1983.

4. Brendan T. Byrne, "Annual Message to the New Jersey Legislature," January 10, 1975.

5. *1983 Annual Report/New Jersey Sports and Exposition Authority*.

6. George Sternlieb and James W. Hughes, *The Atlantic City Gamble* (Cambridge: Harvard University Press, 1983), 59.

7. *Ibid*, 75.

8. *Ibid*, 10–11.

9. Brendan T. Byrne, "Annual Message," 1978.

10. Thomas H. Kean, "Kean Proposes Specific Tax Cut Plans: Aims at Economic Growth," Press Release, April 28, 1981.

11. *Report of the Governor's Commission on Science and Technology for the State of New Jersey*, December 1983.

12. Thomas H. Kean, "Annual Message to the New Jersey Legislature," January 10, 1984.

13. Michael Norman, "Small War Between States Pits New York against New Jersey," *New York Times*, March 27, 1984, Section II, 4.

GERALD M. POMPER

Conclusion

When Governor Richard Hughes sought reelection in 1965, New Jersey was an unimpressive state. To visitors, its most prominent feature was the turnpike, which took them past the foul pig farms of Secaucus, the smoking refineries of Elizabeth, and the empty rural stretches below Camden. To residents, the state government was but a distant presence. Trenton gave little to its constituents by way of services or funds, but then it also asked little by way of taxes or political participation.

To recall New Jersey only two decades ago is to remember what was absent rather than to regret what has been lost. Consider the simple use of leisure. In 1965, Newark's crowded residents did not spend summer weekends at Round Valley, because the dam and recreation area were still undeveloped. No fans cheered major league athletic teams in meadowlands that provided only a corridor for travelers en route to watch the Yankees or Giants or Knicks or Rangers. Ocean swimmers either would find beaches on the New Jersey shore closed to nonresidents or they would have to pay significant fees to enjoy the sand and surf. Nature lovers could wander through the primitive Pinelands, but no state controls existed to prevent the eventual loss of this rich botanical life and these quiet rivers to suburban sprawl. Atlantic City was little more than a museum, its street names reminding visitors of Monopoly games, and its annual Miss America contest a monument to the eroding model of female triviality.

In political life as well, the state was more of a geographical description than a civic commonwealth. To paraphrase Gertrude Stein, in New Jersey there was no "there" there. The sacrosanct principle of home rule left communities largely free to determine the degree of their commitment to public education, to compete for industrial development, to use zoning ordinances to exclude new residents with "undesirable" incomes or color, to foul their neighbors' water and air. Citizens were regularly reminded of their local interests by high property taxes, but the state's limited role was disguised by a revenue system that asked individuals to make only indirect contributions to the state when they bought gasoline or liquor or cigarettes. Altogether, in 1965, the state spent only $182 for governmental services for each New Jerseyan.

Politicians themselves literally stayed at home. Public careers were founded on strong county parties whose power was reinforced by strong voter loyalties to their locally dominant Republican or Democratic organizations. Legislators came to Trenton usually only once a week and concluded their business quickly enough to spend their nights at home. They left Trenton governmentally stunted, without significant legislative staff, without long-term leaders, and with only a limited executive bureaucracy.

How different is New Jersey in 1986, as Governor Thomas Kean begins his second term. In seeking recreation, New Jerseyans now camp in the mountains; swim at the shore; crowd the Meadowlands' stadium, racetrack, and Byrne arena; walk through the Pinelands reserve; and gamble at Atlantic City casinos. These new opportunities did not just happen; they have come through a series of concerted state actions. Reversing the historic deference to localism, the government in Trenton, with the approval of the state's voters, created regional authorities and enacted legislation to promote a vision of the more general interest.

The same assertion of a state interest, rather than a local interest, is evident in many other areas of public policy as well. The historic decision of the state supreme court in *Robinson v. Cahill* revived the long-dormant issue of the state's responsibility to provide a "thorough and efficient" education for every child regardless of the wealth of his or her community. Though implementation of improved educational opportunity has trailed behind principle, the result still has been the state's assumption of a large share of the public schools' costs.

Similarly in economic development, decisions are still made principally by private interests, but these actions are now supplemented and occasionally guided by state efforts to promote the conversion of New Jersey to a center for high technology. Housing patterns are no longer determined only by the wishes of builders and the wishes of municipalities: a state concern for lower-income families also must be heeded. Moreover, New Jersey has learned the basic environmental lesson that even its small portion of the earth must be considered as an interdependent ecological system. Upriver communities can no longer discharge their wastes upon downriver shores, and upwind cities can no longer pollute the lungs of their downwind neighbors. Undergirding all of these new policy directions is a revised financial foundation. With each paycheck and each purchase New Jerseyans are instructed that the state government exists and now is responsible for half of their total nonfederal tax bill.

THE EMERGENCE OF STATE POLITICS

New Jersey has become a state indeed. Although one of the original members of the Union, there is some truth in the observation that New Jersey did not emerge as a full political entity until the last few decades, and that it might even be considered one of the youngest states in the nation. To be a state means more than having a formal government that issues regulations and more than being represented by a star and a stripe on the national flag. Full statehood also requires the mutual involvement of the citizens and the government: the citizens must be interested in and aware of the activities of their public officials and the government should be concerned about and responsive to popular needs. In this sense, New Jersey is only now reaching political maturity.

The process, however, is not complete. Garden Staters do not yet evidence the state pride or state consciousness of Texans or Iowans; Trenton is still less of a going governmental enterprise than Sacramento or Albany; and most legislators still commute no more than twice a week to the capital. New Jersey is a state of contrasts and ambiguities that evidence its transition from past passivity to modern activity. Moreover, there is no assured destination as New Jersey moves through this transition. The possibilities include a reversion to past patterns, or new fragmentation into different groupings, or further strengthening of the state's new cohesion. Whatever happens in the future, however, will depend at least partly on the factors that have recently changed the character of the state, factors such as changing institutions, new patterns of politics and culture, economic development, and fiscal innovations, as well as the significant influence of individual leaders.

FORMAL INSTITUTIONS

Formal governmental institutions do not completely control the realities of politics. They do, however, channel the political process and provide boundaries for what it is possible to achieve. By adopting a new constitution in 1947, New Jersey greatly enlarged these possibilities and provided opportunities for creative leadership.

The new state charter strengthened gubernatorial powers, although no paper document could create the necessary human qualities for real leadership. It permitted two four-year terms (instead of the previous limit of a single three-year tenure), thus facilitating a longer-range view from the executive office. The constitution further enhanced the power of the executive by consolidating the bureaucratic agencies and placing them under the direct control of the governor; by giving the chief executive strong financial powers to prepare the state budget and to delete any specific appropriation; and by arming the governor with the political clout inherent in the conditional veto over legislation.

These bones of a new state constitution, however, still required the muscle and brains of real persons before they could move. Sometimes governors would be content simply to administer the apparatus and to enjoy the pale spotlight that inevitably illuminated the only state official elected by all of New Jersey's voters. Yet all found it necessary to respond in some way to the new expectations for leadership that the 1947 charter created.

In the judiciary the effect of constitutional change was even more apparent. The new constitution eliminated overlapping and competitive jurisdictions and consolidated the legal system under a single hierarchy. Immediately the state supreme court established itself as a leader among the appellate benches of the nation. The court improved legal administration itself and made criminal law. Then it turned to basic policy questions, focusing public and legislative attention on the quality of education, the environment, and housing opportunities. Here again, individual leadership was critical. While the modern state charter provided opportunities for judicial impact, the justices themselves had to make the most of them.

The legislature was the institution least affected by the new structure of government. This is because, when it established the 1947 constitutional convention, the legislature provided multiple defenses against any alteration of its own most treasured feature—representation by one senator for each of the twenty-one counties. County equality had been the norm since the nineteenth century, when a rural New Jersey was divided along north-south lines. In the twentieth century, even as the state became more urban and suburban and a variety of social and ethnic differences created divisions among its residents, the old equal county representation remained, preserving the power of the rural counties in the legislature. Institutional change was limited to increasing the term of legislators and making their election more coincident with that of the governor. By refusing to change its representational base, and by neglecting to alter internal procedures, the legislature remained the least modern branch of the state government and the most severely malapportioned in the nation. Its archaic features consequently hamstrung the modernization of state policy for a long time.

Despite the legislature's reluctance, however, it too eventually changed under the U.S. Supreme Court's mandate of representation on the basis of one person, one vote. In 1966, a new and limited constitutional convention completed the renovation of state government. Counties no longer had direct political representation in Trenton. Instead, legislators in both senate and assembly had to be elected from legislative districts of equal population.

The effects of this change were not immediately obvious, for many Trenton veterans continued to win election in the new districts. With their replacement, however, older customs of the legislature began to pass. Senators and assembly members were less prone to see themselves as the emissaries of their county parties. Acting more as individuals, they might concern themselves only with local interests, but they also learned that they could not gain their ends without considering those of other constituencies as well. The legislature became more professional and more institutionalized. Committee specialization made the members more expert, more aggressive, and more involved in the general problems of the state. Leadership no longer rotated automatically, allowing strong personalities to develop experience and accumulate chips for trading. Staff was hired, providing continuity and expertise in policy-making. And the legislators, sometimes surprisingly and always haltingly, found themselves capable of dealing with major public issues.

THE NEW POLITICS

Aided by these new institutional structures, new patterns of politics also developed in New Jersey and furthered the emergence of the state as a distinct political entity. The changing character of the political parties is illustrative. Earlier, party organizations had been isolated and largely self-sufficient county baronies, engaged with government only when necessary for their own ends, but largely able to fend for themselves. Frank Hague, Democratic boss of Hudson County, or Frank Farley, Republican boss of Atlantic County, ruled communities that were economically viable and politically secure against competition by the opposition party. Patronage jobs were wanted and plentiful; legislators served at the sufferance of the boss; and governors waited in line for nomination to a weak office.

This political situation has changed considerably. The county and local governments now need state assistance, not neglect. Party organizations need the help of state leaders and even of the state party apparatus to raise funds, to develop campaigns, and to defend policy positions. Patronage still exists but the opportunities at the local levels are limited, while the best-paying and most influential political appointments are controlled by the state executive. Nominees for the governorship are no longer beholden to county leaders. Able to raise their own funds, either privately or through public financing, and able to appeal directly to the voters through the media, they have less need to win approval from county organizations. Instead, county organizations seek to clutch at the short coattails of popular politicians, such as Bill Bradley or Tom Kean. Even legislative candidates, now running in districts that do not follow county lines, have less reason to heed the directions of any would-be political boss.

The source of these political changes is to be found in the behavior of the voters, who are more independent and less loyal to their traditional parties than formerly. The national trend to party independence has been not only evident but exaggerated in New Jersey. Until recently, only half of the state's electorate would spontaneously declare itself committed to the Republicans or Democrats, in contrast to at least three-fifths of the electorate in the entire United States. The Garden State appears to have the right social conditions to breed independence—suburban communities and high transiency. Furthermore, without statewide newspapers or television stations voters also lack the consistent cues and arguments that promote long-term loyalties.

The weakening of county organizations and the loosening of party loyalties have provided new opportunities for politicians with different—and sometimes broader—outlooks. Indeed, changed politics has required that politicians adapt to new circumstances. Strong local parties, when they existed, assured candidates a solid base of support, but also exerted a degree of discipline on these candidates through their control of nominations. When the parties weakened, political aspirants were freed from the discipline, but they had to rely more on their own resources. If voters will no longer respond to the call for party loyalty, then office seekers must invoke personal loyalties. If local canvassing no longer effectively mobilizes the electorate, then media advertisements, direct mail, and candidate-centered strategies may do the trick. If the party's coffers are empty, election funds can be obtained from individual contributors and from the proliferating political action committees. These new political techniques already dominate statewide elections and many races for Congress, and are likely soon to affect even the state legislature.

In this altered environment, the party organizations, in their own self-interest, will further the trend toward statewide politics. A more volatile electorate requires greater campaign effort and greater campaign spending, beyond the resources available locally. This increased cost of election encourages local party units to raise and spend funds more centrally. As new campaigning techniques become more prevalent, the parties will seek economies of scale in the use of polls, media advertising, and direct mail solicitation.

Similarly, the popularity of a particular gubernatorial candidate will now affect outcomes in races for freeholder or mayor. The new residents of Leisure Village, for instance, may know nothing about Monroe Township's politics, but their votes may well be influenced by a Brendan Byrne or a Tom Kean, who is responsible for old-age assistance programs. Such appeals give local candidates and organizations a selfish reason to be more concerned about the qualifications and policies of persons at the head of the ticket.

Gubernatorial nominations evidence the party organizations' changed relationship to statewide politics. In the past, these nominations were decided by bargaining among powerful county leaders and only ratified later in primary elections. This tight control was destroyed in the 1970s, when individualist campaigning—aided by state funding—led to open contests, prolific spending, party splits, and even to challenges to incumbent governors, such as Cahill and Byrne.

Today parties are taking at least halting steps towards creating mechanisms to live in the more open environment of gubernatorial nominations. Proposed amendments to the election finance law would decrease potential candidates' access to public funding, and thus limit the number of aspirants. In 1985 Republicans rallied without dissent behind the reelection candidacy of Governor Kean. Democrats still had a primary contest, but party leaders were able to discourage some possible aspirants and to limit competition to three significant contenders. Efforts are also under way to develop a system of party endorsements for statewide candidates through pre-primary conventions. With a broad popular base, such conventions might provide a new means of uniting the parties.

Interest groups also affect New Jersey's shifting politics. Certainly the presence and influence of these groups in Trenton is not new—railroads have lobbied for profitable concessions, teachers have pressed for collective bargaining powers, and businesses have urged low corporate taxation. Nor is there anything novel in the self-interested concerns of these groups. What is new about interest groups in New Jersey is their scope, their methods, and, to some extent, their increased statewide focus. There are more groups represented in Trenton, occupying more buildings on State Street, making more demands, and providing more grist for the legislative and executive mills than there used to be. As recently as 10 years ago, only 165 lobbyists, representing 175 organizations, had officially registered with the state attorney general. By 1985 the numbers had grown to 450 lobbyists working on behalf of nearly 900 organizations.[1] In a mutual interaction, the greater activities of the state stimulate more group efforts, and the increased activities of the groups provide more work for state government.

Not only are there more groups, but they have a wider range of interests as well. Economic and business interests predominate, but there also are associations to promote the needs of the handicapped, to permit or to prohibit the use of bear traps in state forests, to provide aid to cities, to advance the demands of dental associations or professors. As more and more varied interests become involved, lobbying methods become more diverse. Groups no longer confine themselves to lobbying legislators in the corridors of the State House, but now also attempt to use the resources of numbers and money. The legislature frequently endures mass lobbying efforts or mass pilgrimages to Trenton, as large groups converge on the capital to press their demands. Many interests have formed political action committees to collect funds that are contributed to the election campaigns of friendly legislators. Public participation in politics now extends beyond voting to include active electoral mobilization and financial contributions. Even though the contending interests are concerned with relatively narrow objectives, these activities teach New Jerseyans that they have a personal stake in Trenton.

Some groups focus more directly than others on state concerns. There are not only such established associations as the New Jersey Chamber of Commerce, the state AFL-CIO, and the League of Women Voters, but also temporary alliances between various groups and prominent individuals. They all seek changes in a broad range of policies, often through public referenda on bond issues or constitutional amendments. Efforts of this kind have urged state government to broaden the tax base, increase spending on public and higher education, and develop the Green Acres conservation program. These activities promote the growing state awareness by New Jersey's residents.

THE EMERGENCE OF NEW JERSEY

As New Jersey's politics has changed, so has its political culture. For the most part, the underlying culture of a community such as a state is more fundamental than the decisions of its transient public officials. Reflecting the state's traditions, politicians in New Jersey have exemplified an individualist culture in which professional specialists pursue particular interests.[2] But cultures can be changed, usually by external occurrences, but also sometimes from the internal promptings of politicians.

POLITICAL CULTURE

Political culture includes at least three aspects: identification, expectations, and support.[3] New Jersey has been changing in all three respects. There is a greater sense of identity with the state as a political entity. More activity is expected of the people in Trenton. While New Jerseyans remain skeptical of the honesty and competence of their government officials, they seem to be offering more positive support in recent years.

In a remarkably short period of eight years, according to surveys taken between 1977 and 1985, New Jersey has overcome its feelings of inferiority. Four out of five residents now find the Garden State a good or excellent place to live. This level of satisfaction is not unique in the United States, but New Jerseyans at least are no longer *less* satisfied than those living in the rest of the country. That fact is itself remarkable in a state where residence has sometimes drawn the scorn once accorded the vice-presidency: "It isn't a crime exactly. You can't be sent to jail for it, but it's a kind of a disgrace. It's like writing anonymous letters."[4]

The improved self-image of New Jersey parallels a happier view of its state government. Both the governor and the legislature are now evaluated more positively by citizens than in the past. Moreover citizens now give a higher rating to the state than to either their own municipalities or their particular neighborhoods. Previously, the local areas were preferred.[5]

External or nonpolitical factors partially explain this change of attitude. The advent of major league sports, the development of tourism and casino gambling, and economic development have all contributed to the state's enhanced self-image. Yet, being nonpolitical in nature, these causes cannot fully explain political effects. Even winning sports teams (and New Jersey lacks champions) are not necessarily sources of civic satisfaction. Gambling successes and good jobs provide private rewards, but do not in themselves produce public gratification.

Rather an explanation for the marked alteration in New Jersey's political culture must be sought in an understanding of changing political activity. The state has reason to be proud of its leadership in various areas of public policy. Long before environmental protection became a national concern, New Jersey was taking action to control air pollution. It has gone on to protect the other critical resources of seashore and water. In the Pinelands Act the state reserved a fifth of its entire area from unrestricted development, a planning innovation unmatched by any other industrial state. When the national government was reducing its commitment to education, the state drastically altered its tax structure and attempted (although not yet successfully) to equalize schooling for all children. In electoral politics, New Jersey has pioneered in the public financing of election campaigns and in techniques such as postcard registration to increase voter participation.

Through such actions, New Jersey's political leaders have done more than just reflect the state's culture; they have also helped to transform it. In the process they have been civic educators, teaching the state's people that they do have a collective identity and a responsibility to the polity beyond their individual needs and particular interests. A succession of governors from Hughes to Byrne to Kean have taught the need for state programs in transportation, education, and environmental protection. Legislators such as Assembly Speaker William Hamilton assumed the responsibility for restructuring the state's tax system and then went back to their constituents and justified the state's new role. Appointed administrators, aided by unidentified but thoughtful civil servants, have developed new policy goals and techniques. Chief justices such as Arthur Vanderbilt and Joseph Weintraub instructed the electorate in the elements of legal and social justice. These and other leaders have altered the political culture, and the community life, of New Jersey.

ECONOMIC AND FISCAL CHANGE

Paralleling these political changes have been developments in the state's private and public economy. Policy actions depend ultimately on the resources generated by nongovernmental production of goods and services. State governments can neither create money nor borrow beyond their means. Government, however, can affect the uses and distribution of the state's economic resources—and it has done so in New Jersey.

The dominant feature of the state's economic development over the last four decades has been the shift of jobs and wealth out of the cities and into the suburbs and rural areas. The principal lines of communication are no longer the railroads that link Trenton and Newark, but the interstate highways that bring new offices to Morris County and new residents to Monmouth County, as well as the computer and satellite networks that free industry from fixed geographical locations.

This dispersion of industry has stimulated state action in both urban and other areas. The Newark riots of 1967 were only the most dramatic manifestation of the cities' loss of jobs, declining schools, and shrinking tax base. The decline of urban prosperity created needs that could only be met by state or federal action. The state government responded by promoting economic development in the cities, providing direct revenue aid, and even by paying some of the salaries of local firefighters. While these measures have not halted urban decline, they have made the existence of Trenton far more visible and important in these localities and in the lives of their citizens.

In the more prosperous areas economic change has also promoted state involvement, although for different reasons. The state has been active in creating the infrastructure for growth. At first, New Jersey's government was largely concerned with providing physical facilities, such as highways, or aiding businesses in finding suitable locations. A broader role has developed more recently. The state is now concerned as well with providing the human resources and the social conditions required for economic development—conditions such as education, technical research facilities, and recreation. It is also attending to the consequences of development, especially pollution and toxic wastes.

Inherently, these are state rather than local activities. High-speed highways are not limited by municipal and county boundaries. As industry extends along these highways, Trenton must promote regional planning, regulation, and fiscal equity. Similarly, only the state can control the ill effects of chemical dumps or provide the large funding and the large population base required for advanced technology research centers and outstanding higher education.

Economic development and its political response also affect the consciousness of New Jersey's citizens. New Jersey is no longer a state

typified by the bedroom suburban commuter whose work and life–
style is centered in New York or Philadelphia. The overwhelming proportion of residents both live and work within the state, and they are
joined by increasing numbers who commute into New Jersey. As she
drives to work along Interstate 80, the programmer from Leonia sees
not only her local streets, but parts of her state. As he looks for housing, the transferred worker has new choices made available by real estate development guided by state policy. As increased state funding
improves educational opportunities as well as the visibility of Rutgers, more high school graduates attend their own state
university. Through hundreds of experiences like these, New Jerseyans develop more awareness—and perhaps more pride—in
the commonwealth.

Certainly, the new fiscal system promotes a greater state awareness. Taxes are important not only for the revenues they raise, but
also because they teach taxpayers about the relative size and differing
roles of various levels of government. As the property tax declines in
its relative impact, less attention need be given to the local governments and school districts; as sales and income taxes increase, state
government must be given more heed.

This state's residents are surely no more eager than other Americans to pay taxes. Yet, even as many sister states imposed spending
limitations on government, New Jersey adopted an income tax and
then raised both the sales and the new income levies. As the nation
debates federal tax revision, it may well find a model in New Jersey,
which has a simple income tax including mildly progressive rates and
virtually no loopholes. These fiscal changes were made politically feasible by the imposition of budget caps, which promised relief from local taxes and from rising government expenditures at all levels.

The use of the caps illustrates the changed focus of government in
New Jersey. The law makes the state government appear both prudent and generous. School districts and municipalities are held to
small percentage increases in their spending, and both are subject to
strict supervision by state agencies. Trenton's spending, on the other
hand, had been statutorily limited only by the growth of the state's
economic base. This restraint was so inefficacious, however, that it
lapsed without controversy. The state is now legally unrestricted in its
spending increases, even as it maintains restraints on the lower levels
of government.

The state also generously distributes property tax rebates. While
these checks have sometimes been timed to aid the governor's personal standing, their greater significance is that they contrast a benefit

received from the state with a cost imposed by the locality. They reinforce the lesson that New Jerseyans have been learning for twenty years—state government is important.

FRAGMENTATION AND UNCERTAINTY

New Jersey's recent state activism is not a certain harbinger of future innovation. Indeed, for all of the changes that have taken place, the future of the state is still uncertain. Even with new revenue sources and the assumption of new responsibilities, New Jersey's state government spends only an average amount of money for each citizen and still ranks below the national norm in expenditures on some vital functions including education. Similarly, even as they display new state pride, citizens have but overcome past feelings of inferiority; they are yet to be convinced of the superiority of life in the Garden State. The glass of state achievement is just half full; it is also half empty.

Change is a rule of life for a state as much as for individuals. New Jersey now seeks to resolve its collective identity crisis, and thereby shows the contrasts and strains that inevitably accompany such periods of transition. The state may revert to past political patterns, to institutional incohesion, citizen cynicism, functional failures. But the state may also continue its recent movement toward self-confidence and achievement. The future will depend on leadership and on the ability and effort of politicians to chart policies and to convince the public.

These leaders still face obstacles. Fragmentation persists as a major characteristic of New Jersey politics, as it does in American government generally. In fact, some recent developments have increased the divisions in the state, making it even more difficult to achieve coherent public policies. These divisions are evident both in the social structure and the formal institutions of the state.

Ethnic pluralism, for instance, has been characteristic of New Jersey from the days of the first Dutch and Swedish settlers. That pluralism has resisted the homogenization of the "melting pot" and is likely to complicate political action. Political ingenuity will be needed to build coalitions among past powers such as the Irish, the Italian-Americans (now the largest population group in the state) and other emerging factions.

Blacks have become a visible and self-conscious force also, especially within the Democratic party. Governing many of the state's larger cities and mobilizing an enlarged electorate, they demonstrated their growing importance in the impressive votes gained by Kenneth Gibson in the 1981 and 1985 gubernatorial primaries. Bloc voting by blacks, however, can complicate the necessary building of coalitions either within the Democratic party or with Republicans. Hispanics are another significant ethnic group, but their impact has been limited by competition with blacks. Moreover, Hispanics are not always united, since there are considerable political differences between, for example, Cubans and Puerto Ricans.

New Jersey also has a growing generation gap. This state has a large older population and is second only to Florida overall in the median age. At the same time, the state and its high-technology industries are attracting more young people, particularly professionals. Age differences can lead to policy differences. Senior citizens will be more enthusiastic about the allocation of casino revenues for aid to the elderly, while Yuppies will be more favorable toward educational spending. The interests of these groups will sometimes clash directly as in the recent outlawing of mandatory retirement.

Economic differences among groups, however, are likely to remain the most fundamental, and could become significantly magnified. As the economy changes, the social division grows between the cities— poor, aging, and based on declining manufacturing—and the suburbs—wealthy, developing, and based on expanding technology. Of course, class differences have always existed in New Jersey, but in large cities these classes at least saw one another on the streets and in the schools. The new economy separates classes along geographical lines. The same highways that keep traffic moving around the state also allow travelers to avoid the unpleasant sights of urban decay. The same computers that make the home an office, isolate the office worker and insulate the citizen from an awareness of others and of their common lives.

Political institutions are meant to bridge these differences between ethnic groups, generations, geographical areas, and social classes. New Jersey has begun to develop such unifying mechanisms, but barriers remain strong and perhaps invulnerable. Thus, the tradition of home rule even when subordinated continues to influence state politics. The number of children decreases, but 611 school districts maintain their independence, even if some are no more than paper constituencies. The spread of industry along highway networks calls for regional planning, but municipalities continue to compete for the best ratables while avoiding the housing development envisaged by the *Mount Laurel* decision.

Crisis has sometimes forced action. The most obvious example is the change in the fiscal and school systems which followed the decision in *Robinson v. Cahill*. Though the legislature had enacted a new school law in 1975, the lawmakers could not agree on funding it. As Richard Hughes, then Chief Justice remembered, "They dilly-dallied along, and they postponed and postponed." Finally, they faced both the demands of the governor and the pressure of school closure by the courts. Then, but only then, "the Legislature realized they were in real trouble, and they passed an income tax 10 days later."[6] New Jersey's state government cannot be considered effective if it is able to act only in such dire circumstances.

Paradoxically, as the separate institutions of New Jersey's government become stronger, there may be a decline in the overall effectiveness of the state. To some extent, the dynamism of New Jersey under the new constitution resulted from a practical weakness in the theoretical system of the checks and balances. The governor's considerable authority was not matched by an equally strong legislature. Therefore, his control over the budget and final authority over legislation through the conditional veto was not threatened by a vigorous opposition on the other side of the State House. The judiciary, too, could innovate because it could eventually persuade or push the legislature into following its lead in new policy directions such as school finance and land use. Moreover, the executive and judicial branches were sometimes allied against threats to their autonomy from the legislature, as in disputes over the governor's appointive power or bureaucratic regulation.

As the legislature has modernized, it has developed the power to balance more effectively the actions of the governor and the judiciary. In the long run, this change increases the prospect for effective statewide policy. In the short run, however, the legislators' proper concern for their own districts and their favorite interests can retard coherent policy-making. In responding to *Mount Laurel*, for example, the common reaction has been to seek local relief of the burden of low-cost housing, not to formulate a broad and effective policy. In dealing with the budget deficit of 1982 and the budget surplus of 1985 alike, most legislators have been more prone to defend pet appropriations than to look toward a long-range fiscal plan for the state. This emphasis on immediate needs is matched by the executive's effort to dominate policy disputes.

The inherent localism of the legislature and its inevitable clashes with the separate executive branch are reinforced by underlying tendencies in electoral politics. Candidate-centered campaigns provide few incentives for cooperation among legislators and build no bridges

across the formal institutional divisions. The present changed and
centrifugal environment of politics rather encourages independence
by officeholders and intervention by interest groups. With parties still
weak, political action committees become more important. Their role
is most obviously illustrated in campaign finance, where the PACs'
share of spending rose from 17 percent of all legislative contributions
in 1979 to 24 percent in 1981 and then to 39 percent in 1983.[7]

Increased spending in elections is the most visible manifestation of
the growth of interest groups in the state and is itself a testament to
the new power of state government. The direct effect of their activity,
however, is a further fracturing of power as each group seeks its particular goals. Broad visions of the public interest arise only acciden-
tally from the clashes of these groups. Achieving such vision is made
more difficult in the absence of effective statewide media, which are
unlikely to appear in the foreseeable future.

Dispersal of power results as well, ironically, from New Jersey's
policy innovations like the campaign finance law. This legislation has
made party nominations more open and campaigning more honest.
Yet, at the same time, it has restricted the parties, which are the major potential agent for coherent government, in the choice of their
most visible leader, the candidate for governor. The law's limits on expenditures have also promoted a reliance on media campaigning. This
trend may result in more telegenic candidates, but it may also lessen
the chances of electing chief executives who can effectively build support for their policy goals.

The state has also been creative in finding novel devices to raise
funds and promote policy goals, devices such as lotteries, casino gambling, and regional authorities. Each of these techniques, however,
builds its own rigidity into the state budget or removes an area of policy from direct political control. The long-term danger is that too
many sources of revenue will be reserved for too many favored functions and that too many decisions will be made by autonomous authorities. Inevitably, there will be limits to what the state can do and how
much its citizens will pay. At that point the state government may find
itself confined in bonds of its own making.

New Jersey's Future

New Jersey now gets much from its state government and demands
much. The state's future problem may be that its citizens will expect
more than either Trenton or any state agency can deliver. In the past
state politics was less significant, but it was also easier to manage. To-

day, being more important, state politics is more difficult to control and direct.

In the past, there were relatively few active players in the game of New Jersey politics and government. Limited policy initiatives could be undertaken if there was agreement among the state's few leaders —the governor, major corporate executives, and the most powerful county bosses. Now, there are more initiatives but also more players. Mass media observe state government more carefully; party discipline is more difficult to achieve; and many interests must be consulted and conciliated. The politics of small groups has been replaced by the politics of participation, and this is more complicated and often more frustrating, even if it may also be more significant.

Leadership remains the key factor. It was not inevitable that New Jersey would recognize its problems with education, the environment, and economic development, or that it would increase its taxation in order to attempt solutions. No provision of the constitution compelled Richard Hughes to broaden the tax base or William Cahill to foster medical education or Brendan Byrne to preserve open space or Thomas Kean to upgrade the public schools. These and other actions followed from visions and choices deliberately made by these governors and by other political leaders.

Different choices will confront different leaders in the coming years. As the federal government restricts its activities, New Jersey and her sister states will be facing new needs and additional demands. An aging population requires more expensive health care, and a more complex society requires innovative education. A slack economy worsens social distress, just as a booming economy worsens environmental dangers and housing shortages. Citizens will continue to debate the equity of taxation, to invoke governmental power in their own interests, and to define their common identity.

Public officials, whether hesitant or eager, inevitably will shape New Jersey's future. They may respond creatively and achieve long-term successes. They will certainly make errors, produce unexpected consequences, and sometimes delay until crises impend. They will surely need to be people different from their predecessors. They will need to develop skills in media presentation and public presentation and rely less on techniques of individual negotiation and personal persuasion.

One element, however, will remain constant. In New Jersey as elsewhere successful politics will require leaders who have both "passion and perspective," who understand that "man would not have attained the possible unless time and again he had reached out for the impossible."[8] At times, New Jersey has had such leaders; it will need more in the future.

Notes

1. The earlier figures are from Philip Burch, "Interest Groups," in *Politics in New Jersey*, Alan Rosenthal and John Blydenburgh, eds., (New Brunswick: Rutgers University, Eagleton Institute of Politics, 1975), 83. The recent figures are from the Attorney-General's Office of Legislative Information (1985).

2. Daniel Elazar, *American Federalism: A View from the States*, 2nd ed. (New York: Crowell, 1972), 84–126.

3. Alan Rosenthal, "On Analyzing States," in *The Political Life of the American States*, Alan Rosenthal and Maureen Moakley, eds. (New York: Praeger, 1984), 13–17.

4. Finley Peter Dunne, *The World of Mr. Dooley*, Louis Filler, ed. (New York: Collier Books, 1962), 50.

5. The data are summarized in Figures 1.2 and 1.3 and Tables 1.1 and 1.2. See also the discussion by Matthew Kauffman, "New Jersey Looks at Itself," *New Jersey Reporter*, 14 (March 1985): 13–17.

6. Virginia D. Sederis, "Mr. Hughes Remembers," *New Jersey Reporter*, 14 (April 1985): 17.

7. Stephen A. Salmore and Barbara Salmore, *Candidates, Parties and Campaigns: Electoral Politics in America* (Washington: Congressional Quarterly Press, 1985), 201.

8. Max Weber, *Politics as a Vocation* (Philadelphia: Fortress Press, 1965; originally published in 1919), 55.

Appendix: Chronology of Recent Major Events in New Jersey Politics

1947 New state constitution adopted.

1948 Arthur T. Vanderbilt becomes chief justice.

1949 Albert E. Driscoll (R) elected governor.

1952 New Jersey Turnpike completed.

1953 Robert E. Meyner (D) elected governor.

1954 Air Pollution Control Act adopted.

1957 Robert E. Meyner (D) re-elected governor.
Democrats win control of state assembly.
Joseph Weintraub becomes chief justice.

1961 Richard J. Hughes (D) elected governor.

1965 Richard J. Hughes (D) re-elected governor.
Democrats win control of both houses of legislature.

1966 Constitution amended to provide equal representation in both houses of legislature.
State sales tax adopted.

1967 Rioting erupts in Newark.

1969 William Cahill (R) elected governor. Republicans win control of both houses of legislature. Hackensack Meadowland Development Commission created.

1970 Department of Environmental Protection created.

1973 Brendan Byrne (D) elected governor. Democrats win control of both houses of legislature. *Robinson v. Cahill* decision by supreme court. Richard J. Hughes becomes chief justice.

1975   *Mount Laurel I* decision by supreme court. "Thorough and efficient" (T&E) public education law adopted.

1976   Supreme court closes public schools for eight days. Income tax, education funding law, and spending caps adopted. Public financing of gubernatorial elections adopted.

1977   Brendan Byrne (D) re-elected governor.

1978   Casino gambling begins in Atlantic City.

1979   Robert N. Wilentz becomes chief justice. Pinelands Protection Act adopted.

1981   Thomas Kean (R) elected governor.

1982   Television Channel 9 moves to New Jersey.

1983   *Mount Laurel II* decision by supreme court.

1984   High-technology bond issue approved. Alternate teacher certification approved.

1985   Thomas Kean (R) re-elected governor. Republicans win control of state assembly. State establishes minimum teacher salary of $18,500.

Index

Notes on Contributors

Gerald M. Pomper is professor of political science and director of the Center on Political Parties at the Eagleton Institute of Politics, Rutgers University.

Albert Burstein, now a private attorney with Rosen, Weiss, Slattery, and Burstein, is the former chairman of the Education Committee of the New Jersey General Assembly.

James W. Hughes is chair and graduate director of the Department of Urban Planning and Policy Development, Rutgers University.

Eleanor V. Laudicina is director, Master of Public Administration Program, Kean College of New Jersey.

Susan S. Lederman is associate professor and coordinator of the Public Administration Program, Kean College of New Jersey.

Donald Linky is senior vice president of New Jersey Business and Industry Association, and former chief counsel and director of policy and planning during the Byrne administration.

Maureen W. Moakley is assistant professor of political science and a faculty associate at the Eagleton Institute of Politics, Rutgers University.

John C. Pittenger is dean of the Rutgers School of Law at Camden.

Alan Rosenthal is professor of political science and director of the Eagleton Institute, Rutgers University.

Stephen A. Salmore is professor of political science at the Eagleton Institute of Politics, Rutgers University.

George Sternlieb is director of the Center for Urban Policy Research and professor of urban planning and policy development, Rutgers University.

Richard J. Sullivan, former New Jersey commissioner of environmental protection, is a partner in the firm of New Jersey First, Inc.

Carl E. Van Horn is associate professor of political science and director of the
Center for State Politics and Public Policy at the Eagleton Institute of
Politics, Rutgers University.

Cliff Zukin is associate professor of political science and director of the *Star-
Ledger/* Eagleton Poll, Eagleton Institute, Rutgers University.